Udit Narayan

51 Songs' Sargam

A rare collection of 51 Songs'
lyrics in English and its Swarlipi with Taal

Udit Narayan

Notations writer: Vinod Kumar

Notion Press

NOTION PRESS

India. Singapore. Malaysia.

ISBN xxx-x-xxxxx-xx-x

Vinod Kumar

DEDICATION

This book is dedicated to my Parents.

-Vinod Kumar

CONTENTS

Vinod Kumar

BIOGRAPHY OF UDIT NARAYAN

Udit Narayan (born 1 December 1955) is an Indian playback singer whose songs have been featured mainly in Hindi films. He has also sung in various other languages including Telugu, Kannada, Tamil, Bengali, Odia, Bhojpuri, Nepali, Malayalam, Assamese, Bagheli and Maithili. He has won four National Film Awards and five Filmfare Awards with twenty nominations among many others. The Government of India awarded him the Padma Shri in 2009 and the Padma Bhushan in 2016 for his contribution to arts and culture. As many as 21 of his tracks feature in BBC's "Top 40 Bollywood Soundtracks of all time".

He got to sing with Mohammed Rafi in his Hindi playback debut in movie Unees-Bees in 1980 and also with Kishore Kumar in the 1980s. He finally made his mark in the 1988 movie Qayamat Se Qayamat Tak starring Aamir Khan and Juhi Chawla, his song "Papa Kehte Hain" was his notable performance which earned him his first Filmfare Award in the 1980s and he established himself in Bollywood Playback Singing. The soundtrack became one of the highest selling albums in the 1980s. The soundtrack was a breakthrough for the careers of Anand–Milind, as well as T-Series, one of India's leading record labels. after which he was one of the favourites of music directors. In the 1990s he sung for a thousands of songs including Hindi and Nepali languages.

Recognising his contribution, King of Nepal Birendra Bir Bikram Shah Dev awarded him with the Order of Gorkha Dakshina Bahu in 2001 after which for his contribution to Indian cinema and music, and Chitragupta Cineyatra Samman 2015 for his contribution to Bhojpuri cinema. He is the only male singer in the history of the Filmfare Awards to have won in over three decades (the 1980s, 1990s, and 2000s).

Udit Narayan Jha was born in a Maithil Brahmin family in 1955 to Nepali father Harekrishna Jha and Indian mother Bhuvaneshwari Jha. In 2009, He was born in the Baisi village of Supaul district of Bihar at his maternal grandparents' home. Udit Narayan revealed at a ceremony held by the Bihar Jharkhand Association of North America, that he identifies as a Bihari.

Narayan studied at Jageshwar High School, Kunauli, Supaul, Bihar, India, where he finished his SSC and later obtained his intermediate degree from Ratna Rajya Lakshmi Campus, Kathmandu, Nepal. His father Harekrishna Jha was a farmer and his mother Bhuvneshwari Devi was a folk singer who encouraged his career.

Udit Narayan and Deepa were married in 1985. With Deepa Narayan, he has one son, Aditya Narayan, who is also a playback singer.

Narayan is one of the most prominent singers of Bollywood throughout the 1990s and early 2000s. He has been the on-screen singing voice for various Bollywood stars. He has sung for Bollywood actors Amitabh Bachchan, Rajesh Khanna, Dev Anand, Aamir Khan, Shah Rukh Khan, Salman Khan, Akshay Kumar and Ajay Devgn. Most of his duets are with Alka Yagnik. He began his career in 1970 as a Maithili folk singer (staff artist) for Radio Nepal, singing mostly popular folk songs in Maithili and Nepali. Gradually, he started singing modern Nepali songs. After eight years, Narayan moved to Bombay on a musical scholarship for Nepalese from the Indian Embassy in Nepal to study classical music at Bhartiya Vidya Bhavan.

Narayan started his Bollywood career in 1980 when he was noted by music director Rajesh Roshan, who asked Narayan to playback sing for the Hindi film Unees-Bees. Narayan was given the opportunity to sing with the singer Mohammed Rafi. He sang for Devanand a couplet in Swami Dada. His first duet was in the film Sannata. Soon after, Narayan sang for a number of other movies, including Bade Dil Wala in 1983, where he sang a duet with senior singer Lata Mangeshkar, composed by senior music director R. D. Burman. In the same year, Narayan sang with Kishore Kumar in the film Kehdo Pyar Hai. Another singer he sang with was Suresh Wadkar with music composed by Bappi Lahiri. A significant milestone in his career occurred in 1988 when Anand–Milind gave him the opportunity to sing all the songs for the Bollywood movie Qayamat Se Qayamat Tak, with Alka Yagnik, which earned him a Filmfare Award. In a 2014 interview with The Times of India, Narayan said: "The song I've sung, "Manzilein", is the best song of my career after "Pehla Nasha", which gave me superstardom!". Narayan remained prolific through the 2000s, singing numbers in films such as Pukar, Dhadkan, Lagaan, Devdas and Veer-Zaara

In 2002, Narayan sang "Bairi Piya" with newcomer Shreya Ghoshal, from the film Devdas, of which Rediff mentioned: "Narayan successfully captures the eternal romanticism of Devdas". In 2014, Narayan sang a song titled "Naa Hum Jo Kah De" along with Shreya Ghoshal, for the album Women's Day Special: Spreading Melodies Everywhere. The song was composed by Ram Shankar and penned by A. K. Mishra.

He competed with his closest professional rival Kumar Sanu who won five consecutive Filmfare awards in the 1990s.

Narayan's work has been praised by his contemporaries Alka Yagnik, Kavita Krishnamurthy and music director Ankit Tiwari. Mid-Day included him in the list of notable 90s playback singers. Narayan is considered one of the most prominent singers of his generation.

Narayan has performed in many stage shows in India and abroad and is the recipient of many awards. These include Screen Videocon Award, MTV Best Video Award and Pride of India Gold Award. In 2010, Narayan with Madhushree sang for the English independent film When Harry Tries to Marry.

Narayan also sang the title song for the TV show Yeh Duniyan Gazab Ki, with Kumar Sanu. In 2015 he was involved in a mega series campaign Melancholy, where 421 Nepali artists had sung a 33 minutes 49-second long environmental song, in which 365 artists set a Guinness World Record on 19 May 2016 at Radio Nepal Studio, Singhadurbar, Kathamandu. It is written, composed and directed by environmentalist Nipesh DHAKA.

Narayan was on the panel of judges of Indian Idol 3 in 2007 with music composer Anu Malik and playback singer Alisha Chinai on Sony TV.

Narayan was on the panel of judges on Sony TV for Waar Parriwar, a reality show based on the bringing together of a singing gharana (family of singers). He shared judging duties with fellow playback singer Kumar Sanu and Jatin Pandit of the music duo Jatin–Lalit.

Udit Narayan Jha acted in and sang all the songs in a 1985 Nepali movie called Kusume Rumal which is one of the All Time Classics in Nepali movie industry starring himself with Bhuwan K.C. and Tripti Nadakar, which spent 25 weeks on the box office top ten list and became the highest-grossing Nepalese movie of all time until overtaken in 2001 by another Tulsi Ghimire film, Darpan Chaya.

While listening to the always happy-faced Udit Narayan's melodious songs, we wish him good health and bow our heads in his honour.

PREFACE

My hearty greetings and Namaste to Readers. I have written 51 Songs' Sargam books of Mukesh-1,2, Kishor-1,2, Lata, Asha, Manna dey, Yesudas, Kumar Shanu, Rafi-1,2,3,4, Mahendra Kapoor and SD Burman's composed song book in Hindi Language and translated many books in English SARGAM and Western CDEFG. Bhajan Swarlipi 1,2,3,4 and one Gazal Sargam book is also published in Hindi, English and Western notes. All these books are available online. Now I have translated the Udit Narayan book in English as 'Udit Narayan 51 Songs' Sargam'. It is in English Lyrics with notes in SRGM style, so that music lovers can play and sing songs and get enjoyed. A person having basic knowledge of music can play the songs on any instrument.

Mostly song's notations are written in original scale but somewhere you have to transpose +1 or − 1 or ±2 to get original scale. Sa taken is also mentioned in each song's detail. Person who knows western notations can understand as given below:

.नी	.नी	सा	रे	रे	ग	ग	म
.$\underline{N}$	.N	S	$\underline{R}$	R	$\underline{G}$	G	M
.B^b	.B	C	D^b	D	E^b	E	F
.$A^\#$	.B	C	$C^\#$	D	$D^\#$	E	F

मे	प	ध	ध	नी	नी	सां	रे
M*	P	$\underline{D}$	D	$\underline{N}$	N	S'	$\underline{R}$'
G^b	G	A^b	A	B^b	B	C'	$D^{b\prime}$
$F^\#$	G	$G^\#$	A	$A^\#$	B	C'	$C^{\#\prime}$

In this book some symbols are given as (G-) it means you have to play G for two beats duration or matra similarly you have to play for the beats for more number of −(dash), if there are more dashes. When two notes are written adjacending to each other it means you have to play the notes in one beat or matra as MP mapa is played in one beat.

Lower Octave notes are written a dot before them as .G .A .B^b .B
Middle Octave notes are written simple C D E F G A B
Higher Octave notes are written an appostrophy after it C' D' E' etc.

Notations at the beginning of the song are prelude and notations in the middle of the song are interlude. These notations are written by me by my experience. Hope readers shall understand, like and enjoy it.

- "Mukesh 51 Songs' Sargam" Part 1, 2,
- "Lata 51 Songs' Sargam",
- "Kishore 51 Songs' Sargam", Part 1, 2,
- "Md. Rafi 51 Songs' Sargam" Part 1, 2, 3, 4,
- "Asha 51 Songs' Sargam"
- "Singe Sachindev Burman and Yesudas 51 Songs' Sargam"
- "Manna Dey 51 Songs' Sargam"
- "Composer Sachindev Burman 51 Songs' Sargam" (In this book different singers songs sargam are available)
- "Kumar Shanu 51 Songs' Sargam"
- "Superhit 51 Gazals' Sargam"
- "Mahendra Kapoor 51 Songs' Sargam"
- "Sabad and Punjabi Songs Sargam, Part-1"
- "Bhajan Swarlipi" Part-1, 2, 3, 4,
- "Suman Kalyanpur 51 Songs' Sargam"
- "Md. Rafi Superhit Songs"

One has to practice sargam daily and its palte also so that one can become expert in playing difficult notes sequence. People can enjoy your playing instruments and then only your success will be counted.

Care has been taken to provide accuracy still there is no liability of correctness and accuracy of notes and writer, printer, publisher and editor is not responsible for any error or ommissions or mistakes. If any mistake/ommission is found, kindly inform.

For purchasing the books in India, one can visit notionpress.com or flipkart.com or indiamart.com and amazon.in. Kindly review my books at amazon and flipkart and give proper stars after purchasing my books from the above sites. For any query, email to me.

- Vinod Kumar (vinod66vk@gmail.com)

SARGAM

SARGAM swars/sound are derived from voice of animals and birds. C scale is as follows:-

Note Name	Swar	स्वर नाम	Swar full name	स्वर का पूरा नाम हिंदी में	यह स्वर किस पशु पक्षी की आवाज से लिया गया है.
C=	Sa=	सा	Shadaj	षडज	Peacock/ मोर की आवाज़
D=	Re=	रे	Rishabh	रिषभ	Papiha /पपीहा की आवाज़
E=	Ga=	ग	Gandhar	गन्धार	Goat/ बकरा की आवाज़
F=	Ma=	म	Madhyam	मध्यम	Crane/ बगुला की आवाज़
G=	Pa=	प	Pancham	पंचम	Koccoo/Koyal/ कोयल की आवाज़
A=	Dha=	ध	Dhaiwat	धैवत	Frog/ दादुर या मेंढक की आवाज़
B=	Ni=	नी	Nishad	निषाद	Elephant हाथी की आवाज़
C'=	Sa'=	सां	(Higher Sa)		

C#=Re=रे (रे कोमल), D#=Ga=ग (ग कोमल), F#=Ma*=मे (म तीव्र), G#=Dha=ध (ध कोमल), A#=Ni=नी (नी कोमल)

We can write as S R R G G M M* P D D N N S'

All notes underlined are called Komal Swar as Komal Re Komal Ga Komal Dha Komal Ni. One note Ma* is called Tivra Ma. Learn this table to know sequence of the notes-

S	R	R	G	G	M	M*
सा	रे	रे	ग	ग	म	मे
C	D^b	D	E^b	E	F	G^b
C	$C^{\#}$	D	$D^{\#}$	E	F	$F^{\#}$

P	D	D	N	N	S'
प	ध	ध	नी	नी	सां
G	A^b	A	B^b	B	C'
G	$G^{\#}$	A	$A^{\#}$	B	C'

Sa and Pa are Achal (Fixed) Swar they do not have any Komal or Tivra. They are fixed notes as per North Indian music tradition.

Vinod Kumar

OCTAVE

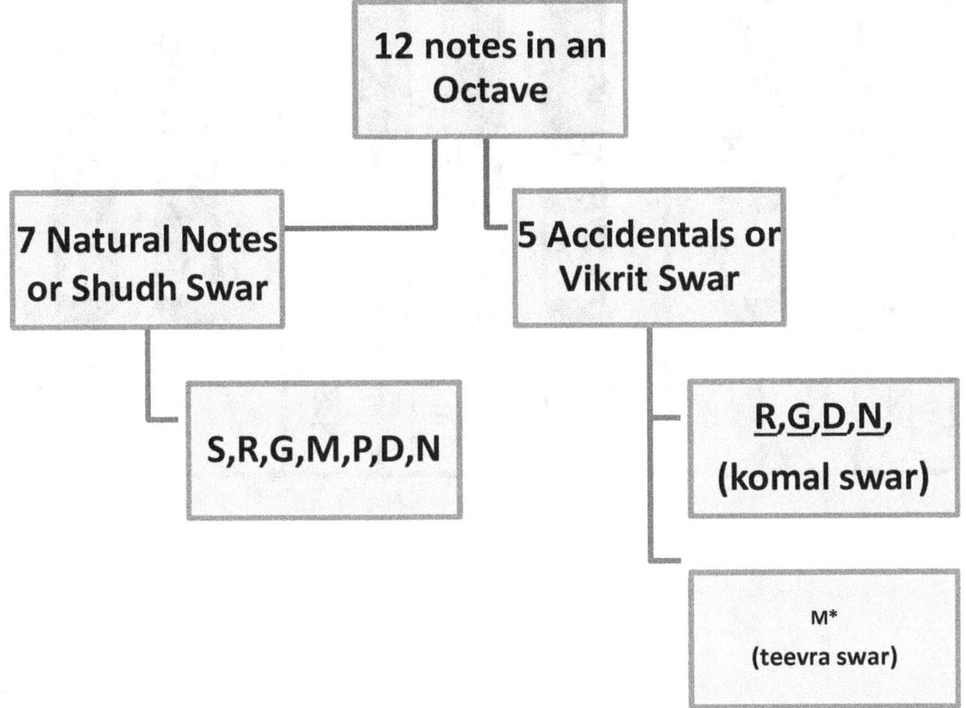

Sequence of the notes on any instrument are:
.D .D .N .N S R R G G M M* P D D N N S' R' R' G' G'

C Scale is given as: SRGMPDNS'

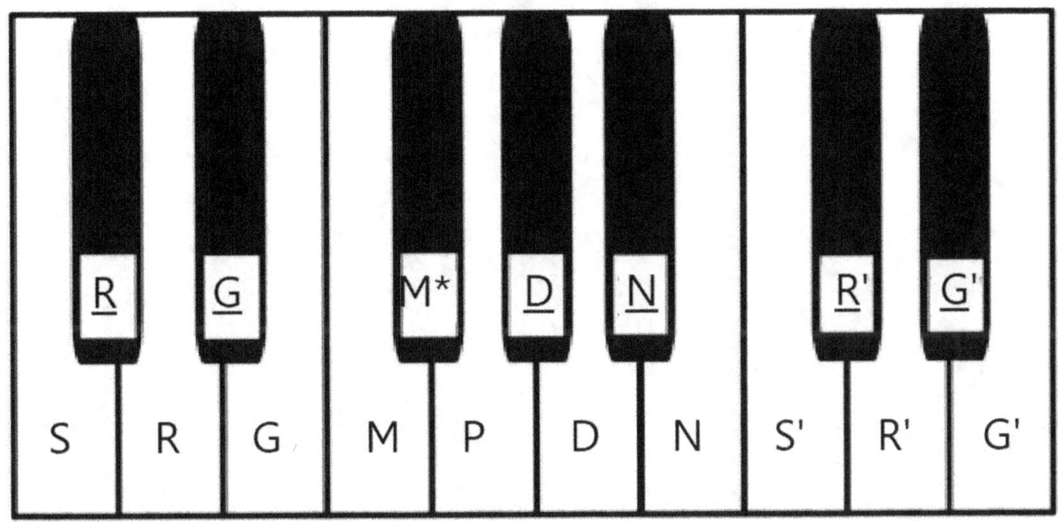

Udit Narayan 51 Songs' Sargam

$C^{\#}$ Scale is given as: SRGMPDNS'

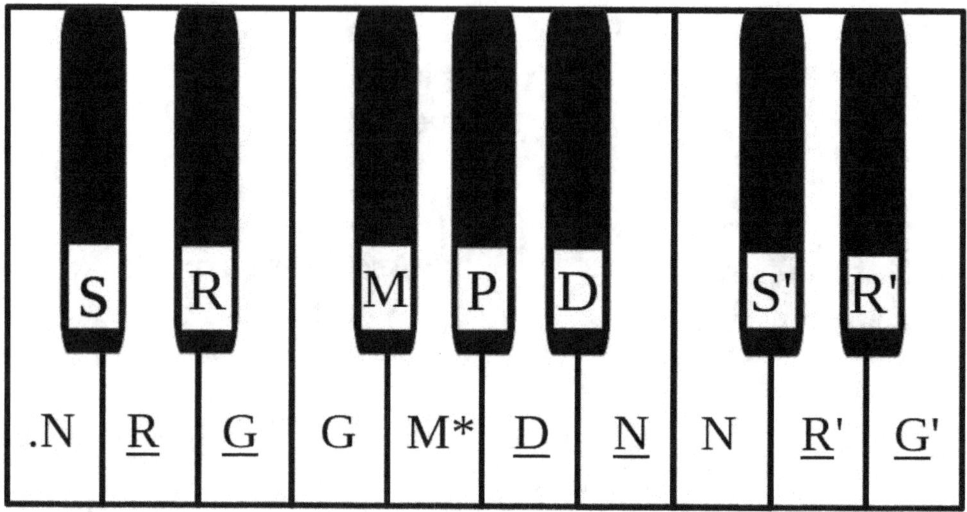

1. AGAR TUM MIL JAO

Film: Zahar (2005)	Music: Annu Malik, Rup Kumar Rathaur
Lyrics: Saeed qadri, shakeel aazmi	Singer: Udit Narayan
Taal: Kaharwa	Chord: SGP RGD S=D

agar tum mil jao, zamaana chhod denge ham -4
tumhen pa kar zamaane bhar se rishta tod denge ham

bina tere koee dilakash nazaara ham na dekhenge
tumhen na ho pasand usako dobaara ham na dekhenge
teree soorat na ho jisamen, hoon -3, vo sheesha tod denge ham

tere dil mein rahenge, tujhako apana ghar bana lenge
tere khvaabon ko gahanon kee tarah khud par saja lenge
qasam teree qasam, hoon -3, taqadeer ka rookh mod denge ham

tumhen ham apane jism-o-jaan mein kuchh aise basa lenge
teree khushaboo apane jism kee khushaboo bana lenge
khuda se bhee na jo toote, hoon -3, vo rishta jod lenge ham

AGAR TUM MIL JAO

dha	ge	n	ti	n	ke	dhi	n	dha	ge	n	ti	n	ke	dhi	n
1	2	3	4	5	6	7	8	1	2	3	4	5	6	7	8

prelude:
DN DN DN DN DN DN DN DM- MPDP-
PD PD PD PD PD PD NDPM GMPM-
S'D P G-S'D G R-
RRG RG SRG- RGP–GRR–
RRG RG SMG- RG PPP GGGR-

RRG RG S RG- RRG PP GG R
agar tum mil jao zamana chhod denge hm

music: S' S' S' – N – P D – P D – P –

dha 1	ge 2	n 3	ti 4	n 5	ke 6	dhi 7	n 8	dha 1	ge 2	n 3	ti 4	n 5	ke 6	dhi 7	n 8
											R	R	G	R	G
											a	g	r	tu	m
S	-	R	-	G	-	-	-	-	-	-	R	R	-	G	-
mi	l	ja	-	o	-	-	-	-	-	-	z	ma	-	na	-
P	-	-	P	G	-	G	-	R	-	-	M	G	G	R	G
chho	-	-	d	den	-	ge	-	hm	-	-	a	g	r	tu	m
S	-	M	-	G	-	-	-	-	-	-	R	R	-	G	-
mi	l	ja	-	o	-	-	-	-	-	-	z	ma	-	na	-
P	-	-	P	G	-	G	-	R	-	-	P	P	-	P	-
chho	-	-	d	den	-	ge	-	hm	-	-	tu	mhe	-	pa	-
D	-	-	D	D	-	D	S'	S'	-	S'	-	D	-	P	-
kr	-	-	z	ma	-	ne	-	bh	r	se	-	ri	sh	ta	-
D	-	-	P	G	-	R	-	G	-	-					
to	-	-	d	den	-	ge	-	hm	-	-					

interlude: P D S'N DPD- G- P- P D S'N DPD- G- P-
D R' - R'G'R' S'NR' S'- G P N S'D M G   G M P M P S' N D –
DS'DPG -3

dha 1	ge 2	n 3	ti 4	n 5	ke 6	dhi 7	n 8	dha 1	ge 2	n 3	ti 4	n 5	ke 6	dhi 7	n 8
											S'	S'	-	S'	-
											bi	na	-	te	-
S'	D	-	D	D	-	D	-	DG	-	-	G	R	-	G	-
re	-	-	ko	ee	-	di	l	ksh	-	-	n	za	-	ra	-
P	-	-	P	G	-	G	-	R	-	-					
hm	-	-	n	de	-	khen	-	ge	-	-					

music: G M G R S M G- G- M G R
S—R G P S'D-

Vinod Kumar

												S'	S'	-	S'	-
												tu	mhe	-	na	-
S'	D	-	D	D	D	D	D	D	G	-	G	R	-	G	-
ho	-	-	p	sn	d	u	s	ko	-	-	do	ba	-	ra	
P	-	-	P	G	-	G	-	R	-	-	R	R	-	R	-
hm	-	-	n	de	-	khen	-	ge	-	-	te	ri	-	su	-
S	S	R	-	G	-	G	G	G	-	-	-	-	-	-	-
r	t	na	-	ho	-	ji	s	me	-	-	-	-	-	-	-
D	-	-	-	G	-	-	-	R	-	-	R	R	-	R	-
hu	-	-	-	-	-	-	-	-	-	-	te	ri	-	su	-
S	S	R	-	G	-	G	G	G	-	-	R	R	-	G	-
r	t	na	-	ho	-	ji	s	me	-	-	vo	shi	-	sha	-
P	-	-	P	G	-	G	-	R	-	-	R	R	-	R	G
to	-	-	d	den	-	ge	-	hm	-	-	a	g	r	tu	m
S	-	R	-	G	-	-	-	-	-	-	G	R	-	G	-
mi	l	ja	-	o	-	-	-	-	-	-	z	ma	-	na	-
P	D	-	P	G	-	G	-	R	-	-					
chho	-	-	d	den	-	ge	-	hm	-	-					

interlude: MG MG MG MG   MG MG MG MG M-
      aa...
      PD- D- N D P D – S'-
flute: G P D-P D-P D-P D-P
    D P D S' --- D P G R S G --- G P---

RRG RG SRG- RRG P –P G G R –
RRG RG SMG- RRG P –P G G R –

											S'	S'	-	S'	-
											te	re	-	di	l
S'	D	-	D	D	-	D	-	D	G	P	G	R	G	-	
me	-	-	r	hen	-	ge	-	tu	jh	ko	-	a	p	na	-
P	-	-	P	G	-	G	-	R	-	-					
ghr	-	-	b	na	-	len	-	ge	-	-					

music: G M G R S M G- G- M G R
      S—R G P S' D -

								S'	S'	-	S'	-
								te	re	-	kha	-

S'	D	D	-	D	P	D	-	D	G	-	G	G	R	G	G
bo	-	ko	-	g	h	no	-	ki	-	-	t	r	h	khu	d

P	-	-	P	G	-	G	-	R	-	-	R	R	-	R	G
par	-	-	s	ja	-	len	-	ge	-	-	q	sm	-	te	-

S	-	-	R	G	-	-	-	-	-	-	-	-	-	-	-
ri	-	-	q	sm	-	-	-	-	-	-	-	-	-	-	-

D	-	-	-	G	-	-	-	R	-	-	R	R	-	R	G
hu	-	-	-	hu	-	-	-	hu	-	-	q	sm	-	te	-

S	-	-	R	G	-	G	G	G	-	-	G	R	-	G	G
ri	-	-	q	sm	-	t	q	di	-	-	r	ka	-	ru	kh

P	-	-	P	G	-	G	-	R	-	-	M	G	-	R	-
mo	-	-	d	den	-	ge	-	hm	-	-	a	g	r	tu	m

S	-	M	-	G	-	-	-	-	-	-	G	R	-	G	-
mi	l	ja	-	o	-	-	-	-	-	-	z	ma	-	na	-

P	-	-	P	G	-	G	-	R	-	-
chho	-	-	d	den	-	ge	-	hm	-	-

interlude: DN DN DN DN DN DN DN DM- MPDP-
PD PD PD PD PD PD NDPM GMPM-
S' D P G - S' D G R-
R R G R G S R G – R R G P – G R R –
R R G R G S M G - R G P P P G G G R –

music: R G P P P D D S' D-

											S'	S'	-	S'	S'
											tu	mhe	-	h	m

D	D	D	-	D	P	D	-	G	-	G	-	R	R	G	-
a	p	ne	-	ji	s	mo	-	jan	-	me	-	ku	chh	ae	-

P	-	-	P	G	-	G	-	R	-	-
se	-	-	b	sa	-	len	-	ge	-	-

music: G M G R S M G- G- M G R
    S—R G P S' D –

											S'	S'	-	S'	S'
											te	ri	-	khu	sh

S'	D	-	-	D	P	D	-	D	-	-	G	G	-	R	G
bu	-	-	-	a	p	ne	-	ji	-	-	sm	ki	-	khu	sh

P	-	-	P	G	-	G	-	R	-	-	R	R	-	R	G
bu	-	-	b	na	-	len	-	ge	-	-	khu	da	-	se	-

S	-	R	-	G	-	G	-	G	-	-	-	-	-	-	-
bhi	-	na	-	jo	-	tu	-	te	-	-	-	-	-	-	-
D	-	-	-	G	-	-	-	R	-	-	R	R	-	R	G
hu	-	-	-	hu	-	-	-	hu	-	-	khu	da	-	se	-
S	-	R	-	G	-	G	-	G	-	-	G	R	-	G	-
bhi	-	na	-	jo	-	tu	-	te	-	-	vo	ri	sh	ta	-
P	-	-	P	G	-	G	-	R	-	-	M	G	-	R	G
jo	-	-	d	len	-	ge	-	hm	-	-	a	g	r	tu	m
S	-	M	-	G	-	-	-	-	-	-	R	R	-	G	-
mi	l	ja	-	o	-	-	-	-	-	-	z	ma	-	na	-
P	-	-	P	G	-	G	-	R	-	-	P	P	-	P	-
chho	-	-	d	den	-	ge	-	hm	-	-	tu	mhe	-	pa	-
D	-	-	D	D	-	D	S'	S'	-	S'	-	D	-	P	-
kr	-	-	z	ma	-	ne	-	bh	r	se	-	ri	sh	ta	-
D	-	-	P	G	-	R	-	G	-	-	M	G	G	R	G
to	-	-	d	den	-	ge	-	hm	-	-	a	g	r	tu	m
S	-	M	-	G	-	-	-	-	-	-	R	R	-	G	-
mi	l	ja	-	o	-	-	-	-	-	-	z	ma	-	na	-
P	-	D	P	G	-	G	-	R	-	-					
chho	-	-	d	den	-	ge	-	hm	-	-					

2. AAYE HO MERI ZINDAGI ME

Film: Raja Hindustani (1996)	Music: Nadeem Shrawan
Lyrics: Sameer	Singer: Udit Narayan,
Taal: Daadra	Chord: <u>G</u>P<u>N</u> P<u>N</u>R' S=C#

aae ho meree zindagee mein tum bahaar ban ke
mere dil mein yoon hee rahana tum pyaar pyaar ban ke
aankhon mein tum base ho sapane hazaar ban ke
mere dil mein yoon hee rahana haay tum pyaar pyaar ban ke,
aae ho meree..

udit naaraayan:
ghoonghat mein har kalee thee, rangon mein na dhalee thee
na shokh thee havaen, na khushaboo manachalee thee
aaya hai ab ke mausam kaisa khumaar ban ke
mere dil mein...

man ka nagar tha khaalee, sookhee padee thee daalee
holee ke rang pheeke, benoor thee divaalee
rimajhim baras pade ho tum to phuhaar ban ke
mere dil mein...

alaka yaagnik:
mere saathee mere saajan, mere saath yoon hee chalana
badalega rang zamaana par tum nahin badalana
meree maang yoon hee bharana taare hazaar ban ke
mere dil mein...

gar main jo rooth jaoon, to tum mujhe manaana
thaama hai haath mera, phir umar bhar nibhaana
mujhe chhod ke na jaana vaade hazaar karke
mere dil mein...

Vinod Kumar

AAYE HO MERI ZINDAGI ME

dha 1	dhi 2	na 3	dha 4	tun 5	na 6	dha 1	dhi 2	na 3	dha 4	tun 5	na 6

D----- N P   R' S' G' R' N D P M
hu --------   hu-----------------

D P M G
Ho………

prelude:
P M G- P M G N D P N D P P M G P M G
P N G'R'-S' N D P M P G-P-M G---

										G aa	- -

| G ye | - - | P ho | M me | P - | M ri | G zin | - - | R d | S gi | - - | R me |
| G tum | - - | P b | M ha | P - | M r | R b | R n | G ke | - | | |

music: N-D-P-M- MPM- GRG-

										N me	N re

N dil	- -	R' me	S' yun	R' -	S' hi	D r	- h	N na	- -	- -	- -
P ha	D ye	- -	P -	- -	- -	- -	- -	- -	- -	N me	N re
N di	- l	R' me	S' yun	R' -	S' hi	D r	D h	P na	- -	P tu	- m
M pya	- -	M r	D pya	- -	D r	P b	P n	M ke	- -	G aa	- -
G ye	- -	P ho	M me	P -	M ri	G zin	- -	R d	S gi	- -	R me
G tum	- -	P b	M ha	P -	M r	R b	- n	G ke	-		

music: N-D-P-M- MPM- GRG-

										G aan	- -

| G kho | - - | P me | M tum | P - | M b | G se | - - | R ho | S - | R s | R p |

<u>G</u>	-	P	M	P	M	R	-	<u>G</u>	-	<u>N</u>	<u>N</u>
ne	-	h	za	-	r	b	n	ke	-	me	re
<u>N</u>	-	R'	S'	R'	S'	D	D	P	-	P	-
dil	-	me	yun	-	hi	r	h	na	-	tu	m
M	-	M	D	-	D	P	P	M	-	<u>G</u>	-
pya	-	r	pya	-	r	b	n	ke	-	aa	-
<u>G</u>	-	P	M	P	M	<u>G</u>	-	R	S	-	R
ye	-	ho	me	-	ri	zin	-	d	gi	-	me
<u>G</u>	-	P	M	P	M	R	-	<u>G</u>	-		
tum	-	b	ha	-	r	b	n	ke	-		

interlude:
shahnaayi: <u>G</u>'--- R' S' S'R'—S' <u>N</u> D –S' <u>N</u>-D P-
       S'—<u>N</u> D <u>N</u>—D P M –D P-M P—
synthe: <u>G</u>DP <u>G</u>DP M<u>G</u>S P- M- <u>G</u>-
sitar: <u>G</u>' R' S'R' S'<u>N</u> R'S'<u>N</u> <u>N</u>S' <u>N</u> D
      S' <u>N</u>D D <u>N</u> D P   P D P M
      MPDPM <u>G</u>P<u>G</u>---

										R'	-
										ghun	-
R'	R'	R'	R'	S'	R'	<u>G</u>'	-	<u>G</u>'	-	P	-
gh	t	me	h	r	k	li	-	bhi	-	rn	-
P	-	<u>D</u>	<u>N</u>	-	P	P	M	M	<u>G</u>	-	-
go	-	me	n	-	dh	li	-	thi	-	-	-

music: R' R'S' <u>N</u>D<u>N</u> <u>N</u>P   P D <u>N</u> R' S' D<u>N</u> <u>N</u>-

										R'	-
										na	-
R'	-	R'	R'	S'	R'	R'	<u>G</u>'	<u>G</u>'	-	P	-
sho	-	kh	thi	-	h	va	-	yen	-	na	-
P	P	<u>D</u>	<u>N</u>	-	P	P	M	M	<u>G</u>	-	-
khu	sh	bu	m	n	ch	li	-	thi	-	-	-

music: P <u>N</u> D <u>N</u> P M P M <u>G</u> --

										<u>G</u>	-
										aa	-
<u>G</u>	-	P	M	P	M	<u>G</u>	-	R	S	R	
ya	-	hai	a	b	ke	mau	-	s	m	kai	-
<u>G</u>	-	P	M	P	M	R	-	<u>G</u>	-	<u>N</u>	<u>N</u>
sa	-	khu	ma	-	r	b	n	ke	-	me	re

Vinod Kumar

N	-	R'	S'	R'	S'	D	D	N	-	-	-
di	l	me	yun	-	hi	r	h	na	-	-	-

P	D	-	P	-
ha	ye	-	e	-

interlude:
piano: P PMG P PMG P PMG P PMG G M M P PMG
       N DP D N S' N S' N -- N R' S' N D N ---
       P PMG P PMG P PMG P PMG G M M P PMG
violin: P – M P M G R –S- GMP --- M P M G R—S—
       S G M—N D N P P-M-R G---

										N	R'
										m	n
R'	-	R'	R'	S'	R'	R'	G'	G'	-	P	-
ka	-	n	g	r	tha	kha	-	li	-	su	-
P	-	D	N	-	P	P	M	M	G	R'	-
khi	-	p	di	-	thi	da	-	li	-	ho	-
R'	-	R'	S'	-	R'	G'	-	G'	-	P	-
li	-	ke	rn	-	g	fii	-	ke	-	be	-
P	-	D	N	-	P	P	M	M	G	G	G
nu	-	r	thi	-	di	va	-	li	-	ri	m
G	-	P	M	P	M	G	-	R	S	R	R
jhi	m	b	r	s	p	de	-	ho	-	tu	m
G	-	P	M	P	M	R	-	G	-	N	N
to	-	fu	ha	-	r	b	n	ke	-	me	re
N	-	R'	S'	R'	S'	D	D	N	-	-	-
dil	-	me	yun	-	hi	r	h	na	-	-	-
P	D	-	P	-	-	-	-	-	-	N	N
ha	ye	-	e	-	-	-	-	-	-	me	re
N	-	R'	S'	R'	S'	D	D	P	-	P	-
dil	-	me	yun	-	hi	r	h	na	-	tu	m
M	-	M	D	-	D	P	-	M	-	G	-
pya	-	r	pya	-	r	b	n	ke	-	aa	-
G	-	P	M	P	M	G	-	R	S	-	R
ye	-	ho	me	-	ri	zin	-	d	gi	-	me

G	-	P	M	P	M	R	-	G	-
tum	-	b	ha	-	r	b	n	ke	-

3. AE AJNABI

Film: Dil Se (1998)	Music: A. R. Rahman
Lyrics: Gulzar	Singer: Udit Narayan, Mahalaxmi Ayyar
Taal: Kaharwa	Chord: GPN S=C

o paakhee paakhee paradesee paakhee paakhee paradesee -5

ai ajanabee too bhee kabhee aavaaz de kaheen se
main yahaan tukadon mein jee raha hoon
too kaheen tukadon mein jee rahee hai, ai ajanabee...

roz-roz resham see hava aate-jaate kahatee hai bata
resham see hava kahatee hai bata
vo jo doodh dhulee maasoom kalee
vo hai kahaan, kahaan hai
vo raushanee kahaan hai
vo jaan see kahaan hai
main adhoora too adhooree jee rahe hain
ai ajanabee...

too to nahin hai lekin teree muskuraahaten hain
chehara kaheen nahin hai, par teree aahaten hain
too hai kahaan, kahaan hai
tera nishaan kahaan hai, mera jahaan kahaan hai
main adhoora too adhooree jee rahe hain
ai ajanabee...

Vinod Kumar

AE AJNABI

dha	ge	n	ti	n	ke	dhi	n	dha	ge	n	ti	n	ke	dhi	n
1	2	3	4	5	6	7	8	1	2	3	4	5	6	7	8

```
N   NR'   R'R'   NR'DM*D
o   pakhi pakhi  pardesi

NR'   R'R'   NR'NDM*-D
pakhi pakhi  pardesi

DN   G'G'   G'G'G'-G'
pakhi pakhi pardesi

G'G'M*'R'   R'N   NNNS'
pa--khi     pakhi pardesi

NN   NN   NNDS'NDNDP
pakhi pakhi pardesi

GG   GG   M*D-DM*PM*G
pakhi pakhi pardesi
```

dha	ge	n	ti	n	ke	dhi	n	dha	ge	n	ti	n	ke	dhi	n
G	-	P	P	G	P	-	-	G	-	P	-	G	P	-	-
ae	-	a	j	n	bi	-	-	tu	-	bhi	-	k	bhi	-	-
G	-	D	-	P	G	-	G	G	-	G	-	-	-	-	-
aa	-	va	-	j	de	-	k	hin	-	se	-	-	-	-	-
N	N	D	-	-	N	N	D	-	D	G'	G'	G'	-	G'	-
main	y	han	-	-	tu	k	do	-	me	jii	r	ha	-	hu	-
N	N	D	-	-	N	N	D	-	D	G'	G'	G'	-	G'	N
main	y	han	-	-	tu	k	do	-	me	jii	r	ha	-	hu	tu
M*'	-	G'	-	-	-	N	N	G'	-	R'	-	-	-	N	D
k	-	hin	-	-	-	tu	k	do	-	me	-	-	-	jii	r
R'	-	-	G'	R'	-	N	D	P	-	-	-	-	-	-	-
hi	-	-	hai	-	-	-	-	-	-	-	-	-	-	-	-

interlude:
```
D P D G' G' G'-- M*' G' R'  R' R' R'-
R' G' G' R'- N D P—
P D N D  D N M*' G' G' –
N N N R' R' R' G' G'   N N N R' R' R' G' G'   N N N R' R' R' G' G'
```

dha	ge	n	ti	n	ke	dhi	n	dha	ge	n	ti	n	ke	dhi	n
N	-	S'	N	-	S'	N	-	N	-	N	D	P	-	-	-
ro	-	z	ro	-	z	re	-	shm	-	si	h	va	-	-	-
N	-	S'	N	-	S'	N	S'	N	-	N	S'	N	-	N	S'
aa	-	te	ja	-	te	k	h	ti	-	hai	b	ta	-	re	-

N	-	N	S'	N	-	N	S'	S'	-	N	D	P	-	-	-
shm	-	si	h	va	-	k	h	ti	-	hai	b	ta	-	-	-
N	-	R'	R'	-	R'	N	N	N	-	R'	R'	-	R'	N	N
vo	-	jo	du	-	dh	dhu	li	ma	-	su	-	-	m	k	li
N	-	G'	-	N	G'	-	N	M*'	-	-	-	G'	G'	-	-
vo	-	hai	-	k	han	-	k	han	-	-	-	hai	-	-	-
N	-	G'	-	N	P'	-	M*'	G'	-	-	-	G'	-	-	-
vo	-	rau	-	sh	ni	-	k	han	-	-	-	hai	-	-	-
N	-	G'	-	N	P'	-	M*'	G'	-	-	-	G'	-	-	-
vo	-	ja	-	n	si	-	k	han	-	-	-	hai	-	-	-
N	-	G'	G'	-	G'	-	-	N	-	R'	R'	-	R'	-	-
main	-	a	dhu	-	ra	-	-	tu	-	a	dhu	-	ri	-	-
R'	-	-	-	-	R'	G'	-	N	D	P	D	P	-	-	-
jii	-	-	-	-	r	hi	-	hai	-	-	-	-	-	-	-
G	-	P	P	G	P	-	-								
ae	-	a	j	n	bi	-									

interlude:

DN	G'G'	G'G'G'-G'
pakhi	pakhi	pardesi

G'G'M*'R'	R'N	NNNS'
pa--khi	pakhi	pardesi

NN	NN	NNDS'NDNDP
pakhi	pakhi	parde--------si-

.NG	GM*	M*D-DM*PM*G
pakhi	pakhi	pardesi

D	-	N	-	-	D	N	-	-	D	N	-	G'	R'	N	D
tu	-	to	-	-	n	hin	-	-	hai	le	-	kin	-	-	-
D	-	N	-	-	D	-	N	G'	-	G'	G'	G'	G'	R'	N
te	-	ri	-	-	mu	-	sku	ra	-	h	te	hain	-	-	-
D	D	N	-	-	D	N	-	-	D	N	-	G'	R'	N	D
che	h	ra	-	-	k	hin	-	-	n	hin	-	hai	-	p	r
D	-	N	-	-	D	-	N	M*'	-	-	-	G'	G'	-	-
te	-	ri	-	-	aa	-	h	te	-	-	-	hain	-	-	-

N	-	G'	-	N	G'	-	N	M*'	-	-	-	G'	-	-	-
tu	-	hai	-	k	han	-	k	han	-	-	-	hai	-	-	-
N	-	G'	-	N	P'	-	M*'	G'	-	-	-	G'	-	-	-
te	-	ra	-	ni	shan	-	k	han	-	-	-	hai	-	-	-
N	-	G'	-	N	P'	-	M*'	G'	-	-	-	G'	-	-	-
me	-	ra	-	j	han	-	k	han	-	-	-	hai	-	-	-
N	-	G'	G'	-	G'	-	-	N	-	R'	R'	-	R'	-	-
main	-	a	dhu	-	ra	-	-	tu	-	a	dhu	-	ri	-	-
R'	-	-	-	-	R'	G'	-	N	D	P	D	P	-	-	-
jii	-	-	-	-	r	hi	-	hai	-	-	-	-	-	-	-
G	-	P	P	G	P	-	-								
ae	-	a	j	n	bi	-									

4. AE MERE HAMSAFAR

Film: Qayamat se Qayamat tak (1988) Lyrics: Majrooh Sultanpuri Taal: Kaharwa	Music: Anand Milind Singer: Udit Narayan, Alka Yagnik Chord: PNR' S=C

ai mere hamasafar, ek zara intazaar
sun sadaen de raheen hai, manzil pyaar kee

ab hai judaee ka mausam, do pal ka mehamaan
kaise na jaega andhera, kyo na thamega toofaan
kaise na milegee, manzil pyaar kee

pyaar ne jahaan pe rakha hai, jhoom ke kadam ek baar
vaheen se khula hai koee rasta, vaheen se giree hai deevaar
roke kab rukee hai, manzil pyaar kee

AE MERE HAMSAFAR

dha	ge	n	ti	n	ke	dhi	n	dha	ge	n	ti	n	ke	dhi	n
1	2	3	4	5	6	7	8	1	2	3	4	5	6	7	8

prelude:
S'R' R'-S'- S'R' R'-S'-
MPMDM S'-D- MP-
D-P D-P D-P D- N-
guitar: R'--- P- D N S' R' G' S' N DP D N M
      S' MM PD M- D D N D P—
      P D N S' R' (PNR')

N	-	D	P	-	-	-	-	N	-	D	P	-	-	-	-
ae	-	me	re	-	-	-	-	hm	-	s	fr	-	-	-	-
N	N	N	R'	-	S'	-	N	DP	DP	M	-	-	-	-	-
i	k	z	ra	-	in	-	t	za	-	-	-r	-	-	-	-
-	M	-	M	D	-	P	M	-	M	-	M	D	-	P	M
-	sun	-	s	da	-	yen	-	-	de	-	r	hin	-	hain	-
R	-	N	-	-	D	-	P	P	-	-	-	-	-	-	-
mn	-	zil	-	-	pya	-	r	ki	-	-	-	-	-	-	-

interlude:
bigul: R'S'R' S' R' M' R' S' N S' D N S'-D-
banjo: P-D N- D- M- M-P D — PM P- -2
synthe: R' M' P' M' R' S' R' M' R' S'
      D-P — D —P-D-P-

P	P	P	R'	S'	N	D	N	S'	-	S'	D	-	-	-	-
a	b	hai	ju	da	-	ee	ka	mau	-	sm	-	-	-	-	-
M	-	M	S'	N	D	P	D	N	-	-	-	-	-	-	-
do	-	p	l	ka	-	me	h	ma	-	-	-	-	-	-	n
P	-	P	R'	S'	N	D	N	S'	-	S'	D	-	-	-	-
kai	-	se	n	ja	ye	ga	an	dhe	-	ra	-	-	-	-	-
M	-	M	S'	N	D	P	D	N	-	-	-	-	-	-	-
kyu	-	n	th	me	ga	tu	-	fa	-	-	-	-	-	-	n

dohrane hetu music: R' D'P'D' P' M' S' D' P' M' R'--

N	-	N	-	-	-	R'	N	S'	-	-	-	D	P	M	-
kai	-	se	-	-	-	n	mi	le	-	-	-	gi	-	-	-
R	-	N	-	-	D	-	P	P	-	-	-	-	-	-	-
mn	-	zil	-	-	pya	-	r	ki	-	-	-	-	-	-	-
N	-	D	P	-	-										
ae	-	me	re	-	-										

Vinod Kumar

interlude: D-P- D-P- R'-P-   D-P- D-P- R'-P-
          P P' D' P' D' P'- M'-   S' M' P' M' R' S'- S' R' <u>G</u>' D
          D R' S' D - D <u>N</u> D P D - M <u>N</u> D P –

P	P	P	R'	S'	<u>N</u>	D	<u>N</u>	S'	-	S'	D	-	-	-	-
pya	-r	ne	j	han	pe	r	-	kha	-	hai	-	-	-	-	-
M	-	M	S'	<u>N</u>	D	P	D	<u>N</u>	-	-	-	-	-	-	-
jhu	-m	ke	q	d	m	i	k	ba	-	-	-	-	-	-	r
P	P	P	R'	S'	<u>N</u>	D	<u>N</u>	S'	S'	S'	D	-	-	-	-
v	hin	se	khu	la	hai	ko	ee	r	s	ta	-	-	-	-	-
M	M	M	S'	<u>N</u>	D	P	D	<u>N</u>	-	-	-	-	-	-	-
v	hin	se	gi	ri	hai	di	-	va	-	-	-	-	-	-	r

dohrane hetu music: R' D'P'D' P' M' S' D' P' M' R'--

N	-	N	-	-	R'	R'	N	S'	-	-	-	D	P	M	-
ro	-	ke	-	-	k	b	ru	ki	-	-	-	hai	-	-	-
R	-	<u>N</u>	-	-	D	-	P	P	-	-	-	-	-	-	-
mn	-	zil	-	-	pya	-	r	ki	-	-	-	-	-	-	-
<u>N</u>	-	D	P	-	-	-	-	<u>N</u>	-	D	P	-	-	-	-
ae	-	me	re	-	-	-	-	hm	-	s	fr	-	-	-	-
<u>N</u>	<u>N</u>	<u>N</u>	R'	-	S'	-	<u>N</u>	DP	DP	M	-	-	-	-	-
i	k	z	ra	-	in	-	t	za	-	-	-r	-	-	-	-
-	M	-	M	D	-	P	M	-	M	-	M	D	-	P	M
-	sun	-	s	da	-	yen	-	-	de	-	r	hin	-	hain	-
R	-	<u>N</u>	-	-	D	-	P	P	-	-	-	-	-	-	-
mn	-	zil	-	-	pya	-	r	ki	-	-	-	-	-	-	-

5. AESA ZAKHM DIYA HAI

Film: Akele Ham Akele Tum (1995) Lyrics: Majrooh Sultanpuri Taal: Kaharwa	Music: Annu Malik Singer: Udit Narayan Chord: DS'G' S=C

aaya hoon yaaron dil apana deke,
aankhon mein chehara kisee ka leke
vo dil ka qaatil dilabar hamaara,
jisake lie main hua aavaara
milate hee jisane chooma tha mujhako,
phir na palat ke dekha dubaara

aisa jakhm diya hai jo na phir bharega
har haseen chehare se ab yah dil darega
ham to jaan dekar yoon hee mar mite the
sun lo ai haseenon ye hamase ab na hoga

raseele honth chhalakate gaal
mastaanee chaal bura kar de haal
palak bhadake ke dil dhadake
umr kee uthaan kadakatee kamaan
qaatil ada zaalim haya mere khuda mere khuda
shola badan bahaka chaman magar yaaron
ham to jaan dekar yoon hee mar mite the
sun lo ai haseenon ye hamase ab na hoga
aisa jakhm diya hai

raseele honth chhalakate gaal
mastaanee chaal bura kar de haal
palak bhadake hai ke dil dhadake
umr kee uthaan kadakatee kamaan
qaatil ada zaalim haya mere khuda o mere khuda
too jo kahe to taaron mein tujhe lekar chaloon
too jo kahe to qadamon mein unhen la daal doon
seene se lagaake yah badan kar doon gulaabee
chehara choom karake main bana doon aafataabee
he he la la la la la ham to jaan dekar
tumape mar mite hain kaun pyaar tumase itana karega
aisa jakhm diya hai jo na phir bharega
har haseen chehare se ab yah yah dil darega
aisa jakhm diya hai

Vinod Kumar

aaya hoon yaaron dil apana leke
aankhon mein chehara kisee ka leke
koee na koee mera bhee hoga
yaheen pe kaheen chhupa hee hoga.

AESA ZAKHM DIYA HAI

dha	ge	n	ti	n	ke	dhi	n	dha	ge	n	ti	n	ke	dhi	n
1	2	3	4	5	6	7	8	1	2	3	4	5	6	7	8
P---MG		M* --- GM*GR													
aa-----		aa----------													
R' D'—P' D' P' – R' G' R'—N P R G-															
aa--------------------------															
											S'	-	N	-	D
											aa	-	ya	-	hu
N	-	S'	-	-	-	-	-	-	-	-	S'	-	N	N	D
ya	-	ro	-	-	-	-	-	-	-	-	di	l	a	p	na
N	-	-	D	-	-	-	-	-	-	-	N	-	D	-	P
de	-	-	ke	-	-	-	-	-	-	-	aan	-	kho	-	me
D	-	N	-	-	-	-	-	-	-	-	N	N	-	P	-
che	h	ra	-	-	-	-	-	-	-	-	ki	si	-	ka	-
D	-	-	G	-	-	-	-	-	-	-	S'	-	N	-	D
le	-	-	ke	-	-	-	-	-	-	-	vo	-	di	l	ka
N	-	S'	-	-	-	-	-	-	-	-	S'	-	N	-	D
qa	-	ti	l	-	-	-	-	-	-	-	di	l	b	r	h
N	-	D	-	-	-	-	-	-	-	-	N	-	D	-	P
ma	-	ra	-	-	-	-	-	-	-	-	ji	s	ke	-	li
D	-	N	-	-	-	-	-	-	-	-	N	N	-	P	-
ye	-	main	-	-	-	-	-	-	-	-	hu	aa	-	aa	-
D	-	-	G	-	-	-	-	-	-	-	G'	-	R'	-	S'
va	-	-	ra	-	-	-	-	-	-	-	mi	l	te	-	hi
R'	-	G'	-	-	-	-	-	-	-	-	G'	-	R'	-	S'
ji	s	ne	-	-	-	-	-	-	-	-	chu	-	ma	-	tha

dhage 12	nti 34	nke 56	dhin 78	dhage 12	nti 34	nke 56	dhin 78	dhage 12	nti 34	nke 56	dhin 78	dhage 12	nti 34	nke 56	dhin 78
R'	-	S'	-	-	-	-	-	-	-	-	R'	-	N	-	D
mu	jh	ko	-	-	-	-	-	-	-	-	fi	r	na	-	p
N	-	P	-	-	-	-	-	-	-	-	S'	-	N	-	D
I	t	ke	-	-	-	-	-	-	-	-	de	-	kha	-	do
N	-	S'	-	-	-	-	-	-	-	-	-	-	-	-	-
ba	-	ra	-	-	-	-	-	-	-	-	-	-	-	-	-

o-- S' N D -2 N D P

dhage 12	nti 34	nke 56	dhin 78	dhage 12	nti 34	nke 56	dhin 78	dhage 12	nti 34	nke 56	dhin 78	dhage 12	nti 34	nke 56	dhin 78
S'	S'	ND	-N	S'	S'	-	-	S'	S'	-P	-G	R	R	-	-
ae	sa	zkh	mdi	ya	hai	-	-	jo	na	-fi	r,bh	re	ga	-	-
N	-D	P	-D	NS'	N	P	-	R	R	P	-R	G	G	-	-
hr	-h	si	-n	cheh	re	se	-	ab	ye	dil	-d	re	ga	-	-
G'	G'	-R'	-S'	R'	G'	-	-	G'	G'	-R'	S'	D	P	-	-
hm	to	-ja	-n	de	kr	-	-	yun	hi	-mr	mi	te	the	-	-
P	P	NS'	ND	P	P	-	P	P	P	-D	DN	D	P	M	G
sun	lo	ae-	-h	si	no	-	ye	hm	se	-a	b,n	ho	ga	-	-
S'	S'	ND	-N	S'R'	S'	-	-								
ae	sa	zkh	mdi	ya-	hai	-	-								
												-	-D	D	D^N
												-	-r	si	le-
^PD	-P	-	-	-	-D	D	N	D	-P	-	-	-	N	N	N
hon-	-th	-	-	-	-chh	lk	te	ga	-l	-	-	-	ms	ta	ni
D^N	-P	-	-	-	NS'	-R'	N	S'	-	-	N	D	-D	D	D
cha-	-l	-	-	-	bura	-kr	de	ha	-	-	-	-l	-p	lk	fd
D	-	-	-	-	-D	D	N	D	-	P	-	-	-N	NN	NN
ke	-	-	-	-	-ke	dil	dhd	ke	-	-	-	-	-u	mr	ki,u
DN	-P	-	-	-	S'	S'	R'S'	N	S'	-	N	D	G	M	P
tha-	-n	-	-	-	k	dk	ti,k	ma	-	-	-	n	qa	til	a
G	-	R	-	-	R	P	R	G	-	-	-	-	-G	-M	-P
da	-	-	-	-	za	lim	h	ya	-	-	-	-	-me	-re	-khu
G	-	R	-	-	-R	-P	-R	G	-	-	-	-	-G	-D	-D
da	-	-	-	-	-me	-re	-khu	da	-	-	-	-	-sho	-la	-b
N	-G	-D	-D	N	-D	D	S'	R'	-	-	-	-	G'	-	-
dn	-bh	-ka	-ch	mn	-m	gr	ya	ro	-	-	-	-	o	-	-

1	2	3	4	5	6	7	8	1	2	3	4	5	6	7	8
G'	G'	-R'	-S'	R'	G'	-	-	G'	G'	-R'	S'	D	P	-	-
hm	to	-ja	-n	de	kr	-	-	yun	hi	-mr	mi	te	the	-	-
P	P	NS'	ND	P	P	-	P	P	P	-D	DN	D	P	M	G
sun	lo	ae-	-h	si	no	-	ye	hm	se	-a	b,n	ho	ga	-	-
S'	S'	ND	-N	S'R'	S'	-	-								
ae	sa	zkh	mdi	ya-	hai	-	-								
	G	-D	-S'	N	NN	-N	-N	D	DD	-D	-N	D	-	-	-
	tu	-jo	-k	he	tota	-ro	-me	tujh	kole	-ke	-ch	lun	-	-	-
-	G	-D	-S'	N	NN	N	-N	DD	-D	-D	-P	M	-	-	-
-	tu	-jo	-k	he	toq	dmo	-me	unhe	-la	-da	-l	dun	-	-	-
S'	-D	-D	-S'	N	-P	-P	-N	D	-P	-M	-G	M	R	-	-
si	-ne	-se	-l	ga	-ke	-ye	-b	dan	-k	r,dun	-gu	la	bi	-	-
N	D	-P	-N	D	-P	-M	-D	P	P	-P	-M	G	G	-	-
cheh	ra	-chu	-m	kr	-ke	-main	-b	na	dun	-aa	-f	ta	bi	-	-

G'	R'
ae	he

R'	P'	R'	G'	R'
la	la	la	la	la

1	2	3	4	5	6	7	8	1	2	3	4	5	6	7	8
G'	G'	-R'	-S'	R'	G'	-	-	G'	G'	-R'	S'	D	P	-	-
hm	to	-ja	-n	de	kr	-	-	tum	pe	-mr	mi	te	hain	-	-
P	-D	N-	-D	P	P	-	-	P	P	-D	N	PD	P	M	G
kau	-n	pya-	-r	tum	se	-	-	it	na	-k	re	ga-	-	-	-
S'	S'	ND	-N	S'R'	S'	-	-								
ae	sa	zkh	mdi	ya-	hai	-	-								
dha	ge	n	ti	n	ke	dhi	n	dha	ge	n	ti	n	ke	dhi	n
1	2	3	4	5	6	7	8	1	2	3	4	5	6	7	8
											S'	-	N	-	D
											aa	-	ya	-	hu
N	-	S'	-	-	-	-	-	-	-	-	S'	-	N	N	D
ya	-	ro	-	-	-	-	-	-	-	-	di	l	a	p	na
N	-	-	D	-	-	-	-	-	-	-	N	-	D	-	P
le	-	-	ke	-	-	-	-	-	-	-	aan	-	kho	-	me

D	-	N	-	-	-	-	-	-	-	-	N	N	-	P	-
che	h	ra	-	-	-	-	-	-	-	-	ki	si	-	ka	-
D	-	-	G	-	-	-	-	-	-	-	G'	-	R'	-	S'
le	-	-	ke	-	-	-	-	-	-	-	ko	-	ee	-	na
R'	-	G'	-	-	-	-	-	-	-	-	G'	-	R'	-	S'
ko	-	ee	-	-	-	-	-	-	-	-	me	-	ra	-	bhi
R'	-	-	S'	-	-	-	-	-	-	-	R'	R'	-	S'	D
ho	-	-	ga	-	-	-	-	-	-	-	y	hin	-	pe	k
N	-	P	-	-	-	-	-	-	-	-	G	G	-	R	-
hin	-	-	-	-	-	-	-	-	-	-	chhu	pa	-	hi	-
GP	-	-	G	-	-	-	-	-	-	-	-				
ho-	-	-	ga	-	-	-	-	-	-	-	-				

6. BIN TERE SANAM

Film: Yara Dildara (1991)	Music: Jatin Lalit
Lyrics: Majrooh Sultanpuri	Singer: Udit Narayan, Kavita Kri.
Taal: Kaharwa	Chord: RMD S=D

bin tere sanam mar mitenge ham, aa meree jindagee
aana hee pada sajana, zaalim hai dil kee lagee

tere hee dam se hogee dil kee muraad pooree
tere bagair jaanam hai jindagee adhooree
ai mere haseen ab na ja kaheen, aa meree jindagee
aana hee pada sajana, jaalim hai dil kee lagee, bin tere sanam …

ye jaanakar balam jee thaamee hai teree baahen
sahanee padengee sabakee kaanto bharee nigaahen
sab sahenge ham aur hansenge ham, aa meree jindagee o ho ho
aana hee pada sajana, jaalim hai dil kee lagee, bin tere sanam …

tum ho mere to ab hai mausam gulaam apana
shabanam ne likh diya hai phoolon pe naam apana
sun hava yahee geet ga rahee, aa meree jindagee
aana hee pada sajana, jaalim hai dil kee lagee, bin tere sanam …

Vinod Kumar

BIN TERE SANAM

dha	ge	n	ti	n	ke	dhi	n	dha	ge	n	ti	n	ke	dhi	n
1	2	3	4	5	6	7	8	1	2	3	4	5	6	7	8

```
R—D—R'—G'R'S'
aa----------------

D  P  G   D  G  D P D  G R
he he he  he he he he he aa ha

R – D  R' R' G'R'S'
aa he he he A he A

D P G  D ----    G – D P DPD--
aa ----- aa ---  aa------------
```

1	2	3	4	5	6	7	8	1	2	3	4	5	6	7	8
R	-	D	M	-	G	R	-	R	-	D	M	-	G	R	-
bi	n	te	re	-	s	n	m	m	r	mi	te	-	ge	h	m
R	-	D	P	-	M	-	P	P	G	-	-	-	-	-	-
aa	-	me	ri	-	zin	-	d	gi	-	-	-	-	-	-	-
D	N	-	D	-	P	P	-	M	P	P	G	-	-	-	-
aa	na	-	hi	-	p	da	-	s	j	na	-	-	-	-	-
G	M	-	G	S	G	-	R	R	-	-	-	-	-	-	-
za	lim	-	hai	dil	ki	-	l	gi	-	-	-	-	-	-	-
D	-	D	-	D	N	-	D	D	-	D	M	-	-	-	-
te	-	re	-	hi	dm	-	se	ho	-	gi	-	-	-	-	-
D	-	D	-	D	S'	-	S'	S'	-	N	-	-	-	-	-
dil	-	ki	-	mu	ra	-	d	pu	-	ri	-	-	-	-	-
G	-	G	-	G	P	-	G	G	-	G	S	-	-	-	-
te	-	re	-	b	gai	-	r	ja	-	nm	-	-	-	-	-
G	-	G	-	G	D	-	D	D	-	R	-	-	-	-	-
hai	-	zin	-	d	gi	-	a	dhu	-	ri	-	-	-	-	-
R	-	D	M	-	G	R	-	R	-	D	M	-	G	R	-
ae	-	me	re	-	h	sii	-	a	b	n	ja	-	k	hin	-
R	-	D	P	-	M	-	P	P	G	-	-	-	-	-	-
aa	-	me	ri	-	zin	-	d	gi	-	-	-	-	-	-	-
D	N	-	D	-	P	P	-	M	P	P	G	-	-	-	-
aa	na	-	hi	-	p	da	-	s	j	na	-	-	-	-	-

G	M	-	G	S	G	-	R	R	-	-	-	-	-	-	-
ja	lim	-	hai	dil	ki	-	l	gi	-	-	-	-	-	-	-
D	-	D	-	D	N̲	-	D	D	-	D	M	-	-	-	-
ye	-	ja	-	n	k	r	b	l	m	jii	-	-	-	-	-
D	-	D	-	D	S'	-	S'	S'	-	N		-	-	-	-
tha	-	mi	-	hain	te	-	ri	ba	-	hen	-	-	-	-	-
P	P	G	-	G	P	-	G	G	G	G	S	-	-	-	-
s	h	ni	-	p	den	-	gi	s	b	ki	-	-	-	-	-
G	-	G	-	G	D	-	D	D	-	R		-	-	-	-
kan	-	ton	-	bh	ri	-	ni	ga	-	hen	-	-	-	-	-
R	-	D	M	-	G	R	-	R	-	D	M	-	G	R	-
s	b	s	hen	-	ge	h	m	au	r	s	hen	-	ge	h	m
R	-	D	P	-	M	-	P	P	G	-		-	-	-	-
aa	-	me	ri	-	zin	-	d	gi	-	-	-	-	-	-	-
D	N̲	-	D	-	P	P	-	M	P	P	G	-	-	-	-
aa	na	-	hi	-	p	da	-	s	j	na	-	-	-	-	-
G	M	-	G	S	G	-	R	R	-	-	-	-	-	-	-
ja	lim	-	hai	dil	ki	-	l	gi	-	-	-	-	-	-	-

G – D- G'- R'- S'- D- R'- S'- D P D S' – D- D S' R'------
aa--

D	-	D	-	D	N̲	-	D	D	-	D	M	-	-	-	-
tu	m	ho	-	me	re	-	to	a	b	hai	-	-	-	-	-
D	-	D	-	D	S'	-	S'	S'	S'	N		-	-	-	-
mau	-	s	m	gu	la	-	m	a	p	na	-	-	-	-	-
P	P	G	-	G	P	P	P	G	-	G	S	-	-	-	-
sh	b	nm	-	ne	li	kh	di	ya	-	hai	-	-	-	-	-
G	-	G	-	G	D	-	D	G	G	R		-	-	-	-
fu	-	lo	-	pe	na	-	m	a	p	na	-	-	-	-	-
R	-	D	M	-	G	R	-	R	-	D	M	-	G	R	-
su	n	h	va	-	y	hi	-	gi	-	t	ga	-	r	hi	-
R	-	D	P	-	M	-	P	P	G			-	-	-	-
aa	-	me	ri	-	zin	-	d	gi	-	-	-	-	-	-	-
D	N̲	-	D	-	P	P	-	M	P	P	G	-	-	-	-
aa	na	-	hi	-	p	da	-	s	j	na	-	-	-	-	-

G	M	-	G	S	G	-	R	R	-	-	-	-	-	-	-
ja	lim	-	hai	dil	ki	-	I	gi	-	-	-	-	-	-	-

7. BOLE CHUDIYAN BOLE KANGANA

Film: Kabhi Khushi Kabhi Gam (2001)	Music: Jatin Lalit
Lyrics: Sameer	Singer: Udit Narayan and others
Taal: Kaharwa	Chord: P̲N̲R' S=C

bole chudiyaan bole kangana, haay main ho gayi teri sajna -2
tere bin jiyu nahiyo lagda main te mar gaiyaan
lai ja lai ja dil lai ja lai ja, lai ja lai ja soneya lai ja lai ja, aa.......

bole chudiyaan bole kangana, haay main ho gayi teri sajna -2
tere bin jiyu nahiyo lagda main te mar gaiyaan
lai ja lai ja soneya lai ja lai ja, lai ja lai ja dil lai ja lai ja ho.......

bole chudiyan bole kangna hay main ho gaya tera sajna
tere bin jiyo nahiyo lagda main te mar javaan
lai ja lai ja soniye lai ja lai ja, dil lai ja lai ja ho.....

haay haay main mar jaavaan mar jaavaan tere bin
ab to meri ratein katati taare gin gin
bas tujhko pukara kare, meri bindiya ishara kare
oye lashkara lashkara teri bindiya ka lashkara
aese chamke jaise chamke chand ke paas sitaara, ho....

meri paayal bulaaye tujhe jo ruthe manaaye tujhe
o sajan ji haan sajan ji
kuchh socho kuch samjho meri baat ko

bole chudiyan bole kangna hay main ho gaya tera sajna
tere bin jiyo nahiyo lagda main te mar javaan
lai ja lai ja soniye lai ja lai ja, dil lai ja lai ja ho.....

apnii maang suhagan ho, aa... sang hamesha saajn ho aa..
aake meri duniya me vaaps na jana
sehra baandh ke maahi tu mere ghar aana

oye soni kitti soni aaj tu lagdi ve
bas mere sath ye jodi teri sajdi ve
rup aesa suhaana tera chaand bhii hai diwana tera

jaa re jaa o jhuthe teri gallan ham na maane
kyon tareefein karta hai tu ham to sab kuchh jaane
o…… o……
mere dil ki duaa yah kahe teri jodi salaamt rahe

o sajan ji haan sajan ji
yun hi beete saara jiivan saath me

bole chudiyan bole kangna hay main ho gaya tera sajna
tere bin jiyo nahiyo lagda main te mar javaan
lai ja lai ja soniye lai ja lai ja, dil lai ja lai ja ho…..

aajaa heeriye, o jaja ranjhna, o aaja heeriye, jaja rahjhna
lai ja lai ja, dil lai ja lai ja
lai ja lai ja soniye lai ja lai ja
na juda honge ham kabhi khushi kabhi gam

BOLE CHUDIYAN BOLE KANGANA

dha	ge	n	ti	n	ke	dhi	n	dha	ge	n	ti	n	ke	dhi	n
1	2	3	4	5	6	7	8	1	2	3	4	5	6	7	8

R'N S'G'R' S'R' NR'S' R' N S'G'R' S'R' NR'S'
bole chudiyan bole kngna hay main ho gyi teri sajna

PP P N DD DDS' N N N S' S' D
tere bin jii niyo lgda main te mr gai yan—

R' P D P R'R'R' R' P N D
lai ja lai ja soneya lai ja lai ja

R' P D P R' R' P N D
lai ja lai ja dil lai ja lai ja,

R' S'N DNP R'--- S'--- S' M'- G' ^{S'}R' ^{S'}R' ^{S'}R'
o----- ----o --- aa------- ---------

| R' | - | N | S' | - | G' | R' | - | - | - | - | - | - | - | - | - |
| bo | - | le | chu | - | di | yan | - | - | - | - | - | - | - | - | - |

| S' | - | R' | N | - | R' | S' | - | - | - | - | - | - | - | - | - |
| bo | - | le | kn | - | g | na | - | - | - | - | - | - | - | - | - |

R'	-	N	S'	-	G'	R'	-	-	-	-	-	-	-	-	-
ha	y	main	ho	-	g	yi	-	-	-	-	-	-	-	-	-
S'	-	R'	N	-	R'	S'	-	-	-	-	-	-	-	-	-
te	-	ri	sa	-	j	na	-	-	-	-	-	-	-	-	-
P	-	-	P	P	-	N	-	D	-	-	D	D	D	S'	-
te	-	-	re	bi	n	jii	-	nai	-	-	u	l	g	da	-
N	-	-	N	N	-	S'	-	S'	-	D	-	-	-	-	-
main	-	-	te	m	r	g	ee	yan	-	-	-	-	-	-	-
R'	-	P	D	-	P	-	-	-	-	-	R'	-	R'	R'	-
lai	-	ja	lai	-	ja	-	-	-	-	-	so	-	ne	ya	-
R'	-	P	N	-	D	-	-	-	-	-	-	-	-	R'	-
lai	-	ja	lai	-	ja	-	-	-	-	-	-	-	-	di	l
R'	-	P	D	-	P	-	-	-	-	-	-	D	S'	N	D
lai	-	ja	lai	-	ja	-	-	-	-	-	-	ho	-	-	-
P	-	-	-	-	-										
o	-	-	-	-	-										
R'	-	N	S'	-	G'	R'	-	-	-	-	-	-	-	-	-
bo	-	le	chu	-	di	yan	-	-	-	-	-	-	-	-	-
S'	-	R'	N	-	R'	S'	-	-	-	-	-	-	-	-	-
bo	-	le	kn	-	g	na	-	-	-	-	-	-	-	-	-
R'	-	N	S'	-	G'	R'	-	-	-	-	-	-	-	-	-
ha	y	main	ho	-	g	ya	-	-	-	-	-	-	-	-	-
S'	-	R'	N	-	R'	S'	-	-	-	-	-	-	-	-	-
te	-	ra	sa	-	j	na	-	-	-	-	-	-	-	-	-
P	-	-	P	P	-	N	-	D	-	-	D	D	D	S'	-
te	-	-	re	bi	n	jii	-	nee	-	-	u	l	g	da	-
N	-	-	N	N	-	S'	-	S'	-	D	-	-	-	-	-
main	-	-	te	m	r	ja	-	na	-	-	-	-	-	-	-
R'	-	P	D	-	P	-	-	-	-	-	R'	-	R'	R'	-
lai	-	ja	lai	-	ja	-	-	-	-	-	so	-	ni	ye	-
R'	-	P	N	-	D	-	-	-	-	-	-	-	-	R'	-
lai	-	ja	lai	-	ja	-	-	-	-	-	-	-	-	di	l

R'	-	P	D	-	P	-	-	-	-	-	-	D	S'	N	D
lai	-	ja	lai	-	ja	-	-	-	-	-	-	ho	-	-	-
P	-	-	-	-	-										
o	-	-	-	-	-										

interlude:
NN S' NS' NS' NS' NS' NS'R'G'---G'M' R' R'G' S'R'N—2
flute: PN PS' S'S' S'R'S'G'—R'- S'-
NNS'- NNS'- N---

MMP MP MP- N DDP- MMP MP MM-
MMP MMD MMP-

														R'	-
														ha	y
S'	-	R'	-	S'	-	N	-	N	-	N	N	N	-	N	-
ha	y	main	-	m	r	ja	-	van	-	m	r	ja	-	van	-
S'	-	R'	-	S'	-	S'	R'	N	R'	S'	-	-	-	R'	R'
te	-	re	-	bin	-	-	-	-	-	-	-	-	-	a	b
S'	-	R'	-	S'	-	N	-	N	-	N	N	N	-	N	-
to	-	me	-	ri	-	ra	-	te	-	k	t	ti	-	ta	-
S'	-	R'	-	S'	-	-	-	-	-	-	-	-	-	S'	S'
re	-	gin	-	gin	-	-	-	-	-	-	-	-	-	b	s
P	P	-	S'	S'	S'	-	S'	R'	S'	N	-	-	-	S'	S'
tujh	ko	-	pu	ka	ra	-	k	ren	-	-	-	-	-	me	ri
P	P	-	S'	S'	S'	-	S'	R'	S'	N	-	R'	-	-	-
bindi	ya	-	i	sha	ra	-	k	re	-	-	-	ho	y	-	-
D	-	N	-	S'	-	N	-	D	-	N	-	S'	-	N	-
l	sh	ka	-	ra	-	l	sh	ka	-	ra	-	te	-	ri	-
D	D	N	-	S'	-	N	-	D	-	N	-	-	-	-	-
bin	di	ya	-	ka	-	l	sh	ka	-	ra	-	-	-	-	-
D	-	N	-	S'	-	N	-	D	-	N	-	S'	-	N	-
ae	-	se	-	ch	m	ke	-	jai	-	se	-	ch	m	ke	-
D	-	N	N	S'	-	N	N	D	-	N	-	-	-	-	N
chan	-	d	ke	pa	-	s	si	ta	-	ra	-	-	-	-	o
M'	-	-	-	-	-	G'	R'	S'	-	-	-	S'	R'	N	R'
o	-	-	-	-	-	au	-	au	-	-	-	o	-	-	-

```
S'   -    -    -  | -    -            |                  |            S'   S'
o    -    -    -  | -    -            |                  |            me   ri

P    P    -    S' | S'   S'   -    S' | R'   S'   N    - | -    -     S'   -
pa   yl   -    bu | la   ye   -    tu | jhe  -    -    - | -    -     jo   -

P    P    -    S' | S'   S'   -    S' | R'   S'   N    N | -    D     D    -
ru   the  -    m  | na   ye   -    tu | jhe  -    -    o | -    s     j    n

P    -    -    N  | -    D    D    -  | P    -    -    D | P    D     M    -
jii  -    -    han| -    s    j    n  | jii  -    -    - | -    -     -    -

M    -    S'   -  | M    -    S'   -  | M    -    S'   - | S'   -     S'   -
ku   chh  so   -  | cho  -    ku   chh| sm   -    jho  - | me   -     ri   -

R'   S'   S'   R' | -    -    S'   -  | N    -    -    - | -    -     -    -
ba   -    -    -  | -    -    t    -  | ko   -    -    - | -    -     -    -

R'   -    N    S' | -    G'   R'   -  | -    -    -    - | -    -     -    -
bo   -    le   chu| -    di   yan  -  | -    -    -    - | -    -     -    -

S'   -    R'   N  | -    R'   S'   -  | -    -    -    - | -    -     -    -
bo   -    le   kn | -    g    na   -  | -    -    -    - | -    -     -    -
```

interlude:
R- P- M G M – S R – P—
hu ------------------------

R N—D P – D – P- MPMPG --
aa------------------------------

sntur: PPP R'R'R' R'G'R' S'R'S' DND NS'NDN
flute: PN R'R'R' G'R' S' S'S' R'M'G'R'R'--

P- R'- S' R'--- S' N D – P-   NS'NDN--
aa--

```
P    P    N    -  | D    -    P    M  | P    -    P    P | P    -     -    -
a    p    ni   -  | man  -    g    su | ha   -    g    n | ho   -     -    -

R    G    M    -  | -    -    G    -  | R    -    -    - | -    -     -    -
aa   -    -    -  | -    -    -    -  | -    -    -    - | -    -     -    -

P    -    D    N  | D    -    M    -  | P    -    P    P | P    -     -    -
sn   -    g    h  | me   -    sha  -  | sa   -    j    n | ho   -     -    -

R    G    M    -  | -    -    P    N  | D    -    -    - | -    -     -    -
aa   -    -    -  | -    -    -    -  | -    -    -    - | -    -     -    -
```

M	-	D	-	D	-	N	-	S'	S'	-	S'	-	-	D	-
aa	-	ke	-	me	-	ri	-	du	ni	-	ya	-	-	me	-
N	-	D	D	P	-	G	-	M	-	-	-	-	-	-	-
va	-	p	s	na	-	ja	-	na	-	-	-	-	-	-	-
M	-	M	-	D	-	D	N	S'	-	-	S'	-	-	S'	-
se	h	ra	-	ban	-	dh	ke	ma	-	-	hi	-	-	tu	-
S'	-	S'	G'	R'	-	S'	-	R'	-	N	-	-	-	R'	-
me	-	re	-	gh	r	aa	-	na	-	-	-	-	-	o	-
S'	-	R'	-	S'	-	N	-	N	-	N	-	N	-	N	N
so	-	ni	-	ki	-	tti	-	so	-	ni	-	aa	-	j	tu
S'	-	R'	-	S'	-	-	-	-	-	-	-	-	-	R'	-
l	g	di	-	ve	-	-	-	-	-	-	-	-	-	b	s
S'	-	R'	-	S'	-	N	N	N	-	N	-	N	-	N	-
me	-	re	-	sa	-	th	ye	jo	-	di	-	te	-	ri	-
S'	S'	R'	-	S'	-	-	-	-	-	-	-	-	-	S'	S'
s	j	di	-	ve	-	-	-	-	-	-	-	-	-	ru	p
P	P	-	S'	S'	S'	-	S'	R'	S'	N	-	-	S'	-	S'
ae	sa	-	su	ha	na	-	te	ra	-	-	-	-	chan	-	d
P	P	-	S'	S'	G'	-	R'	S'	N	-	-	-	-	-	-
bhi	hai	-	di	va	na	-	te	ra	-	-	-	-	-	-	-
N	S'	N	D	N	S'	N	D	N	S'	N	D	N	S'	N	-
D	-	N	-	S'	-	N	-	D	-	N	-	S'	-	N	-
ja	-	re	-	ja	-	o	-	jhu	-	the	-	te	-	ri	-
D	-	N	-	S'	-	N	-	D	-	N	-	-	-	-	-
gl	-	lan	-	h	m	na	-	ma	-	ne	-	-	-	-	-
D	-	N	-	S'	-	N	-	D	-	N	-	S'	-	N	-
kyu	-	ta	-	ri	-	fen	-	k	r	da	-	hai	-	tu	-
D	-	N	-	S'	-	N	-	D	-	N	-	-	-	-	-
h	m	to	-	s	b	ku	chh	ja	-	ne	-	-	-	-	-

M' --- G'R'S' S'R'NR'S'
o——————————————

NDP-- D—NS'NDN
ho——————————————

													S'	S'
													me	re
P	P	-	S'	S'	S'	-	S'	R'	S'	N	-	-	-	S'	S'
dil	ki	-	du	aa	yen	-	k	hen	-	-	-	-	-	te	ri
P	P	-	S'	S'	S'	-	S'	R'	S'	N	N	-	D	D	-
jo	di	-	s	la	mt	-	r	he	-	-	o	-	s	j	n
P	-	-	N	-	D	D	-	P	-	-	D	PD	M	-	-
jii	-	-	han	-	s	j	n	jii	-	-	-	-	-	-	-
M	-	S'	-	M	-	S'	-	M	-	S'	-	S'	-	S'	-
yun	-	hi	-	bi	-	te	-	sa	-	ra	-	jii	-	vn	-
R'	S'	S'	R'	-	-	S'	-	N	-	-	-	-	-	-	-
sa	-	-	-	-	-	th	-	me	-	-	-	-	-	-	-

M S'—M S'—R'S'NS'R' S'- N-
aa-------------------------------------

R'	-	N	S'	-	G'	R'	-
bo	-	le	chu	-	di	yan	-
S'	-	R'	N	-	R'	S'	-
bo	-	le	kn	-	g	na	-

R' P DDP R' R' P NND
aa ja hiriye o ja ja ranjhna -3

R' P D P R'R'R' R' P N D
lai ja lai ja soneya lai ja lai ja

R' P D P R' R' P N D
lai ja lai ja dil lai ja lai ja,

R'	-	P	D	-	P	-	-	-	-	-	R'	-	R'	R'	-
lai	-	ja	lai	-	ja	-	-	-	-	-	so	-	ni	ye	-
R'	-	P	N	-	D	-	-	-	-	-	-	-	-	R'	
lai	-	ja	lai	-	ja	-	-	-	-	-	-	-	-	di	l
R'	-	P	D	-	P	-	-	-	-	-	D	S'	N	D	
lai	-	ja	lai	-	ja	-	-	-	-	-	ho	-	-	-	
P	-	-	-	-	-										
o	-	-	-	-	-										

P D M—D ---- D N S'D N D P --
aa------------ aa----------------

P D M—D ----- D N S'D N R'P --
aa------------ aa----------------

8. BHOLI SI SURAT

Film: Dil to Paagal Hai (1997)	Music: Uttam Singh
Lyrics: Anand Bakshi	Singer: Udit Narayan
Taal: Kaharwa	Chord: RP<u>N</u> S=C#

bholee see soorat aankhon mein mastee, aay hae
are bholee see soorat aankhon mein mastee
door khadee sharmae, aay hae
ek jhalak dikhalaaye kabhee,
kabhee aanchal mein chhup jaaye, aay hae
meree nazar se tum dekho to yaar nazar vo aaye

ladakee nahin hai, vo jaadoo hai aur kaha kya jaaye
raat ko mere khvaab mein aaee vo zulfen bikharaaye
aankh khulee to dil chaaha, phir neend mujhe aa jaaye
bin dekhe ye haal hua, dekhoon to kya ho jaaye

saavan ka pahala baadal usaka kaajal ban jae
mauj uthe saagar mein jaise, aise kadam uthaaye
rab ne jaane kis mitatee se usake ang banaaye
chham se kaash kaheen se mere saamane vo aa jaaye

Vinod Kumar

BHOLI SI SURAT

dha 1	ge 2	n 3	ti 4	n 5	ke 6	dhi 7	n 8	dha 1	ge 2	n 3	ti 4	n 5	ke 6	dhi 7	n 8
prelude: P DN DP M PD PM M R P															
PD N DP MP D PM M RP															
bholi si surt aankho me msti aaye haye															
														P / a	P / re
P	-	D	N	D	-	P	-	M	-	P	D	P	-	M	-
bho	-	li	si	su	-	r	t	aan	-	kho	me	m	s	ti	-
M	-	P	D	P	-	M	-	R	-	P	-	-	-	-	-
du	-	r	kh	di	-	sh	r	ma	-	ye	-	-	-	-	-
-	-	-	-	-	-	D	-	R	-	P	-	-	-	-	-
-	-	-	-	-	-	aa	ye	ha	-	ye	-	-	-	-	-
P	-	D	N	D	D	P	P	M	-	P	D	P	-	M	-
ae	-	k	jh	l	k	di	kh	la	-	ye	k	bhi	-	k	bhi
M	-	P	D	P	-	M	M	R	-	P	-	-	-	-	-
aan	-	ch	l	me	-	chhi	p	ja	-	ye	-	-	-	-	-
-	-	-	-	-	-	D	-	R	-	P	-	-	-	-	-
-	-	-	-	-	-	aa	ye	ha	-	ye	-	-	-	-	-
R'	-	R'	R'	R'	-	D	-	N	-	N	-	D	-	P	-
me	-	ri	n	z	r	se	-	tum	-	de	-	kho	-	to	-
N	-	-	N	D	-	P	-	N	-	D	-	D	-	P	-
ya	-	r	n	z	r	vo	-	aa	-	ye	-	-	-	-	-

interlude:
PM R-P-N-D   D S' N D P P
un---------   la la l la l la

PM R-P-N-D D S' N D P P
aa---------   la la l la l la

music: PNR'- S'G'- R'S'ND P- D-

PM R-P-N-D D S' N D P P P--------
aa---------   la la l la l la un---------

P	-	D	N	D	-	P	-	D	-	N	S'	N	-	D	-
l	d	ki	n	hin	-	hai	-	vo	-	ja	-	du	-	hai	
P	-	D	N	D	-	P	-	M	-	P	-	DP	M	P	-
au	-	r	k	ha	-	kya	-	ja	-	ye	-	-	-	-	-
P	-	D	N	D	-	P	-	D	-	N	S'	N	-	D	-
ra	-	t	ko	me	-	re	-	kha	-	b	me	aa	-	yi	-
P	-	D	N	D	-	P	P	M	-	P	-	DP	M	P	-
vo	-	zu	l	fen	-	bi	kh	ra	-	ye	-	-	-	-	-
S'	-	S'	S'	S'	-	S'	-	S'	-	S'	-	S'	-	S'	S'
aan	-	kh	khu	li	-	to	-	di	l	cha	-	ha	-	fi	r
R'	-	-	S'	N	-	P	-	D	-	N	-	-	-	-	-
nin	-	d	mu	jhe	-	aa	-	ja	-	ye	-	-	-	-	-
R'	-	R'	-	R'	-	D	-	N	-	N	N	D	-	P	-
bi	n	de	-	khe	-	ye	-	ha	-	l	hu	aa	-	de	
N	-	N	-	D	-	P	-	N	-	D	-	-	-	P	-
khu	-	to	-	kya	-	ho	-	ja	-	ye	-	-	-	-	-
P	-	D	N	D	-	P	-	M	-	P	D	P	-	M	-
bho	-	li	si	su	-	r	t	aan	-	kho	me	m	s	ti	-
M	-	P	D	P	-	M	-	R	-	P	-	-	-	-	-
du	-	r	kh	di	-	sh	r	ma	-	ye	-	-	-	-	-
-	-	-	-	-	-	D	-	R	-	P	-	-	-	-	-
-	-	-	-	-	-	aa	ye	ha	-	ye	-	-	-	-	-

interlude:

```
R'R' R' S'G'R'      PP PP P- PDN --- DP ---
la la la la la la      music:

R'  R' R' S' G' R'      PP PP P- PDN --- DP ---
la  la la la la la      music:

S' S' S' P R'- S'      PP PP P- PDN --- DP ---
la la la la la la      music:

N S'R' D N S'P D N DP  M*----
la la la  la la la la  la la aa  aa ---

music: PM R—P—N-D--   D S'--- N D—P P—

PM R—P—N-D--    D S'--- N D— P P—
aa-----------------    la la ---- l la – l la
```

P	-	D	<u>N</u>	D	-	P	-	D	-	<u>N</u>	S'	<u>N</u>	-	D	-
sa	-	v	n	ka	-	p	h	la	-	ba	-	d	l	u	s
P	-	D	<u>N</u>	D	-	P	-	M	-	P	-	-	-	-	-
ka	-	ka	-	z	l	b	n	ja	-	ye	-	-	-	-	-
P	-	D	<u>N</u>	D	-	P	-	D	-	<u>N</u>	S'	<u>N</u>	-	D	-
mau	-	j	u	the	-	sa	-	g	r	me	-	jai	-	se	-
P	-	D	<u>N</u>	D	D	P	P	M	-	P	-	-	-	-	-
ae	-	se	-	q	d	m	u	tha	-	ye	-	-	-	-	-
S'	S'	S'	-	S'	-	S'	-	S'	-	S'	-	S'	-	S'	-
r	b	ne	-	ja	-	ne	-	ki	s	mi	-	tti	-	se	-
S'	-	R'	-	<u>N</u>	-	D	P	D	-	<u>N</u>	-	-	-	-	-
u	s	ke	-	an	-	g	b	na	-	ye	-	-	-	-	-
R'	-	R'	-	R'	-	R'	D	<u>N</u>	-	<u>N</u>	-	D	-	P	-
chh	m	se	-	ka	-	sh	k	hin	-	se	-	me	-	re	-
<u>N</u>	-	<u>N</u>	<u>N</u>	D	-	P	-	<u>N</u>	-	D	-	D	-	P	-
sa	-	m	ne	vo	-	aa	-	ja	-	ye	-	-	-	-	-
P	-	D	<u>N</u>	D	-	P	-	M	-	P	D	P	-	M	-
bho	-	li	si	su	-	r	t	aan	-	kho	me	m	s	ti	-
M	-	P	D	P	-	M	-	R	-	P	-	-	-	-	-
du	-	r	kh	di	-	sh	r	ma	-	ye	-	-	-	-	-
-	-	-	-	-	-	P	-	R	-	P	-	-	-	-	-
-	-	-	-	-	-	aa	ye	ha	-	ye	-	-	-	-	-

9. CHOTI SI PYARI SI NANHI SI

Film: Anadi (1993)	Music: Anand Milind
Lyrics: Sameer	Singer: Udit Narayan
Taal: Daadra	Chord: GPN RM*D S=C

chhotee see pyaaree see nanhee see, aaee koee paree
bholee see nyaaree see achchhee see, aaee koee paree

paalane mein aise hee jhoolatee rahe
khushiyon kee baaharon mein jhoomatee rahe
gaate muskuraate sangeet kee tarah
yah to lage raama ke geet kee tarah
raara ru ra ra raara ru -2

saragam jaanoon na
jaane kaise fanakaar ban gaya
sabase nyaaree hai naatedaaree hai
jisako chaahe vah yaar ban gaya
mujhako to jo diya rab ne hee diya
aaya jo dil mein vah mainne ga liya -2
gaate muskuraate sangeet kee tarah
duniya lage raama ke geet kee tarah
raara ru ra ra raara ru -2

CHOTI SI PYARI SI NANHI SI

dha	dhi	na	dha	tun	na	dha	dhi	na	dha	tun	na
1	2	3	4	5	6	1	2	3	4	5	6
prelude: NPG NPG M*M*P DPG – 4											
G	N	D	P	D	P	M*	M*	-	G	-	R
chho	ti	si	pya	ri	si	nn	hi	-	si	-	-
R	G	M*	P	-	M*	G	-	-	-	-	-
aa	yi	ko	ee	-	p	ri	-	-	-	-	-
G	N	D	P	D	P	M*	M*	-	G	-	R
bho	li	si	nya	ri	si	a	chchhi	-	si	-	-
R	G	M*	P	-	M*	G	-	-	-	-	-
aa	yi	ko	ee	-	p	ri	-	-	-	-	-

N	-	N	N	G'	G'	G'	-	R'	-	R'	-
pa	-	l	ne	-	me	ae	-	se	-	hi	-

R'	-	R'	N	-	D	N	-	-	-	-	-
jhu	-	l	ti	-	r	he	-	-	-	-	-

N	N	N	G'	-	G'	G'	-	R'	-	R'	-
khu	shi	yon	ki	-	b	ha	-	ro	-	me	-

R'	-	R'	N	-	D	N	-	-	D	P	G
jhu	-	m	ti	-	r	he	-	-	-	-	-

G	-	P	D	-	N	N	-	M*	-	M*	-
ga	-	te	mu	-s	ku	ra	-	te	-	san	-

D	-	M*	P	-	M*	G	-	-	-	-	-
gi	-	t	ki	-	t	rha	-	-	-	-	-

G	-	P	D	N	-	N	-	M*	-	M*	P
ye	-	to	l	ge	-	ra	-	ma	-	ke	-

D	-	M*	P	-	M*	G	-	-	-	-	-
gi	-	t	ki	-	t	rha	-	-	-	-	-

R	R	-	M*	-	-	-	-	N	N	N	-
ra	ra	-	ru	-	-	-	-	ra	ra	ra	-

M*	M*	-	G	-	-	-	-	-	-	-	-
ra	ra	-	ru	-	-	-	-	-	-	-	-

R	R	-	D	M*	-	-	-	N	N	N	-
ra	ra	-	ru	-	-	-	-	ra	ra	ra	-

M*	M*	-	G	-	-	-	-	-	-	-	-
ra	ra	-	ru	-	-	-	-	-	-	-	-

interlude: $^{R'}$G'- G' R'G'R'- N $^{R'}$G'- G' R'G'R'- N
     M*'-R' M*'-R'   ND-P N GP N D   P N R' R'
     N N R' G'-   N N G' N R' G'---
     NNN NNN NNN NNN

		N	N	N	-	N	N	-	D	P	-
		khu	shi	yan	-	de	ti	-	hai	-	-

-	-	N	N	N	-	N	N	-	D	P	-
-	-	du	kh	h	r	le	ti	-	hai	-	-

-	-	R'	-	R'	-	R'	R'	R'	-	R'	-
-	-	ma	-	ki	-	m	m	ta	-	ka	-

G'	-	R'	R'	-	R'	N	-	-	D	-	P
mo	-	l	na	-	ko	ee	-	-	-	-	-
N	-	N	N	N	-	N	N	-	D	P	-
-	-	n	g	me	-	ga	ti	-	hai	-	-
-	-	N	N	N	N	N	N	-	D	P	-
-	-	su	kh	b	r	sa	ti	-	hai	-	-
-	-	R'	-	R'	-	R'	-	R'	-	R'	-
-	-	ma	-	ke	-	jai	-	sa	-	to	-
G'	-	R'	R'	-	R'	N	-	-	-	-	-
bo	-	l	na	-	ko	ee	-	-	-	-	-
N	-	R'	G'	-	-	N	-	R'	G'	-	-
u	-	mr	bhr	-	-	main	-	k	run	-	-
G'	-	R'	N	R'	N	D	P	-	-	-	-
ma	-	ki	bn	-	d	gi	-	-	-	-	-
N	-	R'	G'	-	-	N	-	R'	G'	-	-
ma	-	te	re	-	-	na	-	m	hai	-	-
G'	-	R'	N	R'	N	D	P	-	-	-	-
me	-	ri	zin	-	d	gi	-	-	-	-	-
R'	-	R'	R'	-	N	N	R'	R'	N	D	-
ma	-	te	re	-	-	na	-	m	hai	-	-
N	-	N	D	-	P	D	-	-	P	G	-
me	-	ri	zin	-	d	gi	-	-	-	-	-
G	-	P	D	-	N	N	-	M*	-	M*	-
ga	-	te	mu	-s	ku	ra	-	te	-	san	-
D	-	M*	P	-	M*	G	-	-	-	-	-
gi	-	t	ki	-	t	rha	-	-	-	-	-
G	-	P	D	N	-	N	-	M*	-	M*	P
ye	-	to	l	ge	-	ra	-	ma	-	ke	-
D	-	M*	P	-	M*	G	-	-	-	-	-
gi	-	t	ki	-	t	rha	-	-	-	-	-
R	R	-	M*	-	-	-	-	N	N	N	-
ra	ra	-	ru	-	-	-	-	ra	ra	ra	-

M*	M*	-	G	-	-	-	-	-	-	-	-
ra	ra	-	ru	-	-	-	-	-	-	-	-
R	R	-	D	M*	-	-	-	N	N	N	-
ra	ra	-	ru	-	-	-	-	ra	ra	ra	-
M*	M*	-	G	-	-	-	-	-	-	-	-
ra	ra	-	ru	-	-	-	-	-	-	-	-

10. DIL TO PAGAL HAI

Film: Dil to Paagal Hai (1997)	Music: Uttam Singh
Lyrics: Anand Bakshi	Singer: Udit Narayan, Lata
Taal: Kaharwa	Chord: P̲N̲R' S=C

dil to paagal hai, dil deevaana hai
pahalee pahalee baar milaata hai yahee, seene mein phir aag lagaata hai
dheere dheere pyaar sikhaata hai yahee, hansaata hai yahee, yahee rulaata hai,
dil to paagal hai, dil deevaana hai

saaree saaree raat jagaata hai yahee, ankhiyon se neend churaata hai
sachche jhoothe khvaab dikhaata hai yahee, hansaata hai yahee, yahee rulaata hai,
dil to paagal hai, dil deevaana hai

is dil kee baaton mein jo aate hain, vo bhee deevaane ho jaate hain
manzil to raahee dhoondh lete hain, raste magar kho jaate hain
dil to paagal hai, dil deevaana hai

soorat se main na pahachaanoongee, naam se bhee na usako jaanoongee
dekhoongee kuchh na main sochoongee, dil jo kahega vahee maanoongee
dil to paagal hai, dil deevaana hai

dil ka kahana ham sab maane, dil na kisee kee maane
jaan dee hamane, jaan gaye sab, ek vo hee na jaane
dil to paagal hai, dil deevaana hai

rahane do chhodo ye kahaaniyaan, deevaane pan kee sab nishaaniyaan
logon kee saaree pareshaaniyaan, is dil kee hain ye meharabaaniyaan
ho dil to paagal hai, dil deevaana hai

DIL TO PAGAL HAI

dhage	nti	nke	dhin	dhage	nti	nke	dhin	dhage	nti	nke	dhin	dhage	nti	nke	dhin
12	34	56	78	12	34	56	78	12	34	56	78	12	34	56	78

prelude: M* P<u>N</u>D M* P<u>N</u> <u>N</u> D- P- x3

P <u>N</u> G' R' R'
tu ru ru tu tu

S' R' <u>G'</u> P' M' <u>G'</u> R'
tu ru ru t tu ru ru

P <u>N</u> <u>G'</u> R' R'
tu ru ru tu tu

<u>N</u> S' R' M' D
tu ru ru tu tu

P <u>N</u> <u>G'</u> R' R'
tu ru ru tu tu

S' R' <u>G'</u> P' M' <u>G'</u> R'
tu ru ru t tu ru ru

P <u>N</u> <u>G'</u> R' R'
tu ru ru tu tu

<u>N</u> S' R' R' S' <u>N</u> D P
tu ru ru tu tu ru tu tu

														<u>N</u>	D
														dil	to
P	-D	-	M	-	-	<u>N</u>	D	P	-D	-	P	-	-	<u>N</u>	D
pa	-g	-l	hai	-	-	dil	di	va	-na	-	hai	-	-	dil	to
P	-D	-	M	-	<u>N</u>	<u>N</u>	D	P	-D	-	P	-	-	-	-
pa	-g	-l	hai	-	-	dil	di	va	-na	-	hai	-	-	-	-

music: P <u>NN</u> <u>NNN</u> P <u>NN</u> <u>NNN</u> P <u>NN</u> <u>NNN</u>

P	<u>N</u>	G'	R'	R'	-	-	S'	<u>N</u>	S'	S'	R'	R'	-	-	-
ph	li	ph	li	ba	-	-r	mi	la	ta	hai	y	hi	-	-	-
P	<u>N</u>	G'	R'	R'	-	-	M'	R'	<u>N</u>	D	-	-	-	-	-
si	ne	me	fir	aa	-	-g	l	ga	ta	hai	-	-	-	-	-
P	<u>N</u>	<u>G'</u>	R'	R'	-	-	S'	<u>N</u>	S'	S'	R'	R'	-	-	P
dhi	re	dhi	re	pya	-	-r	si	kha	ta	hai	y	hi	-	-	hn

P	N	G'	R'	R'	-	-	M'	R'	N	D	N	P	-	N	D
sa	ta	hai	y	hi	-	-	y	hi	ru	la	ta	hai	-	dil	to
P	D	M	-	-	-	N	D	P	D	P	-	-	-	N	D
pa	gl	hai	-	-	-	dil	di	va	na	hai	-	-	-	dil	to
P	-D	-	M	-	N	N	D	P	-D	-	P	-	-	-	-
pa	-g	-l	hai	-	-	dil	di	va	-na	-	hai	-	-	-	-
P	N	G'	R'	R'	-	-	S'	N	S'	S'	R'	R'	-	-	-
sa	ri	sa	ri	ra	-	-t	j	ga	ta	hai	y	hi	-	-	-
P	N	G'	R'	R'	-	-	M'	R'	N	D	-	-	-	-	-
an	khi	yon	se	nin	-	-d	chu	ra	ta	hai	-	-	-	-	-
P	N	G'	R'	R'	-	-	S'	N	S'	S'	R'	R'	-	-	P
sach	che	jhu	the	kha	-	-b	di	kha	ta	hai	y	hi	-	-	hn
P	N	G'	R'	R'	-	-	M'	R'	N	D	N	P	-	N	D
sa	ta	hai	y	hi	-	-	y	hi	ru	la	ta	hai	-	dil	to
P	D	M	-	-	-	N	D	P	D	P	-	-	-	N	D
pa	gl	hai	-	-	-	dil	di	va	na	hai	-	-	-	dil	to
P	-D	-	M	-	N	N	D	P	-D	-	P	-	-	-	-
pa	-g	-l	hai	-	-	dil	di	va	-na	-	hai	-	-	-	-

interlude:

R'-- S' N R'- S' R' P' R'
R'-- S' N R' S' S' R' G' M'-- G' R'-- S' G' R'

N D S' N   S' R'G' S'
tu ru ru ru   ru ru ru ru

G' R' S'G' R'   D N S' N
ru ru ru ru ru   ru ru ru ru

N S' N D N
tu ru ru ru ru

P	PD	N	R'	P	PD	N	R'	S'R'	S'N	S'	-	S'R'	S'N	S'	-
la	ll	la	la	-	-	-	-	lala	ll	la	-	-	-	-	-
P	PD	N	R'	P	PD	N	R'	N	D	N	D	P	-	-	-
la	ll	la	la	-	-	-	-	la	la	la	la	la	-	-	-
	N	D	P	M	P	D	N	D	P	P	-	-	-	-	-
	is	dil	ki	ba	to	me	jo	aa	te	hain	-	-	-	-	-

-	N	D	P	M	P	D	R'	S'	N	D	-	-	-	-	-
-	vo	bhi	di	va	ne	ho	-	ja	te	hain	-	-	-	-	-
-	R'	R'	R'	S'	R'	M'	-S'	N	R'	S'	-	-	-	-	-
-	mn	zil	to	ra	hi	dhun	-dh	le	te	hain	-	-	-	-	-
-	R'	S'	N	R'	S'	D	P	M	-D	-	P	-	-	N	D
-	rs	te	m	g	r	kho	-	ja	-te	-	hain	-	-	dil	to
P	D	M	-	-	-	N	D	P	D	P	-	-	-	N	D
pa	gl	hai	-	-	-	dil	di	va	na	hai	-	-	-	dil	to
P	-D	-	M	-	-	N	D	P	-D	-	P	-	-	-	-
pa	-g	-l	hai	-	-	dil	di	va	-na	-	hai	-	-	-	-

music:
P D NS' NS'- D-
PD DNDP DR'D-
N- G'- R'G'R' S'R'S' NS'N DND PDP M- P-

	N	D	P	M	P	D	N	D	P	P	-	-	-	-	-
	su	rt	se	main	na	p	h	cha	nu	gi	-	-	-	-	-
-	N	D	P	M	P	D	R'	S'	N	D	-	-	-	-	-
-	na	-m	se	bhi	na	us	ko	ja	nu	gi	-	-	-	-	-
-	R'	R'	R'	S'	R'	M'	-S'	N	R'	-	S'	-	S'	R'	-
-	de	kho	ke	khud	se	na	main	so	chun	-	gi	-	-	-	-
-	R'	S'	N	R'	S'	D	P	M	-P	-	P	-	-	N	D
-	dil	jo	k	he	ga	vo	hi	ma	-nu	-	gi	-	-	dil	to
P	D	M	-	-	-	N	D	P	D	P	-	-	-	N	D
pa	gl	hai	-	-	-	dil	di	va	na	hai	-	-	-	han	ye
P	-D	-	M	-	-	N	D	PD	-N	R'	P	-	-	-	-
pa	-g	-l	hai	-	-	han	di	va	-na	-	hai	-	-	-	-

interlude: R' S' N D S' N D
DN D- P- D R'--- MR M- P-
DN D- P- D R'--- M' S'----
DN D- P- D R'--- MR M- P-
PDNS'R'G' M'—R' S' R' M'-- R' N R' M'
G'----- S' D S' G'----
R' G' M'----
G' R' G'M' R' N---- N D P N---
S'---- R'---- R'----
flute: PN DN DN P—
R M- P PN DN P R' R'---

```
R'---- S'  N  S' R'        S'---- N  D  N  S'
hu---- aa  ha ha ha        hu---- aa ho ho ho
```

flute:
```
PN DN DN P—
R M- P PN DN P R' R'---
```

```
      N    S'   R'  | S'   N    N    -   | -    R'   S'   R'  | S'   N    N    -
      dil  -    ka  | k    h    na   -   | -    hm   s    b   | ma   -    ne   -

 -    N    S'   R'  | S'   -    N    -   | S'   -    R'   -   | -    -    G'R'  S'
 -    dil  na   ki  | si   -    ki   -   | ma   -    ne   -   | -    -    -     -

 -    S'   -R'  G'  | R'   -    S'   -   | -    D    -N   S'  | N    -    D     D
 -    ja   -n   ke  | hm   -    ne   -   | -    ja   -n   g   | ye   -    s     b

 -    R'   -    R'  | R'   N    -    D   | N    D    P    -   | N    -    N     D
 -    e    -    k   | vo   hi   -    n   | ja   -    ne   -   | -    -    dil   to

 P    D    M    -   | -    -    N    D   | P    D    P    -   | -    -    N     D
 pa   gl   hai  -   | -    -    dil  di  | va   na   hai  -   | -    -    dil   to

 P    -D   -    M   | -    -    N    D   | PN   -R'  -    P   | -    -    -     -
 pa   -g   -l   hai | -    -    dil  di  | va   -na  -    hai | -    -    -     -
```

interlude:
```
PNR'----- S'- R'G' R'- S'-
S' R' G' P' G' R'   R'G'R' S'R'S'  NS'N DNP
```

```
      N    D    P   | M    P    D    N   | D    P    P    -   | -    -    -     -
      rh   ne   do  | chho do   ye   k   | ha   -ni  yan  -   | -    -    -     -

 -    N    D    P   | M    P    D    R'  | S'   N    D    -   | -    -    -     -
 -    di   va   ne  | pn   ki   sb   ni  | sha  -ni  yan  -   | -    -    -     -

 -    R'   R'   R'  | S'   R'   M'   -S' | N    R'   S'   -   | -    -    -     -
 -    lo   go   ki  | sa   ri   p    re  | sha  -ni  yan  -   | -    -    -     -

 -    R'   S'   N   | R'   S'   D    P   | M    -D   -    P   | -    -    N     D
 -    is   dil  ki  | hai  ye   me   hr  | ba   -ni  yan  -   | -    -    dil   to

 P    D    M    -   | -    -    N    D   | P    D    P    -   | -    -    N     D
 pa   gl   hai  -   | -    -    dil  di  | va   na   hai  -   | -    -    dil   to

 P    -D   -    M   | -    -    N    D   | P    -D   -    P   | -    -    -     -
 pa   -g   -l   hai | -    -    dil  di  | va   -na  -    hai | -    -    -     -

 P    N    G'   R'  | R'   -    -    S'  | N    S'   S'   R'  | R'   -    -     -
 sa   ri   sa   ri  | ra   -    -t   j   | ga   ta   hai  y   | hi   -    -     -

 P    N    G'   R'  | R'   -    -    M'  | R'   N    D    -   | -    -    -     -
 an   khi  yon  se  | nin  -    -d   chu | ra   ta   hai  -   | -    -    -     -
```

P	N	G'	R'	R'	-	-	S'	N	S'	S'	R'	R'	-	-	P
dhi	re	dhi	re	pya	-	-r	si	kha	ta	hai	y	hi	-	-	hn
P	N	G'	R'	R'	-	-	M'	R'	N	D	N	P	-	N	D
sa	ta	hai	y	hi	-	-	y	hi	ru	la	ta	hai	-	dil	to
P	D	M	-	-	-	N	D	P	D	P	-	-	-	N	D
pa	gl	hai	-	-	-	dil	di	va	na	hai	-	-	-	dil	to
P	-D	-	M	-	-	N	D	P	-D	-	P	-	-	N	D
pa	-g	-l	hai	-	-	dil	di	va	-na	-	hai	-	-	dil	to
P	-D	-	M	-	-	N	D	P	-D	-	P	-	-		
pa	-g	-l	hai	-	-	dil	di	va	-na	-	hai	-	-		

11. DIL NE YE KAHA HAI DIL SE

Film: Dhadkan (2000)	Music: Nadeem Shrawan
Lyrics: Sameer	Singer: Udit Narayan, Alka
Taal: Kaharwa	Chord: PNR' S=C

dil ne ye kaha hai dil se mohabbat ho gaee hai tumase
meree jaan mere dilabar mera aitabaar kar lo
jitana bekaraar hoon main khud ko bekaraar kar lo
meree dhadakanon ko samajho tum bhee mujhase pyaar kar lo
meree jaan mere dilabar...

tum jo kah do to, chaand-taaron ko, tod laoonga main
in havaon ko, in ghataon ko, mod laoonga main
kaisa manzar hai meree aankhon mein, kaisa ehasaas hai
paas dariya hai, door sahara hai, phir bhee kyoon pyaas hai
kadamon mein jahaan ye rakh doon mujhase aankhen chaar kar lo
jitana bekaraar hoon main...

meree yaadon mein, mere khvaabon mein, roz aate ho tum
is tarah bhala, meree jaan mujhe, kyoon sataate ho tum
teree baahon se, teree raahon se, yoon na jaoonga main
ye iraada hai, mera vaada hai, laut aaoonga main
duniya se tujhe chura loon thoda intazaar kar lo
jitana bekaraar hoon main...

kaise aankhen chaar kar loon kaise aitabaar kar loon
apanee dhadakanon ko kaise itana bekaraar kar loon
kaise tujhako dil main de doon kaise tujhase pyaar kar loon

DIL NE YE KAHA HAI DIL SE

dha 1	ge 2	n 3	ti 4	n 5	ke 6	dhi 7	n 8	dha 1	ge 2	n 3	ti 4	n 5	ke 6	dhi 7	n 8

```
P D S' DP M* D P
dil ne ye kha hai dil se

PPD      S' DP M* D P
mohobbt ho gyi hai tum se

music:  P P P M*-R,
M M M G-R

P P P M*-R, M M M G-R
        aa-------
P P P M*-R, M M M G-R
        hu-------
```

dha 1	ge 2	n 3	ti 4	n 5	ke 6	dhi 7	n 8	dha 1	ge 2	n 3	ti 4	n 5	ke 6	dhi 7	n 8
												P	-	D	-
												dil	-	ne	-
S'	-	D	P	-	M*	D	-	P	-	-	P	P	-	D	-
ye	-	k	ha	-	hai	di	l	se	-	-	mo	ho	-	b	t
S'	-	D	P	-	M*	D	-	P	-	-	-	P	-	D	-
ho	-	g	yi	-	hai	tu	m	se	-	-	-	me	-	ri	
N	-	R'	S'	-	N	S'	R'	S'	-	-	-	P	-	D	-
ja	-	n	me	-	re	di	l	br	-	-	-	me	-	ra	-
N	-	S'	N	-	D	N	S'	N	-	-	-	P	P	D	-
ae	-	t	ba	-	r	k	r	lo	-	-	-	ji	t	na	-
N	-	R'	S'	-	N	S'	R'	S'	-	-	-	P	P	D	-
be	-	q	ra	-	r	hu	-	main	-	-	-	khu	d	ko	-
N	-	S'	N	-	D	N	S'	N	-	-	-	M	-	P	-
be	-	q	ra	-	r	k	r	lo	-	-	-	me	-	ri	-
P	-	N	D	-	P	N	-	D	-	-	-	D	-	P	-
dh	d	k	no	-	ko	s	m	jho	-	-	-	tum	-	bhi	-
M*	-	M*	M*	-	D	D	-	P	-	-	P	-	P	-	P
mu	jh	se	pya	-	r	k	r	lo	-	-	la	-	la	-	l
M*	-	R	M	-	M	-	M	G	-	R	P	-	P	-	P
la	-	-	la	-	la	-	l	la	-	-	la	-	la	-	l

```
M*   -   R   M   |   -   M   -   M   G   -   R
la   -   -   la  |   -   la  -   l   la  -   -

P  D  S' DP  M* D  P   G'R'S'   R'S'N   G'R'S'   R'S'N
aa------------------   aa------  aa------  aa------  aa------

P P P M*-R,  M M M G-R
aa---------------------

interlude:
P D N S' R'-S' R'-S' N D
S'-N S'-N D P  N-D N-D P M*D-
P D N S' R'-S' R'-S' N D
S'-N S'-N D P  N-D N-D P M* P PP-
synthe: DP M –R- G-R- M-R- G-R-  S S R– G- R-
M- R- G- R- M- R- G- R- S S R– G- R-   PDNR'---
```

R'	-	S'	S'	-	N	-	N	R'	-	S'	S'	-	N	-	N
tum	-	jo	k	h	do	-	to	chan	-	d	ta	-	ro	-	ko

R'	-	S'	S'	-	N	S'	N	D	-	D	N	S'	D	-	-
to	-	d	la	-	un	-	ga	main	-	-	-	-	-	-	-

S'	-	N	N	-	D	-	D	S'	-	N	N	-	D	-	D
i	n	h	va	-	on	-	ko	i	n	gh	ta	-	on	-	ko

S'	-	N	D	-	D	N	D	P	-	-	-	-	-	-	-
mo	-	d	la	-	un	-	ga	main	-	-	-	-	-	-	-

```
P D S'D P M* D P    P P D S'D P M* D P
aa------------------------------------
```

R'	-	S'	S'	-	N	-	N	R'	-	S'	S'	-	N	-	N
kai	-	sa	mn	-	z	r	hai	me	-	ri	aan	-	kho	-	me

R'	-	S'	S'	-	N	S'	N	D	-	D	N	S'	D	-	-
kai	-	sa	a	h	sa	-	s	hai	-	-	-	-	-	-	-

S'	-	N	N	-	D	-	D	S'	-	N	N	-	D	-	D
pa	-	s	d	ri	ya	-	hai	du	-	r	se	h	ra	-	hai

S'	-	N	D	-	D	N	D	P	-	-	-	P	P	D	-
fi	r	bhi	kyu	-	pya	-	s	hai	-	-	-	q	d	mo	-

N	-	R'	S'	-	N	S'	R'	S'	-	G'R'	S'	P	P	D	-
me	-	j	han	-	ye	r	kh	dun	-	-	-	mu	jh	se	-

N	-	S'	N	-	D	N	S'	N	-	-	-	P	P	D	-
aan	-	khen	cha	-	r	k	r	lo	-	-	-	ji	t	na	-

N	-	R'	S'	-	N	G'	R'	S'	-	G'R'	S'	P	P	D	-
be	-	q	ra	-	r	hu	-	main	-	-	-	khu	d	ko	-
N	-	S'	N	-	D	N	S'	N	-	G'R'	S'	M	-	P	-
be	-	q	ra	-	r	k	r	lo	-	-	-	me	-	ri	-
P	-	N	D	-	P	N	-	D	-	-	-	D	-	P	-
dh	d	k	no	-	ko	s	m	jho	-	-	-	tum	-	bhi	-
M*	-	M*	M*	-	D	D	-	P	-	-	P	-	P	-	P
mu	jh	se	pya	-	r	k	r	lo	-	-	la	-	la	-	l
M*	-	R	M	-	M	-	M	G	-	R	P	-	P	-	P
la	-	-	la	-	la	-	l	la	-	-	la	-	la	-	l
M*	-	R	M	-	M	-	M	G	-	R	-	P	-	D	-
la	-	-	la	-	la	-	l	la	-	-	-	dil	-	ne	-
S'	-	D	P	-	M*	D	-	P	-	-	P	P	-	D	-
ye	-	k	ha	-	hai	di	l	se	-	-	mo	ho	-	b	t
S'	-	D	P	-	M*	D	-	P	-	-	-				
ho	-	g	yi	-	hai	tu	m	se	-	-	-				

M'	R'	N	M'	P'	M'	G'	R'	S'	G'
he	he	he	he	ha	ha	ha	ha	ha	ha

G'	S'	D	G'	G'	P'	P'	R'
he	he	he	he	aa	ha	ha	aa

music: P P D N S' N D N S' N
      M P P N D P N D
      D P M* M* M* D D P ---

R'	-	S'	S'	-	N	-	N	R'	-	S'	S'	-	N	-	N
me	-	ri	ya	-	do	-	me	me	-	re	kha	-	bo	-	me
R'	-	S'	S'	-	N	S'	N	D	-	D	N	S'	D	-	-
ro	-	z	aa	-	te	-	ho	tum	-	-	-	-	-	-	-
S'	-	N	N	-	D	D	-	S'	-	N	N	-	D	D	-
i	s	t	rha	-	bh	la	-	me	-	ri	jan	-	mu	jhe	-
S'	-	N	D	-	D	N	D	P	-	-	-	-	-	-	-
kyu	-	s	ta	-	te	-	ho	tum	-	-	-	-	-	-	-
R'	-	S'	S'	-	N	-	N	R'	-	S'	S'	-	N	-	N
te	-	ri	ba	-	hon	-	se	te	-	ri	ra	-	hon	-	se

R'	-	S'	S'	-	N	S'	N	D	-	D	N	S'	D	-	-
yun	-	n	ja	-	un	-	ga	main	-	-	-	-	-	-	-
S'	-	N	N	-	D	-	D	S'	-	N	N	-	D	-	D
ye	-	i	ra	-	da	-	hai	me	-	ra	va	-	da	-	hai
S'	-	N	D	-	D	N	D	P	-	-	-	P	P	D	-
lau	-	t	aa	-	un	-	ga	main	-	-	-	du	ni	ya	-
N	-	R'	S'	-	N	R'	-	S'	R'	R'	R'	P	-	D	-
se	-	tu	jhe	-	chu	ra	-	lun	-	-	-	tho	-	da	-
N	-	S'	N	-	D	N	S'	N	N	N	N	P	P	D	-
in	-	t	za	-	r	k	r	lo	-	-	-	ji	t	na	-
N	-	R'	S'	-	N	G'	R'	S'	R'	R'	R'	P	P	D	-
be	-	q	ra	-	r	hu	-	main	-	-	-	khu	d	ko	-
N	-	S'	N	-	D	N	S'	N	N	N	N	M	-	P	-
be	-	q	ra	-	r	k	r	lo	-	-	-	me	-	ri	-
P	-	N	D	-	P	N	-	D	-	-	-	D	-	P	-
dh	d	k	no	-	ko	s	m	jho	-	-	-	(tum	-	bhi	-
M*	-	M*	M*	-	D	D	-	P	-	-	P	-	P	-	P
mu	jh	se	pya	-	r	k	r	lo)3	-	-	la	-	la	-	l
M*	-	R	M	-	M	-	M	G	-	R	P	-	P	-	P
la	-	-	la	-	la	-	l	la	-	-	la	-	la	-	l
M*	-	R	M	-	M	-	M	G	-	R		P	-	D	-
la	-	-	la	-	la	-	l	la	-	-		kai	-	se	-
N	-	R'	S'	-	N	S'	R'	S'	-	-	-	P	-	D	-
aan	-	khen	cha	-	r	k	r	lun	-	-	-	kai	-	se	-
N	-	S'	N	-	D	N	S'	N	-	-	-	P	P	D	-
ae	-	t	ba	-	r	k	r	lun	-	-	-	a	p	ni	-
N	-	R'	S'	-	N	S'	R'	S'	-	-	-	P	P	D	-
dh	d	k	no	-	ko	kai	-	se	-	-	-	i	t	na	-
N	-	S'	N	-	D	N	S'	N	-	-	-	M	-	P	-
be	-	q	ra	-	r	k	r	lun	-	-	-	kai	-	se	-
P	-	N	D	-	P	N	-	D	-	-	-	D	-	P	-
tu	jh	ko	dil	-	main	de	-	dun	-	-	-	kai	-	se	-

M*	-	M*	M*	-	D	D	-	P	-	-		P	-	D	-
tu	jh	se	pya	-	r	k	r	lun	-	-	-	dil	-	ne	-
S'	-	D	P	-	M*	D	-	P	-	-	P	P	-	D	-
ye	-	k	ha	-	hai	di	l	se	-	-	mo	ho	-	b	t
S'	-	D	P	-	M*	D	-	P	-	-	-	P	-	D	-
ho	-	G	yi	-	hai	tu	M	se	-	-	-	me	-	ri	-
N	-	R'	S'	-	N	S'	R'	S'	-	-	-	P	-	D	-
ja	-	n	me	-	re	di	l	br	-	-	-	me	-	ra	-
N	-	S'	N	-	D	N	S'	N	-	-	-	P	P	D	-
ae	-	t	ba	-	r	k	r	lo	-	-	-	ji	t	na	-
N	-	R'	S'	-	N	S'	R'	S'	-	-	-	P	P	D	-
be	-	q	ra	-	r	hu	-	main	-	-	-	khu	d	ko	-
N	-	S'	N	-	D	N	S'	N	-	-	-	M	-	P	-
be	-	q	ra	-	r	k	r	lo	-	-	-	me	-	ri	-
P	-	N	D	-	P	N	-	D	-	-	-	D	-	P	-
dh	d	k	no	-	ko	s	m	jho	-	-	-	tum	-	bhi	-
M*	-	M*	M*	-	D	D	-	P	-	-	P	-	P	-	P
mu	jh	se	pya	-	r	k	r	lo	-	-	la	-	la	-	l
M*	-	R	M	-	M	-	M	G	-	R					
la	-	-	la	-	la	-	l	la	-	-					

12. DEKHO DEKHO JAANAM HAM

Film: Ishq (1997) Lyrics: Raahat Indauri Taal: Kaharwa	Music: Annu Malik Singer: Udit Narayan, Alka Chord: SGD MDS' S=C#

dekho dekho janam ham, dil apana, tere lie laaye
socho socho duniya mein, kyon aaye, tere lie aaye
ab too hamen chaahe, ab too hamen bhoole,
ham to bane rahenge tere saaye
ree papapa pa, ree papapa -2

yah kya hamen hua yah kya tumhen hua
saanson ke dariya mein gudamud see hone lagee
nayee hai yah saza, saja mein hai maza,
chaahat ko chaahat kee shabanam bhigone lagee
ab aur kya chaahen ab aur kya dekhen
dekha tumhen to dil se nikalee haaye
he dekho dekho janam ham, dil apana, tere lie laaye
socho socho duniya mein, kyon aaye, tere lie aaye
ya yay ya, ya yay ya ya -2

suno zara suno, chuno hamen chuno
aankhon ne aankhon se sharma ke kuchh kah diya
suna mainne suna, chuna tumhen chuna
sheeshe ne sheeshe se takara ke kuchh kah diya
hai pal muraadon ke, ye pal hai yaadon ke,
ab meree jaan rahe ya chalee jaaye
he dekho dekho janam ham, dil apana, tere lie laaye
socho socho duniya mein, kyon aaye, tere lie aaye.......

DEKHO DEKHO JAANAM HAM

dha	ge	n	ti	n	ke	dhi	n	dha	ge	n	ti	n	ke	dhi	n
1	2	3	4	5	6	7	8	1	2	3	4	5	6	7	8

prelude: Chord (SGD) (MDS')
flute:
D- D- NS'NDPM-M-
MGMPN D- D- NS'NDPM-M-
MDPM
bigul: G S'- N D P M -, G S'- N D P M M –
        G R'- S' N N D D P D R' S'-
        S' N D P- M-

Vinod Kumar

G	G	G	G	G	-	D	-	M	-	-	-	M	M	G	G
de	kho	de	kho	ja	-	nm	-	hm	-	-	-	di	l	a	p
S	-	-	-	G	M	R	G	S	-	G	-	-	-	-	-
na	-	-	-	te	re	li	ye	la	-	ye	-	-	-	-	-
N	S'	-	N	D	N	-	D	G	G	G	G	G	G	D	-
-	-	-	-	-	-	-	-	so	cho	so	cho	du	ni	ya	-
M	-	-	-	M	-	G	-	S	-	-	-	G	M	R	G
me	-	-	-	kyu	-	aa	-	ye	-	-	-	te	re	li	ye
S	-	G	-	-	-	N	S'	-	N	D	N	-	D	G	G
aa	-	ye	-	-	-	-	-	-	-	-	-	-	-	a	b
S'	-	-	N	D	-	P	-	M	-	-	-	-	-	G	G
tu	-	-	h	me	-	cha	-	he	-	-	-	-	-	a	b
S'	N	S'	N	D	-	M	-	P	M	-	-	-	-	G	G
tu	-	-	h	me	-	bhu	-	le	-	-	-	-	-	h	m
R'	-	-	S'	N	-	-	N	N	-	N	-	P	-	D	-
to	-	-	b	ne	-	-	r	hen	-	ge	-	te	-	re	-
R'	-	S'	-	-	-	-	-	-	-	-	-	-	-	-	-
sa	-	ye	-	-	-	-	-	-	-	-	-	-	-	-	-

interlude:
S- G M P P S- G M P G'
ri – p p pa pa ri – p p pa ya

bigul: S G N D G' R'G' R'G' G'M'- S'-
       G' R' S' N- D-
S- G M P P S- G M P G'
ri – p p pa pa ri – p p pa ya

															S'
															ye
N	S'	-	-	-	-	-	D	N	-	D	D	-	-	-	S'
kya	-	-	-	-	-	-	h	me	-	hu	aa	-	-	-	ye
N	S'	-	-	-	-	-	D	N	-	D	D	-	-	-	-
kya	-	-	-	-	-	-	tu	mhe	-	hu	aa	-	-	-	-
M	N	-	N	M	N	-	N	M	N	-	N	D	N	-	S'
saan	so	-	ke	dri	ya	-	me	gud	mud	-	si	ho	ne	-	l
N	S'	-	-	N	D	-	-	-	-	-	-	-	-	-	S'
gi	-	-	-	-	-	-	-	-	-	-	-	-	-	-	n

N	S'	-	-	-	-	-	D	N	-	D	D	-	-	-	S'
yi	-	-	-	-	-	-	hai	ye	-	s	za	-	-	-	s

N	S'	-	-	-	-	-	D	N	-	D	D	-	-	-	-
za	-	-	-	-	-	-	me	hai	-	m	za	-	-	-	-

M	N	-	N	M	N	-	N	M	N	-	N	D	N	-	S'
cha	ht	-	ko	cha	ht	-	ki	shb	nm	-	bhi	go	ne	-	l

N	S'	-	-	N	D	-	-	-	-	-	-	-	-	G	G
gi	-	-	-	-	-	-	-	-	-	-	-	-	-	a	b

S'	-	-	N	D	-	P	-	M	-	-	-	-	-	G	G
au	-	-	r	kya	-	cha	-	hen	-	-	-	-	-	a	b

S'	N	S'	N	D	-	M	-	P	M	-	-	-	-	G	-
au	-	-	r	kya	-	de	-	khen	-	-	-	-	-	de	-

R'	-	-	S'	N	-	N	-	D	-	D	-	P	P	D	-
kha	-	-	tum	hen	-	to	-	di	l	se	-	ni	k	li	-

R'	-	S'	-	-	-	-	-	-	-	-	-	R'	-	-	-
ha	-	ye	-	-	-	-	-	-	-	-	-	he	-	-	-

G	G	G	G	G	-	D	-	M	-	-	-
de	kho	de	kho	ja	-	nm	-	hm	-	-	-

interlude: D D D D D D D D D

G'—S' G' M'— M' S' G' M' G'
ya—y y ya-   ya—y y ya- ya-

S' N S' R' S' - S' N G' S' —
bigul: G S'- N D P M -, G S'- N D P M M —
      G R'- S' N N D D P D R' S'-
      S' N D P- M-

															S'
															su

N	S'	-	-	-	-	-	D	N	-	D	D	-	-	-	S'
no	-	-	-	-	-	-	z	ra	-	su	no	-	-	-	chu

N	S'	-	-	-	-	-	D	N	-	D	D	-	-	-	S'
o	-	-	-	-	-	-	h	me	-	chu	no	-	-	-	-

M	N	-	N	M	N	-	N	M	N	-	N	D	N	-	S'
aan	kho	-	ne	aan	kho	-	se	shr	ma	-	ke	kuchh	k	h	di

N	S'	-	-	N	D	-	-	-	-	-	-	-	-	-	S'
ya	-	-	-	-	-	-	-	-	-	-	-	-	-	-	su
N	S'	-	-	-	-	D	-	N	-	D	D	-	-	-	S'
na	-	-	-	-	-	main	-	ne	-	su	na	-	-	-	chu
N	S'	-	-	-	-	-	D	N	-	D	D	-	-	-	-
na	-	-	-	-	-	-	tum	hen	-	chu	na	-	-	-	-
M	N	-	N	M	N	-	N	M	N	-	N	D	N	-	S'
shi	she	-	ne	shi	she	-	se	tk	ra	-	ke	kuchh	k	h	di
N	S'	-	-	N	D	-	-	-	-	-	-	-	-	G	-
ya	-	-	-	-	-	-	-	-	-	-	-	-	-	hai	-
S'	-	-	N	D	-	P	-	M	-	-	-	-	-	G	-
pal	-	-	mu	ra	-	do	-	ke	-	-	-	-	-	ye	-
S'	N	S'	N	D	-	M	-	P	M	-	-	-	-	G	G
pal	-	-	hain	ya	-	do	-	ke	-	-	-	-	-	a	b
R'	-	-	S'	N	-	-	N	D	-	P	-	-	P	D	-
me	-	-	ri	jan	-	-	r	he	-	ya	-	-	ch	li	-
R'	-	S'	-	-	-	-	-	-	-	-	-	R'	-	-	-
ja	-	ye	-	-	-	-	-	-	-	-	-	he	-	-	-
G	G	G	G	G	-	D	-	M	-	-	-				
de	kho	de	kho	ja	-	nm	-	hm	-	-	-				

13. DHARTI SUNAHRI AMBAR NILA

Film: Veer Zara (2004)	Music: Madan Mohan
Lyrics: Javed Akhtar	Singer: Udit Narayan, Lata and others
Taal: Kaharwa	Chord: .NSM SMD S=F

ambar hethaan dharatee vasadee, ethe har rut hansadee,
kinna sona des hai mera
dharatee sunaharee ambar neela, har mausam rangeela, aisa des hai mera
bole papeeha koyal gaaye, saavan ghir-ghir aaye, aisa des hai mera

genhoo ke kheton mein kanghee jo kare havaen
rang-birangee kitanee chunariyaan ud-ud jaen
panaghat par panahaaran jab gagaree bharane aaye
madhur-madhur taanon mein kaheen bansee koee bajae,
lo sun lo, qadam-qadam pe hai mil jaanee, koee prem kahaanee,
aisa des hai mera...

baap ke kandhe chadh ke jahaan bachche dekhen mele
melon mein nat ke tamaashe, kulfee ke chaat ke thele
kaheen milatee meethee golee, kaheen chooran kee hai pudiya
bhole-bhole bachche hain, jaise gudde aur gudiya, aur inako,
roz sunaaye daadee naanee, ik pariyon kee kahaanee,
aisa des hai mera...

sadake sadake jandiye mutiyare ni
kanda chubha tere pare bankiye lade ni
ni adiye kanda chubha tere pare bankiye lade ni
kaun kade tera kandana mutiare ni
kaun sahe teri piir bankiye lade ni
ni adiye kaun sahe teri peer bankiye lade ni

mere des mein mehamaanon ko bhagavaan kaha jaata hai
vo yaheen ka ho jaata hai, jo kaheen se bhee aata hai
tere des ko mainne dekha, tere des ko mainne jaana
jaane kyoon ye lagata hai, mujhako jaana pahachaana,
yahaan bhee, vahee shaam hai, vahee savera -2
aisa hee des hai mera, jaisa des hai tera

Vinod Kumar

DHARTI SUNAHRI AMBAR NILA

dha	ge	n	ti	n	ke	dhi	n	dha	ge	n	ti	n	ke	dhi	n
1	2	3	4	5	6	7	8	1	2	3	4	5	6	7	8

prelude:
P D S'--- N S' R' -- S' N D –P N—S'—S'—N D – PM-
ho--

D D   P D   DD PPD
ambr hethan dhrti vsdi

PP   D P MM   P---D- P-M-
aethe hr rut hnsdi ho----------

RD   PD   MP D PM- GPM<u>GR</u> -
kinna sona <u>des hai mera</u> -3

<u>.N</u>.N SS   RR S   SS
kinna sona <u>des hai   mera</u> -5

music: S-S M-M M S-S P-P P
      S-S <u>N-N N</u>   D- S' <u>N</u>DP-M-
      S-S M-M M S-S P-P P
      S-S <u>N-N N</u>   D-

S	-	S	M	M	-	M	-	M	-	P	D	P	-	M	-
dh	r	ti	su	n	h	ri	-	am	-	b	r	ni	-	la	-
M	-	-	-	-	-	-	-	<u>G</u>	-	-	-	M	-	S	-
aa	-	-	-	-	-	-	-	ho	-	-	-	o	-	o	-
S	-	S	M	M	-	M	-	M	-	P	D	P	-	M	-
dh	r	ti	su	n	h	ri	-	am	-	b	r	ni	-	la	-
M	-	M	-	<u>G</u>	-	<u>R</u>	-	S	-	<u>G</u>	-	<u>R</u>	-	S	-
h	r	mau	-	s	m	rn	-	gi	-	la	-	ae	-	sa	-
<u>.N</u>	-	<u>.N</u>	S	S	-	S	-	<u>G</u>	-	-	-	<u>R</u>	-	S	-
de	-	s	hai	me	-	ra	-	ho	-	-	-	ae	-	sa	-
<u>.N</u>	-	<u>.N</u>	S	S	-	S	-	-	-	-	-	<u>R</u>	-	S	-
de	-	s	hai	me	-	ra	-	-	-	-	-	ae	-	sa	-
<u>.N</u>	-	<u>.N</u>	S	S	-	S	-	<u>G</u>	-	-	-	<u>R</u>	-	S	-
de	-	s	hai	me	-	ra	-	ho	-	-	-	ae	-	sa	-
<u>.N</u>	-	<u>.N</u>	S	S	-	S	-	-	-	-	-	-	-	-	-
de	-	s	hai	me	-	ra	-	-	-	-	-	-	-	-	-

Udit Narayan 51 Songs' Sargam

S	-	S	M	M	-	M	-	M	-	P	D	P	-	M	-
bo	-	le	p	pi	-	ha	-	ko	-	y	l	ga	-	ye	-
M	-	-	-	-	-	-	-	G	-	-	-	M	-	S	-
ae	-	-	-	-	-	-	-	ae	-	-	-	-	-	-	-
S	-	S	M	M	-	M	-	M	-	P	D	P	-	M	-
bo	-	le	p	pi	-	ha	-	ko	-	y	l	ga	-	ye	-
M	-	M	G	G	-	R	-	S	-	G	-	R	-	S	-
sa	-	v	n	ghi	r	ghi	r	aa	-	ye	-	ae	-	sa	-
.N	-	.N	S	S	-	S	-	G	-	-	-	R	-	S	-
de	-	s	hai	me	-	ra	-	ho	-	-	-	ae	-	sa	-
.N	-	.N	S	S	-	S	-	-	-	-	-	-	-	-	-
de	-	s	hai	me	-	ra	-	-	-	-	-	-	-	-	-

interlude: flute: S-S M-M M S-S P-P P
S-S N-N N   D-S' NDPM-

M	-	M	-	P	-	D	-	P	-	D	-	-	-	D	-
ge	-	hu	-	ke	-	khe	-	to	-	me	-	-	-	kn	-
P	-	D	-	P	M	-	G	G	-	M	-	S	-	-	-
ghi	-	jo	-	k	ren	-	h	va	-	yen	-	-	-	-	-
M	-	M	M	P	-	D	-	P	P	D	-	-	-	-	D
rn	-	g	bi	rn	-	gi	-	ki	t	ni	-	-	-	-	chu
P	P	D	-	P	M	M	G	G	-	M	-	S	-	-	-
n	ri	yan	-	u	d	u	d	ja	-	yen	-	-	-	-	-
M	-	M	-	P	-	D	-	P	-	D	-	-	-	D	-
p	n	gh	t	p	r	p	ni	ha	-	rn	-	-	-	j	b
P	P	D	-	P	M	M	-	G	-	M	-	S	-	-	-
g	g	ri	-	bh	r	ne	-	aa	-	ye	-	-	-	-	-
M	M	-	M	P	-	D	-	P	-	D	-	-	-	D	D
m	dhu	r	m	dhu	r	ta	-	no	-	me	-	-	-	k	hin
P	-	D	-	P	M	-	G	G	-	M	S'	S'	-	S'	-
bn	-	si	-	ko	ee	-	b	ja	-	ye	to	su	n	lo	-
S	S	-	M	M	-	M	-	M	P	P	D	P	-	M	-
q	d	m	q	d	m	pe	-	hai	-	mi	l	ja	-	ni	-
M	-	-	-	-	-	M	P	G	-	-	-	M	-	S	-
ee	-	-	-	-	-	h	-	ee	-	y	l	-	-	-	-

Vinod Kumar

```
 S    S    -    M  | M    -    M    -  | M    P    P    D  | P    -    M    -
 q    d    m    q  | d    m    p    r  | hai  -    mi   l  | ja   -    ni   -

 P    -    M    -  | G    -    G    R  | S    -    G    -  | R    -    S    -
 ko   -    ee   -  | pre  -    m    k  | ha   -    ni   -  | ae   -    sa   -

 .N   -    .N   S  | S    -    S    -  | G    -    -    -  | R    -    S    -
 de   -    s    hai| me   -    ra   -  | ho   -    -    -  | ae   -    sa   -

 .N   -    .N   S  | S    -    S    -  | G    -    -    -  | R    -    S    -
 de   -    s    hai| me   -    ra   -  | han  -    -    -  | ae   -    sa   -

 .N   -    .N   S  | S    -    S    -  | -    -            |
 de   -    s    hai| me   -    ra   -  | -    -            |

S' ---- N R' S' R' S'-S' N- N- S' S' N N D P M-
o---------------------------------------------
```

```
                                                            D    D    D
                                                            ho   me   ri

 D    D    D    D  | D    -    D    P  | N    -    D    -  | D    D    D    -
 ju   g    ni   de | dha  -    ge   -  | p    -    gge  -  | ju   g    ni   -

 N    -    -    D  | D    -    D    -  | M    -    M    -  | D    -    D    -
 o    -    s    di | nu   -    to   -  | t    -    bbe  -  | ji   -    nnu  -

 D    -    D    D  | -    D    D    -  | P    -    D    -  | M*   -    M    -
 s    -    tt   i  | -    shq  di   -  | l    -    gge  -  | o    ye   san  ee

 M    M    M    M  | M*   D    D    -  | -    -    -    -  | -    -    M    -
 me   re   ya   o  | ju   g    ni   -  | -    -    -    -  | -    -    vii  r

 M    M    M    M  | M*   D    D    -  | M*   -    M*   -  | M    -    M    -
 me   re   ya   o  | ju   g    ni   -  | ken  h    di   -  | ae   -    o    ye

 M    -    -    M  | M*   -    D    -  | M*   -    M*   -  | M    -    -    -
 na   -    m    san| ee   -    da   -  | len  -    di   -  | ae   -    -    -

 D    -    -    -  | -    -    -    -  | D    -    -    -  | -    -    -    -
 o    ye   -    -  | -    -    -    -  | o    ye   -    -  | -    -    -    -

 M    -    M    M  | P    -    D    -  | P    -    D    -  | -    -    D    -
 ba   -    p    ke | kn   -    dhe  -  | ch   dh   ke   -  | -    -    j    b

 P    -    D    -  | P    -    M    -  | G    M    M    -  | S    -    M    -
 b    ch   che  -  | de   -    khen -  | me   -    le   -  | -    -    me   -
```

M	-	M	-	P	-	P	D	P	-	D	-	-	-	D	-
lo	-	me	-	n	t	ke	t	ma	-	she	-	-	-	ku	I
P	-	D	-	P	-	M	M	G	-	M	-	S	-	-	-
fii	-	ke	-	cha	-	t	ke	the	-	le	-	-	-	-	-
														M	M
														k	hin
M	-	M	-	P	-	D	-	P	-	D	-	-	-	D	-
mi	I	ti	-	mi	-	thi	-	go	-	li	-	-	-	k	hin
P	-	D	-	P	-	M	-	G	M	M	-	S	-	M	-
chu	-	r	n	ki	-	hai	-	pu	di	ya	-	-	-	bho	-
M	-	M	-	P	-	D	-	P	-	D	-	-	-	D	-
le	-	bho	-	le	-	b	ch	che	-	hain	-	-	-	jai	-
P	-	D	-	P	-	M	-	G	M	M	S'	S'	-	S'	-
se	-	gu	d	de	-	au	r	gu	di	ya	aur	i	n	ko	-
S	-	S	M	M	-	M	-	M	-	P	D	P	-	M	-
ro	-	z	su	na	-	yen	-	da	-	di	-	na	-	ni	-
M	-	-	-	-	-	M	P	G	-	-	-	M	-	S	-
ee	-	-	-	-	-	-	-	ho	-	-	-	o	-	o	-
S	-	S	M	M	-	M	-	M	-	P	D	P	-	M	-
ro	-	z	su	na	-	yen	-	da	-	di	-	na	-	ni	-
P	P	M	M	G	-	R	S	S	-	G	-	R	-	S	-
i	k	p	ri	yon	-	ki	k	ha	-	ni	-	ae	-	sa	-
.N	-	.N	S	S	-	S	-	G	s	s	-	R	-	S	-
de	-	s	hai	me	-	ra	-	ho	-	-	-	ae	-	sa	-
.N	-	.N	S	S	-	S	-	-	-	-	-	R	-	S	-
de	-	s	hai	me	-	ra	-	-	-	-	-	ae	-	sa	-
.N	-	.N	S	S	-	S	-	G	s	s	-	R	-	S	-
de	-	s	hai	me	-	ra	-	han	-	-	-	ae	-	sa	-
.N	-	.N	S	S	-	S	-	-	-	-	-	-	-	-	-
de	-	s	hai	me	-	ra	-	-	-	-	-	-	-	-	-

music: S--- M- S--- M- S---

R	G	G	-	G	R	R	-	S	-	-	R	S	-	.N	.N
s	d	ke	-	s	d	ke	-	jan	-	-	di	ye	-	mu	ti

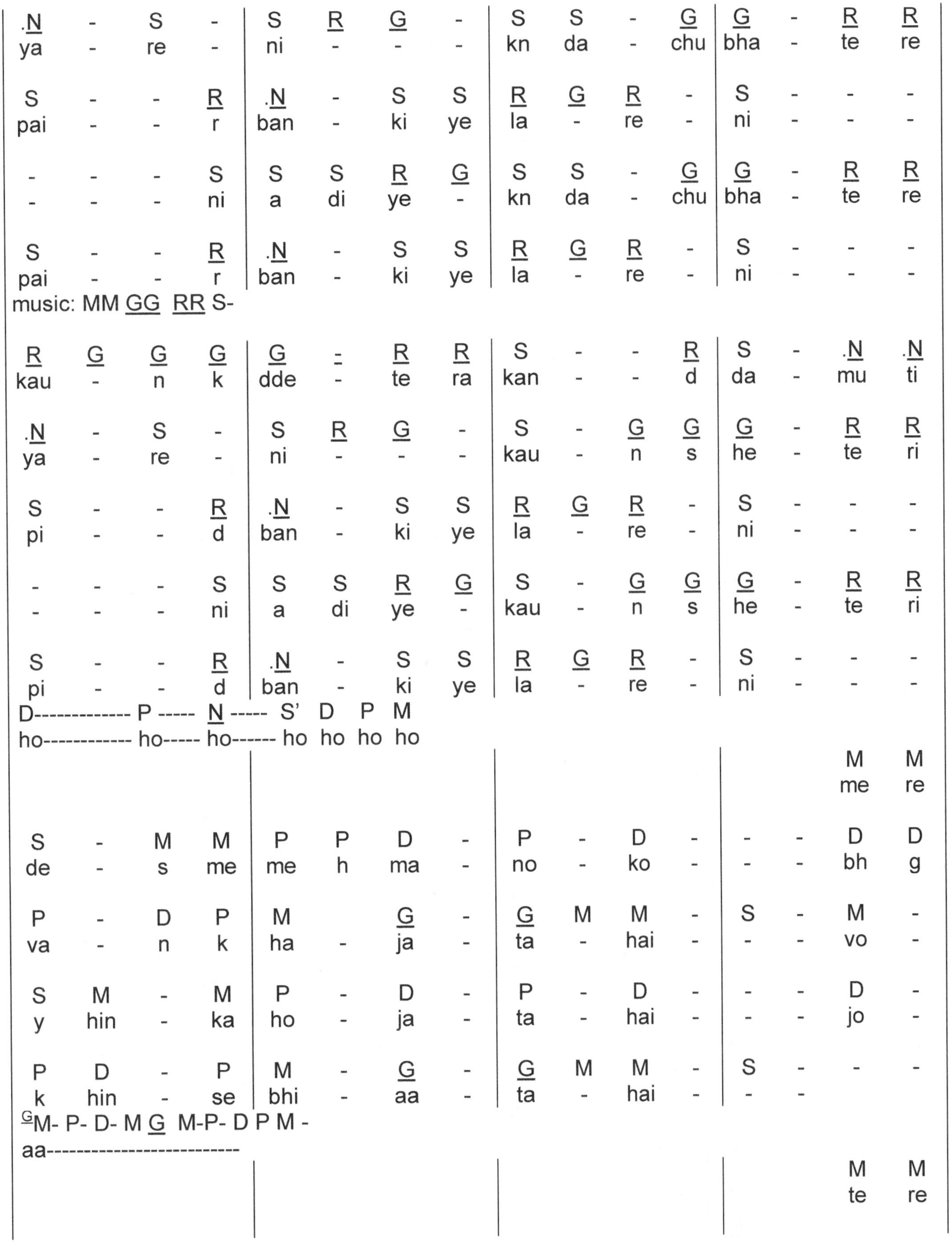

Vinod Kumar

.N	-	S	-	S	R	G	-	S	S	-	G	G	-	R	R
ya	-	re	-	ni	-	-	-	kn	da	-	chu	bha	-	te	re
S	-	-	R	.N	-	S	S	R	G	R	-	S	-	-	-
pai	-	-	r	ban	-	ki	ye	la	-	re	-	ni	-	-	-
-	-	-	S	S	S	R	G	S	S	-	G	G	-	R	R
-	-	-	ni	a	di	ye	-	kn	da	-	chu	bha	-	te	re
S	-	-	R	.N	-	S	S	R	G	R	-	S	-	-	-
pai	-	-	r	ban	-	ki	ye	la	-	re	-	ni	-	-	-

music: MM GG RR S-

R	G	G	G	G	-	R	R	S	-	-	R	S	-	.N	.N
kau	-	n	k	dde	-	te	ra	kan	-	-	d	da	-	mu	ti
.N	-	S	-	S	R	G	-	S	-	G	G	G	-	R	R
ya	-	re	-	ni	-	-	-	kau	-	n	s	he	-	te	ri
S	-	-	R	.N	-	S	S	R	G	R	-	S	-	-	-
pi	-	-	d	ban	-	ki	ye	la	-	re	-	ni	-	-	-
-	-	-	S	S	S	R	G	S	-	G	G	G	-	R	R
-	-	-	ni	a	di	ye	-	kau	-	n	s	he	-	te	ri
S	-	-	R	.N	-	S	S	R	G	R	-	S	-	-	-
pi	-	-	d	ban	-	ki	ye	la	-	re	-	ni	-	-	-

D------------ P ----- N ----- S' D P M
ho------------ ho----- ho------ ho ho ho ho

														M	M
														me	re
S	-	M	M	P	P	D	-	P	-	D	-	-	-	D	D
de	-	s	me	me	h	ma	-	no	-	ko	-	-	-	bh	g
P	-	D	P	M	-	G	-	G	M	M	-	S	-	M	-
va	-	n	k	ha	-	ja	-	ta	-	hai	-	-	-	vo	-
S	M	-	M	P	-	D	-	P	-	D	-	-	-	D	-
y	hin	-	ka	ho	-	ja	-	ta	-	hai	-	-	-	jo	-
P	D	-	P	M	-	G	-	G	M	M	-	S	-	-	-
k	hin	-	se	bhi	-	aa	-	ta	-	hai	-	-	-		

GM- P- D- M G M-P- D P M -
aa-------------------------

														M	M
														te	re

S	-	M	M	P	-	D	-	P	-	D	-	-	-	D	D
de	-	s	ko	main	-	ne	-	de	-	kha	-	-	-	te	re
P	-	D	P	M	-	G	-	G	-	M	-	-	-	-	-
de	-	s	ko	main	-	ne	-	ja	-	na	-	-	-	-	-

D – P N—S' D – P M – M P G – M D P M -
aa---

														M	M
														te	re
S	-	M	M	P	-	D	-	P	-	D	-	-	-	D	D
de	-	s	ko	main	-	ne	-	de	-	kha	-	-	-	te	re
P	-	D	P	M	-	G	-	G	-	M	-	-	-	M	-
de	-	s	ko	main	-	ne	-	ja	-	na	-	-	-	ja	-
S	-	M	-	P	-	D	D	P	-	D	-	-	-	D	P
ne	-	kyu	-	ye	-	l	g	ta	-	hai	-	-	-	mu	jh
P	-	D	-	P	-	M	G	G	-	M	M	G	-	M	-
ko	-	ja	-	n	-	p	h	cha	-	na	y	han	-	bhi	-
S	S	-	M	-	M	M	-	M	P	-	D	P	-	M	-
v	hi	-	sha	-	m	hai	-	v	hi	-	s	ve	-	ra	-
M	-	-	-	-	-	-	-	G	-	-	-	M	-	S	-
aa	-	-	-	-	-	-	-	ho	-	-	-	-	-	-	-
S	S	-	M	-	M	M	-	M	P	-	D	P	-	M	-
v	hi	-	sha	-	m	hai	-	v	hi	-	s	ve	-	ra	-
P	-	M	M	G	-	R	S	S	-	G	-	R	-	S	-
ae	-	sa	hi	de	-	s	hai	me	-	ra	-	jai	-	sa	-
.N	-	.N	S	S	-	S	-	-	-	-	-	R	-	S	-
de	-	s	hai	te	-	ra	-	-	-	-	-	jai	-	sa	-
.N	-	.N	S	S	-	S	-	G	-	-	-	R	-	S	-
de	-	s	hai	te	-	ra	-	han	-	-	-	jai	-	sa	-
.N	-	.N	S	S	-	S	-	-	-	-	-	R	-	S	-
de	-	s	hai	te	-	ra	-	-	-	-	-	ae	-	sa	-
.N	-	.N	S	S	-	S	-	G	-	-	-	R	-	S	-
de	-	s	hai	me	-	ra	-	ho	-	-	-	jai	-	sa	-
.N	-	.N	S	S	-	S	-	-	-	-	-				
de	-	s	hai	te	-	ra	-	-							

14. FIR BHI DIL HAI HINDUSTANI

Film: Fir bhi Dil hai Hindustani (2000)	Music: Jatin Lalit
Lyrics: Javed Akhtar	Singer: Udit Narayan
Taal: Kaharwa	Chord: P$\underline{N}$R' DS'G' S=C

ham logon ko samajh sako to
ham logon ko samajh sako to samajho dilabar jaanee
jitana bhee tum samajhoge utanee hogee hairaanee
apanee chhataree tumako de den kabhee jo barase paanee
kabhee nae paikat me bechen tumako cheez puraanee
(phir bhee dil hai hindustaanee) x 4

thode anaadee hai thode khilaadee,
ruk ruk ke chalatee hai apanee gaadee
hamen pyaar chaahie, aur kuchh paise bhee,
ham aise bhee hain, ham hain vaise bhee
ham logon ko samajh sako to samajho dilabar jaanee
ultee seedhee jaisee bhee hai apanee yahee kahaanee
thodee hamamen hushiyaaree hai thodee hai naadaanee,
thodee hamamen sachchaee hai thodee beeemaanee
(phir bhee dil hai hindustaanee) x 4

aankhon mein kuchh aansoo hai kuchh sapane hain,
aansoo aur sapane donon hee apane hain
dil dukha hai lekin, toota to nahin hai,
ummeed ka daaman, chhoota to nahin hai
ham logon ko samajh sako to samajho dilabar jaanee
thodee majabooree hai lekin thodee hai manamaanee
thodee too too main main hai aur thodee kheencha taanee
ham mein kaaphee baaten hain jo lagatee hain deevaanee
(phir bhee dil hai hindustaanee) x 10

FIR BHI DIL HAI HINDUSTANI

dhage	nti	nke	dhin	dhage	nti	nke	dhin	dhage	nti	nke	dhin	dhage	nti	nke	dhin
12	34	56	78	12	34	56	78	12	34	56	78	12	34	56	78

prelude:

G'---- P' M*'--- G' R' G'- - R' S' R'
aa---------------------------

S' R' G' R' S'- R' S'R'S'N D— S'N D—

D S' G'- R'- S'-
D S' R'-S'- N-
P D S'- N- PD –

P G' R' – G' R'G'R'S' R'
NS'G'S' R'S' D ---

D	D	D	D	D	D	D	D	D	D	D	D	D	P	-	-
hm	lo	go	ko	sm	jhs	ko	to	sm	jho	dil	br	ja	ni	-	-
P	P	P	P	P	P	S'	S'	S'	S'	S'	N	D	D	-	-
jit	na	bhi	tum	sm	jho	ge	ut	ni	ho	gi	hai	ra	ni	-	-
D	D	D	D	D	D	D	D	D	D	D	D	D	P	-	-
ap	ni	chht	ri	tum	ko	de	den	kbhi	-jo	br	se	pa	ni	-	-
P	P	P	P	P	P	S'	S'	S'	S'	S'	NN	D	D	D	D
kbhi	-n	ye	pai	ket	me	be	chen	tum	ko	chi	zpu	ra	ni	fir	bhi
D	D	D	D	D	P	P	P	S'	S'	S'	N	D	D	D	D
dil	hai	hin	dus	ta	ni	fir	bhi	dil	hai	hin	dus	ta	ni	fir	bhi
D	D	D	D	S'	D	P	P	S'	S'	S'	N	D	D		
dil	hai	hin	dus	ta	ni	fir	bhi	dil	hai	hin	dus	ta	ni		

interlude:
P' P'D' P'D' G' G' G'M' G'R' S' PS' PS' R'- G' M' G' R' G'-

P' P'P' D' G'   G' G' G'R' S'
| | | la la | | | | | la

PS' PS' R'   G' M' G' R' P' P'
| la | la la | | | | la

S'N P- R'- S'- R'- G'M' G'R' P'- G''--R' S'NDP D- G'----

G'	G'	G'	G'	-	R'	R'	S'	R'R'	S'	R'	-	-	-	-
tho	de	a	na	-	di	hain	tho	dekhi	la	di	-	-	-	-

-	R'	R'	R'	R'	-	S'	S'	N	S'	N	S'	-	-	-	R'
-	ruk	ruk	ke	chl	-	ti	hai	ap	ni	ga	di	-	-	-	hme
R'	R'N	-D	D	-	-	-	R'	R'	R'	N	D	-	-	-	D
pya	rcha	-hi	ae	-	-	-	aur	kuchh	pai	se	bhi	-	-	-	hm
P	S'	N	S'	-	-	-	D	P	D	D	D	-	-	-	-
ae	se	bhi	hain	-	-	-	hm	hain	vai	se	bhi	-	-	-	-
D	D	D	D	D	D	D	D	D	D	D	D	D	P	-	-
hm	lo	go	ko	sm	jhs	ko	to	sm	jho	dil	br	ja	ni	-	-
P	P	P	P	P	P	S'	S'	S'	S'	NS'	N	D	D	-	-
ul	ti	si	dhi	kai	si	bhi	hai	ap	ni	yhi	-k	ha	ni	-	-
D	D	D	D	D	D	D	D	D	D	D	D	D	P	-	-
tho	di	hm	me	hushi	ya	ri	hai	tho	di	hai	na	da	ni	-	-
P	P	P	P	P	P	S'	S'	S'	S'	S'	N	D	D	D	D
tho	di	hm	me	sch	cha	ee	hai	tho	di	be	ee	ma	ni	fir	bhi
D	D	D	D	D	P	P	P	S'	S'	S'	N	D	D	D	D
dil	hai	hin	dus	ta	ni	fir	bhi	dil	hai	hin	dus	ta	ni	fir	bhi
P	-S'	-	-	-	-	S'	N	D	-D	-	-	-	-	-	-
dil	-hai	-	-	-	-	hin	dus	ta	-ni	-	-	-	-	-	-

interlude:
DN S' S'N S'G' N S' ---
DN S' S'N S'G' N S'R' NS' ---
PDN ND N ND NR' N NS'G' D----
flute: N DP D –

DN S'—ND-   R'—S'N P—D NS' NS' D---
aa aa –aaa – aa –aaa   aa-a aaa aaa aa---

-	G'	G'	G'	G'	-	R'	R'	S'	R'R'	S'	R'	-	-	-	-
-	aan	kho	me	kuchh	aan	su	hain	kuchh	sp	ne	hain	-	-	-	-
-	R'	R'	R'	R'	R'	S'	N	D	S'	N	S'	-	-	-	R'
-	aan	su	aur	sp	ne	do	no	hi	ap	ne	hain	-	-	-	dil
S'R'	-S'	-D	D	-	-	-	R'	R'	S'N	D	D	-	-	-	D
dukha	-hai	le	kin	-	-	-	tu	ta	ton	hin	hai	-	-	-	un
P	PS'	N	S'	-	-	-	D	P	DN	D	D	-	-	-	-
mi	dka	da	mn	-	-	-	chhu	ta	ton	hin	hai	-	-	-	-
D	D	D	D	D	D	D	D	D	D	D	D	D	P	-	-
hm	lo	go	ko	sm	jhs	ko	to	sm	jho	dil	br	ja	ni	-	-

P	P	P	P	P	P	S'	S'	S'	S'	S'	<u>N</u>	D	D	-	-
tho	di	mj	bu	ri	hai	le	kin	tho	di	hai	mn	ma	ni	-	-
D	D	D	D	D	D	D	D	D	D	D	D	D	P	-	-
tho	di	tu	tu	main	main	hai	aur	tho	di	khi	cha	ta	ni	-	-
P	P	P	P	P	P	S'	S'	S'	S'	S'	<u>N</u>	D	D	D	D
hm	me	ka	fii	ba	te	hai	jo	lg	ti	hain	di	va	ni	fir	bhi
D	D	D	D	D	P	P	P	S'	S'	S'	<u>N</u>	D	D	D	D
dil	hai	hin	dus	ta	ni	fir	bhi	dil	hai	hin	dus	ta	ni	fir	bhi
P	-S'	-	-	-	-	S'	<u>N</u>	D	-D	-	-	-	-	-	-
dil	hai	-	-	-	-	hin	dus	ta	-ni	-	-	-	-	-	-

15. GHAR SE NIKALTE HI

Film: Papa Kahte Hain (1996)	Music: Rajesh Raushan
Lyrics: Javed Akhtar	Singer: Udit Narayan
Taal: Kaharwa	Chord: RMD MDS' S=C

ghar se nikalate hee kuchh door chalate hee, raste mein hai usaka ghar
kal subah dekha to baal banaatee vo, khidakee mein aaee nazar

maasoom chehara, neechee nigaahen, bholee see ladakee, bholee adaen
na apsara hai, na vo paree hai, lekin ye usakee jaadoogaree hai
deevaana kar de vo, ek rang bhar de vo, sharma ke dekhe jidhar

karata hoon usake ghar ke main phere
hansane lage hain ab dost mere
sach kah raha hoon usakee kasam hai
main phir bhee khush hoon bas ek gam hai
jise pyaar karata hoon main jisape marata hoon
usako nahin hai khabar

ladakee hai jaise koee pahelee
kal jo milee mujhako usakee sahelee
mainne kaha usako ja ke ye kahana
achchha nahin hai yoon door rahana
kal shaam nikale vo ghar se tahalane ko
milana jo chaahe agar

Vinod Kumar

GHAR SE NIKALTE HI

dha 1	ge 2	n 3	ti 4	n 5	ke 6	dhi 7	n 8	dha 1	ge 2	n 3	ti 4	n 5	ke 6	dhi 7	n 8
											G	M	R	-	G
											gh	r	se	-	ni
M	-	-	-	G	P	-	M	-	-	-	D	D	D	-	S'
kl	-	-	-	-	te	-	hi	-	-	-	ku	chh	du	-	r
P	-	-	-	-	G	P	M	-	-	-	N	S'	M'	-	G'
chl	-	-	-	-	te	-	hi	-	-	-	r	s	te	-	me
S'	-	-	-	-	P	P	P	D	-	-	-	-	-	-	-
hai	-	-	-	-	u	s	ka	ghr	-	-	-	-	-	-	-
S'	-	-	ᴰP	-	-	M	-	-	-	-	M	-	G	R	G
-	-	-	-	-	-	-	-	-	-	-	k	l	su	b	h
M	-	-	-	G	P	-	M	-	-	-	D	-	D	-	S'
de	-	-	-	-	kha	-	to	-	-	-	ba	-	l	-	b
P	-	-	-	-	G	P	M	-	-	-	S'	-	M'	-	G'
na	-	-	-	-	ti	-	vo	-	-	-	khi	d	ki	-	me
S'	-	-	-	-	P	-	P	D	-	-	-	-	-	-	-
aa	-	-	-	-	yi	-	n	zr	-	-	-	-	-	-	-
S'	-	-	ᴰP	-	-	M	-	-	-	-	G	M	R	-	G
-	-	-	-	-	-	-	-	-	-	-	gh	r	se	-	ni
M	-	-	-	G	P	-	P	M	-	-					
kl	-	-	-	-	te	-	hi	-							

interlude:
PDS'P-- M-G P-   PDS'P-- M-G M- 2

D S' M' G' --- R' --- N N---   D D R M D P - N S' D----
aa-----------aa -----------   music:

dha 1	ge 2	n 3	ti 4	n 5	ke 6	dhi 7	n 8	dha 1	ge 2	n 3	ti 4	n 5	ke 6	dhi 7	n 8
											D	-	N	-	R'
											ma	-	su	-	m

```
R'   -   R'  -   | -   R'  -   -   | -   -   -   D   | -   N̲  -   R'
che  -   h   -   | -   ra  -   -   | -   -   -   ni  | -   chi -   ni

S'   -   -   -   | -   S'  -   -   | -   -   -   D   | -   N̲  -   G'
ga   -   -   -   | -   hen -   -   | -   -   -   bho | -   li  -   si

R'   -   R'  -   | -   R'  -   -   | -   -   -   D   | -   N̲  -   R'
l    -   d   -   | -   ki  -   -   | -   -   -   bho | -   li  -   a

S'   -   -   -   | -   S'  -   -   | -   -   -   N   | -   N   -   N
da   -   -   -   | -   yen -   -   | -   -   -   na  | -   a   p   s

N    -   -   -   | -   S'  -   D   | -   -   -   D   | N̲  S'  -   N̲
ra   -   -   -   | -   hai -   -   | -   -   -   na  | -   vo  -   p

D    -   -   -   | -   D   -   -   | -   -   -   P   | -   P   -   P
ri   -   -   -   | -   hai -   -   | -   -   -   le  | -   ki  n   ye

P    -   P   -   | P   -   -   -   | -   -   -   R   | -   M   -   M
u    -   s   -   | ki  -   -   -   | -   -   -   ja  | -   du  -   g

M    -   -   -   | M   -   -   -   | -   -   -   G   | M   R   -   G
ri   -   -   -   | hai -   -   -   | -   -   -   di  | -   va  -   na

M    -   -   -   | G   P   -   M   | -   -   -   D   | D   D   -   S'
kr   -   -   -   | -   de  -   vo  | -   -   -   i   | k   rn  -   g

P    -   -   -   | -   G   P   M   | -   -   -   S'  | S'  M'  -   G'
bhr  -   -   -   | -   de  -   vo  | -   -   -   sh  | r   ma  -   ke

S'   -   -   -   | -   P   -   P   | D   -   -   -   | -   -   -   -
de   -   -   -   | -   khe -   ji  | dhr -   -   -   | -   -   -   -

S'   -   -   ᴰP  | -   -   M   -   | -   -   -   G   | M   R   -   G
-    -   -   -   | -   -   -   -   | -   -   -   gh  | r   se  -   ni

M    -   -   -   | G   P   -   M   | -   -   -   D   | D   D   -   S'
kl   -   -   -   | -   te  -   hi  | -   -   -   ku  | chh du  -   r

P    -   -   -   | -   G   P   M   | -   -   -   N   | S'  M'  -   G'
chl  -   -   -   | -   te  -   hi  | -   -   -   r   | s   te  -   me

S'   -   -   -   | -   P   P   P   | D   -   -   -   | -   -   -   -
hai  -   -   -   | -   u   s   ka  | ghr -   -   -   | -   -   -   -
```

interlude:
PDS'P-- M-G P-   PDS'P-- M-G M- 2

```
D S' M' G' --- R' --- N̲ N---   D̲ D  R M D P - N S' D--
aa-----------   aa -----------   music:
```

											D k	- r	<u>N</u> ta	- -	R' hu
R' u	- -	R' s	- -	R' ke	- -	- -	- -	- -	- -	- -	D gh	- r	<u>N</u> ke	- -	R' main
S' fe	- -	- -	- -	S' re	- -	- -	- -	- -	- -	- -	D hn	D s	<u>N</u> ne	- -	G' l
R' ge	- -	- -	- -	R' hain	- -	- -	- -	- -	- -	- -	D a	D b	<u>N</u> do	- s	R' t
S' me	- -	- -	- -	S' re	- -	- -	- -	- -	- -	- -	N s	N ch	N k	- h	N r
N ha	- -	- -	- -	S' hu	- -	- -	- -	D -	- -	- -	D u	<u>N</u> s	S' ki	- -	<u>N</u> k
D sm	- -	- -	- -	D hai	- -	- -	- -	- -	- -	- -	P main	- -	P fi	- r	P bhi
P khu	- -	P sh	- -	- -	P hu	- -	- -	- -	- -	- -	R b	R s	M e	- -	M k
M gm	- -	- -	- -	- -	M hai	- -	- -	- -	- -	- -	G ji	M se	R pya	- -	G r
M kr	- -	- -	- -	G -	P ta	- -	M hu	- -	- -	- -	D main	- -	D ji	D s	S' pe
P mr	- -	- -	- -	- -	G ta	P -	M hu	- -	- -	- -	S' u	S' s	M' ko	- -	G' n
S' hin	- -	- -	- -	- -	P hai	- -	P kh	D br	- -	- -	- -	- -	- -	- -	- -
S' -	- -	- -	[D]P -	- -	- -	M -	- -	- -	- -	- -	G gh	M r	R se	- -	G ni
M kl	- -	- -	- -	G -	P te	- -	M hi	- -	- -	- -	D ku	D chh	D du	- -	S' r
P chl	- -	- -	- -	- -	G te	P -	M hi	- -	- -	- -	N r	S' s	M' te	- -	G' me
S' hai	- -	- -	- -	- -	P u	P s	P ka	D ghr	- -	- -	- -	- -	- -	- -	- -

interlude:
PDS'P-- M-G P-   PDS'P-- M-G M- 2

D S' M' G' ---   R' --- N̲ N---   D̲ D̲ R M D P - N S' D--
aa-----------   aa -----------   music:--------------

M1				M2				M3				M4			
								- -	- -	- -	D l	- d	N̲ ki	- -	R' hai
R' jai	- -	- -	- -	- -	R' se	- -	- -	- -	- -	- -	D ko	- -	N̲ ee	- -	R' p
S' he	- -	- -	- -	- -	S' li	- -	- -	- -	- -	- -	D k	- l	N̲ jo	- -	G' mi
R' li	- -	- -	- -	R' mu	R' jh	R' ko	- -	- -	- -	- -	D u	D s	N̲ ki	- -	R' s
S' he	- -	- -	- -	- -	S' li	- -	- -	- -	- -	- -	N main	- -	N ne	- -	N k
N ha	- -	- -	- -	N u	N s	S' ko	- -	- -	D -	- -	D ja	N̲ -	S' ke	- -	N̲ ye
D k	- -	D h	- -	- -	D na	- -	- -	- -	- -	- -	P a	- ch	P chha	- -	P n
P hin	- -	- -	- -	- -	P hai	- -	- -	- -	- -	- -	R yun	- -	M du	- -	M r
M r	- -	M h	- -	- -	M na	- -	- -	- -	- -	- -	G k	M l	R sha	- -	G m
M ni	- -	M k	- -	- -	P le	- -	M vo	- -	- -	- -	D gh	D r	D se	- -	S' t
P h	- -	P l	- -	- -	G ne	P -	M ko	- -	- -	- -	S' mi	S' l	M' na	- -	G' jo
S' cha	- -	- -	- -	- -	P he	- -	P a	D gr	- -	- -	- -	- -	- -	- -	- -
S' -	- -	- -	ᴰP -	- -	- -	M -	- -	- -	- -	- -	G gh	M r	R se	- -	G ni
M kl	- -	- -	- -	G -	P te	- -	M hi	- -	- -	- -	D ku	D chh	D du	- -	S' r
P chl	- -	- -	- -	- -	G te	P -	M hi	- -	- -	- -	N r	S' s	M' te	- -	G' me

Vinod Kumar

| S' | - | - | - | - | P | P | P | D | - | - | - | - | - | - | - |
| hai | - | - | - | - | u | s | ka | ghr | - | - | - | - | - | - | - |

16. GORE 2 MUKHDE PE KALA 2 CHASHMA

Film: Suhag (1994)	Music: Anand Milind
Lyrics: Sameer	Singer: Udit Narayan
Taal: Kaharwa	Chord: PNR' S=C

gore gore mukhade pe kaala kaala chashma -2
tauba khuda khair kare khoob hai karishma, khoob hai karishma
gore gore mukhade pe kaala kaala chashma

dekho isako gaur se ladakee hai ke hoor hai
jaadoo isake roop mein ye kitanee magaroor hai
dekhoon jab dekhoon ise dil dhadake
tadape javaanee daee aankh phadake
tauba khuda khair kare khoob hai karishma, khoob hai karishma
gore gore mukhade pe kaala kaala chashma

aadat apanee chhod de kahana mera maan le
jaane main kya cheez hoon too mujhako pahachaan le
ja re ja anaadee aise baaten na bana
jaanoon main to jaanoon teree marzee hai kya
toone meree jaan mera dekha na karishma, dekha na karishma
gore gore mukhade pe kaala kaala chashma

Vinod Kumar

GORE 2 MUKHDE PE KALA 2 CHASHMA

dha 1	ge 2	n 3	ti 4	n 5	ke 6	dhi 7	n 8	dha 1	ge 2	n 3	ti 4	n 5	ke 6	dhi 7	n 8

prelude:
P' P'M' P' P'M' P' P'M' P'D'P'M' M'R'—
PNN PNN PNN D-P P MPDP
PDPDP---   PDPDP---

N	N	N	N	D	D	D	P	M	P	D	P	P	P	P	P
go	re	go	re	mu	kh	de	pe	ka	la	ka	la	ch	sh	ma	-
R'	-	R'	-	-	R'	R'	-	R'	-	G'	-	G'	G'	G'	R'
tau	-	ba	-	-	khu	da	-	khai	-	-	-	r	k	re	-
S'	-	S'	-	S'	S'	-	S'	S'	-	R'	-	R'	S'	N	
-	-	khu	-	b	hai	-	k	ri	-	sh	-	ma	-	-	-
-	-	R'	-	N	D	-	D	P	-	D	-	D	P	M	
-	-	khu	-	b	hai	-	k	ri	-	sh	-	ma	-	-	-
N	N	N	N	D	D	D	P	M	P	D	P	P	P	P	-
go	re	go	re	mu	kh	de	pe	ka	la	ka	la	ch	sh	ma	

interlude: P' P' M' R' P' P' M' R' S'R' S'R' – 2
R'R'R' S'S' D M' M' M' M' P' R'—
R' S'S'S' S' DD P- PDS'R'---

R'	-	R'	-	R'	G'	G'	-	R'	-	-	R'	R'	-	-	-
de	-	kho	-	i	s	ko	-	gau	-	-	r	se	-	-	-
R'	-	R'	-	R'	G'	G'	-	R'	-	-	R'	R'	-	-	-
l	d	ki	-	hai	-	ke	-	hu	-	-	r	hai	-	-	-
R'	-	N	-	D	-	P	-	P	D	M	P	D	-	-	-
ja	-	du	-	i	s	ke	-	ru	-	-	p	me	-	-	-
M	-	P	P	D	-	D	P	P	-	-	P	P	-	-	-
ye	-	ki	t	ni	-	m	g	ru	-	-	r	hai	-	-	-
M	P	D	P	M	P	D	P	M	P	D	R'	S'	-	-	-
de	khu	j	b	de	khu	u	se	di	l	dh	d	ke	-	-	-
R'	S'	S'	N	D	D	P	P	M	P	D	P	P	-	-	-
s	r	pe	j	va	ni	da	yin	aan	kh	f	d	ke	-	-	-
R'	-	R'	-	-	R'	R'	-	R'	-	G'	-	G'	G'	G'	R'
tau	-	ba	-	-	khu	da	-	khai	-	-	-	r	k	re	-

S'	-	S'	-	S'	S'	-	S'	S'	-	R'	-	R'	S'	N	-
-	-	khu	-	b	hai	-	k	ri	-	sh	-	ma	-	-	-
-	-	R'	-	N	D	-	P	P	-	D	-	D	P	M	-
-	-	khu	-	b	hai	-	k	ri	-	sh	-	ma	-	-	-
N	N	N	N	D	D	D	P	M	P	D	P	P	P	P	-
go	re	go	re	mu	kh	de	pe	ka	la	ka	la	ch	sh	ma	-

interlude: P' P' M' R' P' P' M' R' S'R' S'R' – 2
R'R'R' S'S' D M' M' M' M' P' R'—
R' S'S'S' S' DD P- PDS'R'---

R'	-	R'	-	R'	G'	G'	-	R'	-	-	R'	R'	-	-	-
aa	-	d	t	a	p	ni	-	chho	-	-	d	de	-	-	-
R'	-	R'	-	R'	G'	G'	-	R'	-	-	R'	R'	-	-	-
k	h	na	-	me	-	ra	-	ma	-	-	n	le	-	-	-
R'	-	N	-	D	-	P	-	P	D	M	P	D	-	-	-
ja	-	ne	-	main	-	kya	-	chi	-	-	z	hu	-	-	-
M	-	P	P	D	-	D	P	P	-	-	P	P	-	-	-
tu	-	mu	jh	ko	-	p	h	cha	-	-	n	le	-	-	-
M	P	D	P	M	P	D	P	M	P	D	R'	S'	-	-	-
ja	re	ja	a	na	di	ae	si	ba	te	na	b	na	-	-	-
R'	S'	S'	N	D	D	P	P	M	P	D	P	P	-	-	-
ja	nu	main	to	ja	nu	te	ri	m	r	zi	hai	kya	-	-	-
R'	-	R'	-	-	R'	-	R'	R'	-	G'	G'	G'	-	G'	R'
tu	-	ne	-	-	me	-	ri	ja	-	-	n	me	-	ra	-
S'	-	S'	-	S'	S'	-	S'	S'	-	R'	-	R'	S'	N	-
-	-	de	-	kha	n	-	k	ri	-	sh	-	ma	-	-	-
-	-	R'	-	N	D	-	P	P	-	D	-	D	P	M	-
-	-	de	-	kha	n	-	k	ri	-	sh	-	ma	-	-	-
N	N	N	N	D	D	D	P	M	P	D	P	P	P	P	-
go	re	go	re	mu	kh	de	pe	ka	la	ka	la	ch	sh	ma	-

Vinod Kumar

17. HAM PYAR KARNE WALE

Film: dil (1990)	Music: Anand Milind
Lyrics: Sameer	Singer: Udit Narayan, Anuradha
Taal: Kaharwa	Chord: PNR' GPN S=C#

ham pyaar karane vaale, duniya se na darane vaale -2
duniya se na darane vaale
yaar jalane vaalon ko jalaenge, pyaar mein jiyenge mar jaenge -2

rok sake jo, dilavaalon ko, aisee koee jel nahin -2
dil ka lagaana, is duniya mein, logo koee khel nahin -2
baandha hai kisane paagal hava ko?
roka hai kisane udatee ghata ko?
tod ke pinjara, ud jaenge, haath nahin ham aaenge
yaar jalane vaalon ko jalaenge, pyaar mein jiyenge mar jaenge -2

laila nahin ham, majanoon nahin ham,
zulmo-sitam jo hans ke sahen -2
roke kisake, ham to ruke na, apana milaan to hoke rahe -2
pyaar kiya hai pyaar karenge
ham to zamaane se na darenge
apanee mohabbat, kee taaqat se, duniya ko jhukaenge
yaar jalane vaalon ko jalaenge,
pyaar mein jiyenge mar jaenge -2

HAM PYAR KARNE WALE

dhage	nti	nke	dhin	dhage	nti	nke	dhin	dhage	nti	nke	dhin	dhage	nti	nke	dhin
12	34	56	78	12	34	56	78	12	34	56	78	12	34	56	78

prelude: sitar:-
G' G'G' G'G' G'G' R'R'S' R'R'S'- 2
P S'S' S'S' S'S' P R'R' R'R' R'R'
P G'G' G'G' G'G' P M'M' M'M' M'M'
P'M' P'M' G'M'G'R' G'R'S' R'S'N S'N-
M'G' M'G' R'G'R'S' S'R'S'NS' NDP
R'S' R'S' S'R'S'N S'ND S'DS'NDP

R'S' R'S' R'S' R'S' N N- N R'S' R'S' R'S' R'S'
R'S' R'S' R'S' R'S' N N- N R'S' R'S' R'S' R'S'

```
P'  M'G'  M'G'  R'G'S'-
aa----------------

D N S'R' S' N D
aa---------------

P D N D N R' S'
aa---------------

D P D N S' S' -2
```

														G'	-
														hm	-
S'	G'	-	-	S'	S'	-	N	S'	-	S'	-	-	-	G'	G'
pya	-	-	-	r	kr	-	ne	va	-	le	-	-	-	du	ni
S'	G'	G'	-	S'	S'	-	N	S'	-	S'	-	-	-	S'	S'
ya	-	se	-	na	dr	-	ne	va	-	le	-	-	-	du	ni
S'	N	N	-	D	D	-	P	N	-	-	-	D	-	P	-
ya	-	se	-	na	dr	-	ne	va	-	-	-	le	-	-	-
P	-D	D	P	P	R'	R'	N	N	-	D	P	M	-	-	-
ya	-r	jl	ne	va	lo	ko	j	la	-	yen	-	ge	-	-	-
M	-P	P	M	M	N	-N	-N	D	-	P	-	P	-	-	-
pya	-r	me	jii	yen	ge	-m	-r	ja	-	yen	-	ge	-	-	-

```
interlude:
NS' NS' NS'  N N N  S'- 2
N N S' R' R'R' R'R' R'R'
D DD DD DD
R' R'R' R'R' R'R' G'R'R' M'G'G'  P'M'M' P'M'R'G' S'-

G' R' G' M' G' R' G' S'-
aa----------------

G' R' G' M' G' S' N D
aa----------------

P P D N S' R' N D P-  P P D P M P D P-  -2
P'-R'S' -4  M P D N S' R' G' M' P'---
```

	S'	-S'	-S'	R'	-	S'	-	-	S'	-S'	-	R'	S'	S'	-
	ro	-k	-s	ke	-	jo	-	-	dil	-va	-	lo	-	ko	-
-	M'	-	R'	S'	-	N	-	R'	R'	-	S'	S'	-	-	-
-	ae	-	si	ko	-	ee	-	je	-l	n	hin	-	-	-	-

```
music: sitar: R'R'S' R'R'S'  S'R'S'NS'R'S'----
```

R'S'	R'S'	N	N	S'N	S'N	D	D	P	P	M	G	D	-P	P	-
dil	kal	ga	na	is	duni	ya	me	lo	go	ko	ee	khe	ln	hin	-
-	P	-M	-G	N	N	N	-	-	D	-P	-M	D	-	P	-
-	ban	-dha	-hai	ki	s	ne	-	-	pa	-gl	-h	va	-	ko	-
-	P	-M	-G	N	N	N	-	-	D	-P	-M	D	-	P	-
-	ro	-ka	-hai	ki	s	ne	-	-	ud	-ti	-h	va	-	ko	-
-	G'	-G'	-R'	G'	G'	G'	-	-	R'R'	-S'	N	S'	-	N	-
-	to	-d	-ke	pin	j	ra	-	-	ud	-ja	-	yen	-	ge	-
-	N	-N	-N	G'	-	S'	-	N	-	D	P	N	-	D	P
-	ha	-th	-n	hin	-	hm	-	aa	-	yen	-	ge	-	-	-
P	-D	D	P	P	R'	R'	N	N	-	D	P	M	-	-	-
ya	-r	jl	ne	va	lo	ko	j	la	-	yen	-	ge	-	-	-
M	-P	P	M	M	N	-N	-N	D	-	P	-	P	-	-	-
pya	-r	me	jii	yen	ge	-m	-r	ja	-	yen	-	ge	-	-	-

interlude:
N S' R' G' P'--- 2
S'S'S'S' S'S'S'S' R'R'R'R' R'R'R'R'
MPDNS'R'G'M'P'--
PDDPPR'R'NN- DPM--
MPPMMNN- DPP—

PDDPPR'R'NN DPM—
aa---------------------------

MPPMMNN DPP—
aa-------------------------

	S'	-S'	-S'	R'	-	S'	-	-	S'S'	-S'	- S'	R'	-	S'	-
	lai	-la	-n	hin	-	hm	-	-	mj	-nu	-n	hin	-	hm	-
-	M'	-R'	-S'	S'	-	N	-	R'	R'R'	-S'	-S'	S'	-	-	-
-	jul	-mo	-si	tm	-	jo	-	-	hns	-ke	-s	hen	-	-	-

music: sitar: R'R'S' R'R'S' S'R'S'NS'R'S'----

R'S'	R'S'	N	N	S'N	S'N	D	D	DD	DP	M	G	D	DP	P	-
ro-	keki	si	ke	hm	toru	ke	na	ap	nami	ln	to	ho	ker	he	-
-	P	-M	-G	N	-	N	-	-	D	-P	-M	D	-	P	-
-	pya	-r	-ki	ya	-	hai	-	-	pya	-r	-k	ren	-	ge	-
-	P	-M	-G	N	-	N	-	-	D	-P	-M	D	-	P	-
-	hm	-to	-z	ma	-	ne	-	-	se	-na	-d	ren	-	ge	-

-	G'G'	-G'	-R'	G'	-	G'	G'	-	R'	-S'	N	S'	S'	N	-
-	ap	-ni	-mo	ho	-	b	t	-	ki	-ta	-	k	t	se	-
-	N	-N	N	G'	-	-	S'	N	-	D	P	N	-	D	P
-	duni	-ya	-	ko	-	-	jhu	ka	-	yen	-	ge	-	-	-
P	-D	D	P	P	R'	R'	N	N	-	D	P	M	-	-	-
ya	-r	jl	ne	va	lo	ko	j	la	-	yen	-	ge	-	-	-
M	-P	P	M	M	N	-N	-N	D	-	P	-	P	-	-	-
pya	-r	me	jii	yen	ge	-m	-r	ja	-	yen	-	ge	-	-	-

```
P R' N M   M N D P—
aa--------   aa------------
```

18. HAM YAAR HAIN TUMHARE

Film: Haan maine bhi pyar kiya (2002)	Music: Nadeem Shrawan
Lyrics: Sameer	Singer: Udit Narayan, Alka and others
Taal: Kaharwa	Chord: MDS' DS'G' S=C

ham yaar hain tumhaare, diladaar hain tumhaare
hamase mila karo, hamase mila karo
koee shikava agar ho aur shikaayat agar ho
hamase gila karo, hamase gila karo
ja mainne bhee pyaar kiya hai
haan mainne bhee pyaar kiya hai
ham yaar hain tumhaare...

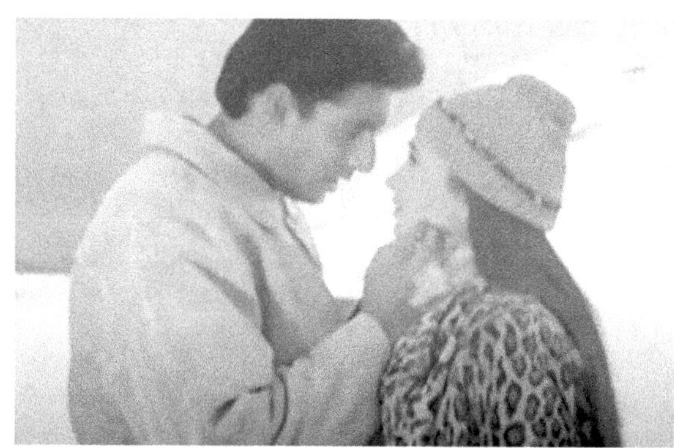

zulphon ko gira ke, palakon ko jhukaana
seekha hai kahaan se, ye jaadoo chalaana
aata hai tumhen to, yoon baaten banaana
jao jee hato bhee, chhodo yoon sataana
chha rahee hai khumaaree, badh rahee beqaraaree
yoon na hansa karo, yoon na hansa karo
koee shikava agar ho...

deevaanon ke jaise, karate ho sharaarat
hamako to pata hai, tere dil kee hakeekat
samajho na zara tum, mausam ka ishaara
aise to akele, na hoga guzaara
aise aahen bharo na, mastiyaan yoon --karo na
zid na kiya karo, ki zid na kiya karo
koee shikava agar ho...

Vinod Kumar

HAM YAAR HAIN TUMHARE

dha 1	ge 2	n 3	ti 4	n 5	ke 6	dhi 7	n 8	dha 1	ge 2	n 3	ti 4	n 5	ke 6	dhi 7	n 8
prelude:															
D N S'--- N D G'--- R' S' N D															
D N S'----- N P D—															
														N	-
														hm	-
N	S'	NS'	-	-	N	-	D	D	-	D	P	-	-	N	-
ya	-	-	-	r	hain	-	tu	mha	-	re	-	-	-	dil	-
N	S'	NS'	-	-	N	-	D	D	-	D	P	-	D	-	N
da	-	-	-	r	hain	-	tu	mha	-	re	-	-	hm	-	se
N	D	-	P	P	M	-	-	-	-	-	-	M	-	P	N
mi	la	-	k	ro	-	-	-	-	-	-	-	hm	-	se	-
N	N	-	D	D	-	-	-	-	-	-	-	-	-	N	N
mi	la	-	k	ro	-	-	-	-	-	-	-	-	-	ko	ee
S'	-	S'	-	-	N	-	D	D	-	D	P	-	N	-	N
shi	-	k	-	-	va	-	a	g	r	ho	-	-	au	r	shi
N	S'	-	-	-	N	-	D	D	-	D	P	-	D	-	N
ka	-	-	-	-	y	t	a	g	r	ho	-	-	hm	-	se
N	D	-	P	P	M	-	-	-	-	-	-	M	-	P	N
gi	la	-	k	ro	-	-	-	-	-	-	-	hm	-	se	-
N	N	-	D	D	-	-	-	-	-	-	-	-	-	-	-
gi	la	-	k	ro	-	-	-	-	-	-	-	-	-	-	-
G'	-	-	-	-	-	R'	G'	M'	-	M'	-	-	-	-	-
ja	-	-	-	-	-	main	-	ne	-	bhi	-	-	-	-	-
N	-	-	-	-	S'	M'	-	G'	-	-	-	-	-	-	-
pya	-	-	-	r	ki	ya	-	hai	-	-	-	-	-	-	-
G'	-	-	-	-	-	R'	G'	G'	M'	M'	-	-	-	-	-
han	-	-	-	-	-	main	-	ne	-	bhi	-	-	-	-	-
N	-	-	-	-	S'	M'	-	G'	-	S'	N	D	-		
pya	-	-	-	r	ki	ya	-	hai	-	-	-	-	-		
interlude:															

S'---- NDN---- DPD--- PD--- PM—
DNS'---- NDN--- DPD—PD--- PD---
M'—G'M' – G'R'---
G'—R'G'--- R'S'---
R'--- S'R'--- S'N—
M'--- G'R'S'ND—
S'---- NDN---- DPD--- PD--- PM—
DNS'---- NDN--- DPD—PD--- PD---

														S'	-
														zu	l
D	-	S'	-	-	G'	R'	G'	G'	S'	-	-	-	-	S'	-
fo	-	ko	-	-	gi	ra	-	ke	-	-	-	-	-	p	l
D	-	S'	-	-	G'	R'	G'	G'	S'	-	-	-	-	D	-
kon	-	ko	-	-	jhu	ka	-	na	-	-	-	-	-	si	-
N	-	N	-	-	R'	R'	-	R'	N	-	-	-	-	N	-
kha	-	hai	-	-	k	han	-	se	-	-	-	-	-	ye	-
N	-	M'	-	-	N	S'	-	D	-	-	-	-	-	S'	-
ja	-	du	-	-	ch	la	-	na	-	-	-	-	-	aa	-
D	-	S'	-	-	G'	R'	-	G'	S'	-	-	-	-	S'	-
ta	-	hai	-	-	tum	hen	-	to	-	-	-	-	-	yun	-
D	-	S'	-	-	G'	R'	-	G'	S'	-	-	-	-	D	-
ba	-	te	-	-	b	na	-	na	-	-	-	-	-	ja	-
N	-	N	-	-	R'	R'	-	R'	N	-	-	-	-	N	-
o	-	jii	-	-	h	to	-	bhi	-	-	-	-	-	chho	-
N	-	M'	-	-	N	S'	-	D	-	-	-	-	-		
do	-	yun	-	-	s	ta	-	na	-	-	-	-	-		

interlude:

M'— R' S' N   N--- S' M' G'
aa------------   aa-----------

G'----- R' G' M'   S'N—S' M' G'   S'ND-
aa------------   aa------------

												N	N
												chha	r
S'	-	-	-	-	N	-	D	D	-	D	P	-	N	-	N
hi	-	-	-	-	hai	-	khu	ma	-	ri	-	-	b	dh	r
S'	-	-	-	-	N	-	D	D	-	D	P	-	D	-	N
hi	-	-	-	-	be	-	q	ra	-	ri	-	-	yun	-	na

Vinod Kumar

N	D	-	P	P	M	-	-	-	-	-	-	M	-	P	N
hn	sa	-	k	ro	-	-	-	-	-	-	-	yun	-	na	-

N	N	-	D	D	-	-	-	G'	R'	S'	R'	D	-	N	N
hn	sa	-	k	ro	-	-	-	o	-	-	-	-	-	ko	ee

S'	-	S'	-	-	N	-	D	D	-	D	P	-	N	-	N
shi	-	k	-	-	va	-	a	g	r	ho	-	-	au	r	shi

S'	-	-	-	-	N	N	D	D	-	D	P	-	D	-	N
ka	-	-	-	-	y	t	a	g	r	ho	-	-	h	m	se

N	D	-	P	P	M	-	-	-	-	-	-	M	-	P	N
gi	la	-	k	ro	-	-	-	-	-	-	-	h	m	se	-

N	N	-	D	D	-	-	-	-	-	-	-	-	-	-	-
gi	la	-	k	ro	-	-	-	-	-	-	-	-	-	-	-

interlude:
D --- G'R'--- S'N—PD—
G' R' G' R' G' R' R' S' S'NDP PD –
D --- G'R'--- S'N—PD—
G' R' G' R' G' R' R' S' S'NDP PD –
G' M' D'---- M' G' R' G'—
D --- G'R'--- NS'—ND—

D --- G'R'--- NS'—ND—
ho – hoho   hoho hoho

														S'	-
														di	-

D	-	S'	-	-	G'	R'	G'	G'	S'	-	-	-	-	S'	-
va	-	no	-	-	ke	jai	-	se	-	-	-	-	-	k	r

D	-	S'	-	-	G'	R'	G'	G'	S'	-	-	-	-	D	-
te	-	ho	-	-	sh	ra	-	r	t	-	-	-	-	h	m

D	-	N	-	-	G'	R'	-	R'	N	-	-	-	-	N	N
ko	-	to	-	-	p	ta	-	hai	-	-	-	-	-	te	re

N	-	M'	-	-	N	S'	-	N	D	-	-	-	-	S'	-
di	l	ki	-	-	h	qi	-	k	t	-	-	-	-	s	m

D	-	S'	-	-	G'	R'	-	G'	S'	-	-	-	-	S'	-
jho	-	na	-	-	z	ra	-	tum	-	-	-	-	-	mau	-

D	-	S'	-	-	G'	R'	-	G'	S'	-	-	-	-	D	-
sm	-	ka	-	-	i	sha	-	ra	-	-	-	-	-	ae	-

N	-	N	-	-	G'	R'	-	R'	N	-	-	-	-	N	-
se	-	to	-	-	a	ke	-	le	-	-	-	-	-	na	-
N	-	M'	-	-	N	S'	-	D	-	-	-	-	-	-	
ho	-	ga	-	-	gu	za	-	ra	-	-	-	-	-	-	

M'— R' S' N   N--- S' M' G'
aa-------------   aa-----------

G'----- R' G' M'   S'N—S' M' G' S'ND-
aa-------------   aa-------------

												-	N	-	N
													ae	-	se
S'	-	-	-	-	N	-	D	D	-	D	P	-	N	-	N
aa	-	-	-	-	hen	-	bh	ro	-	na	-	-	m	s	ti
S'	-	-	-	-	N	-	D	D	-	D	P	-	D	D	N
yan	-	-	-	-	yun	-	k	ro	-	na	-	-	zi	d	na
N	D	-	P	P	M	-	-	-	-	-	P	P	P	P	N
ki	ya	-	k	ro	-	-	-	-	-	-	ke	zi	d	na	-
N	N	-	D	D	-	-	-	-	-	-	-	-	N	-	N
ki	ya	-	k	ro	-	-	-	-	-	-	-	-	ko	-	ee
S'	-	S'	-	-	N	-	D	D	-	D	P	-	N	-	N
shi	-	k	-	-	va	-	a	g	r	ho	-	-	au	r	shi
S'	-	-	-	-	N	N	D	D	-	D	P	-	D	-	N
ka	-	-	-	-	y	t	a	g	r	ho	-	-	h	m	se
N	D	-	P	P	M	-	-	-	-	-	-	M	-	P	N
gi	la	-	k	ro	-	-	-	-	-	-	-	h	m	se	-
N	N	-	D	D	-	-	-	-	-	-	-	-	-	N	-
gi	la	-	k	ro	-	-	-	-	-	-	-	-	-	h	m
R'	S'	NS'	-	-	N	-	D	D	-	D	P	-	-	N	-
pya	-	-	-	r	hain	-	tu	mha	-	re	-	-	-	di	l
R'	S'	NS'	-	-	N	-	D	D	-	D	P	-	D	-	N
da	-	-	-	r	hain	-	tu	mha	-	re	-	-	hm	-	se
N	D	-	P	P	M	-	-	-	-	-	-	M	-	P	N
mi	la	-	k	ro	-	-	-	-	-	-	-	hm	-	se	-

Vinod Kumar

N	N	-	D	D	-	-	-	-	-	-	-	-	-
mi	la	-	k	ro	-	-	-	-	-	-	-	-	-
G'	-	-	-	-	-	R'	G'	G'	M'	M'	-	-	-	-	-
han	-	-	-	-	-	main	-	ne	-	bhi	-	-	-	-	-
N	-	-	-	-	S'	M'	-	G'	-	-	-	-	-	-	-
pya	-	-	-	r	ki	ya	-	hai	-	-	-	-	-	-	-

19. HAM SE TUM DOSTI KAR LO

Film: Narsimha (1991)	Music: Lakshmikant Pyarelal
Lyrics: Javed Akhtar	Singer: Udit Narayan, Alka
Taal: Kaharwa	Chord: P$\underline{N}$R' S=C#

ham se tum dostee kar lo, yah haseen galatee kar lo -2
aao na, haath milao na, o bebee aao na, baat suno, na na na

dostee jo pyaar bane hairat nahin-3
kyon kee zindagee mohabbat hain nafarat nahin-3
dhadake jo, to dil ko dhadakane do
bhadake to, yah shola bhadakane do
raahon mein do baahen baahon mein,
o bebee aao na saath chalo na na na
ham se tum dostee kar lo yah haseen galatee kar lo

hamako aisee baaton ka yakeen kaise ho-3
kaise ham maan le tum itane achchhe ho-3
logo ne, hamen yah bataaya hain
pyaar to, bas ik pal kee chhaaya hain
jao na hamen bahakao na
o baaba jao na jaane bhee do, na na na
tumase kyon dostee kar len, ham yah kyon galatee kar len

vah dil bhee koee dil hain bhala,
jis dil mein kisee ka pyaar na ho
ik roz to vah din aaega, jis din tum bhee hamase yah kaho
ham se tum dostee kar lo

ye phaasale yah dooree kab tak ab aa bhee jao baahon mein
ham raah tumhaaree takate hain kab se in pyaar kee raahon mein
ham se tum dostee kar lo

79

in baaton mein kho jaungee main kya se kya ho jaungee

ab lagata hai dil khona hai jo hona hai vo hona hai

aao na haath milao na o bebee aao na baat suno haan haan haan

hamane yah dostee kar lee, yah haseen galatee kar lee

ham se tum dostee kar lo, yah haseen galatee kar lo

aao na haath milao na, o bebee aao na baat suno haan haan haan.

HAM SE TUM DOSTI KAR LO

dhage 12	nti 34	nke 56	dhin 78	dhage 12	nti 34	nke 56	dhin 78	dhage 12	nti 34	nke 56	dhin 78	dhage 12	nti 34	nke 56	dhin 78
P	-	-	R	P	-D	-	N	S'	-S'	-	N	-	-	-	-
hm	-	-	se	tum	-do	-	s	ti	-k	-r	lo	-	-	-	-
M*	-	-	R	M*	-P	-	P	D	-D	-	P	-	-	-	-
ye	-	-	hn	si	-g	-	l	ti	-k	-r	lo	-	-	-	-
S'	-R'	-	G'	-	-R'	-	-S'	S'	-R'	-	G'	-	R'	R'	R'
aa	-o	-	na	-	-ha	-th	mi	la	-o	-	na	-	o	be	bi
S'	R'R'	-	D	-	D	-S'	S'	R'	-	S'	-	N	-	D	-
aa	-o	-	na	-	ba	-t	su	no	-	na	-	na	-	na	-
P	-	-	R	P	-D	-	N	S'	-S'	-	N	-	-	-	-
hm	-	-	se	tum	-do	-	s	ti	-k	-r	lo	-	-	-	-
M*	-	-	R	M*	-P	-	P	D	-D	-	P	-	-	-	-
ye	-	-	hn	si	-g	-	l	ti	-k	-r	lo	-	-	-	-
R'	R'	R'	R'	S'	-S'	S'	S'	N	-S'	-S'	S'	R'-	-	-	-
do	s	ti	jo	pya	-r	b	ne	hai	-r	-t	n	hin	-	-	-
P	-R	-R	R	D	-	-	-	R	-D	-D	D	P	-	R'	R'
hai	-r	-t	n	hin	-	-	-	hai	-r	-t	n	hin	-	kyu	ki
R'	R'	R'	R'	S'	-	S'S'	S'	NN	-S'	-S'	S'	R'-	-	-	-
zin	-d	gi	mo	ho	-	bt	hai	nf	-r	-t	n	hin	-	-	-
PP	-R	-R	R	D	-	-	-	RR	-D	-D	D	P	-	-	-
nf	-r	-t	n	hin	-	-	-	nf	-r	-t	n	hin	-	-	-
P	-D	-	N	-	R'S'	-D	-P	PD	-D	-	M*	-	-	-	-
dhd	-ke	-	jo	-	todil	-ko	-dh	dk	-ne	-	do	-	-	-	-

M*	-P	-	D	-	DD	-P	-R	RD	-D	-	P	-	-	-	-
fd	-ke	-	to	-	yesho	-la	-f	dk	-ne	-	do	-	-	-	-
S'	-R'	-	G'	-	R'	R'	S'	S'	-R'	-	G'	-	R'	R'	R'
ra	-hon	-	me	-	ba	hen	hon	ba	-hon	-	me	-	o	be	bi
S'	R'R'	-	D	-	D	-S'	S'	R'	-	S'	-	N	-	D	-
aa	-o	-	na	-	sa	-th	ch	lo	-	na	-	na	-	na	-
P	-	-	R	P	-D	-	N	S'	-S'	-	N	-	-	-	-
hm	-	-	se	tum	-do	-	s	ti	-k	-r	lo	-	-	-	-
M*	-	-	R	M*	-P	-	P	D	-D	-	P	-	-	-	-
ye	-	-	hn	si	-g	-	l	ti	-k	-r	lo	-	-	-	-
R'	R'	R'	R'	S'	-S'	S'	S'	N	-N	-S'	S'	R'-	-	-	P
hm	ko	ae	si	ba	-t	ka	y	ki	-n	kai	se	ho	-	-	y
P	-R	-P	P	D	-	-	P	R	-D	-D	D	P	-	-	-
ki	-n	kai	se	ho	-	-	y	ki	-n	kai	se	ho	-	-	-
R'	R'	R'	R'	S'	-S'	S'	S'	N	-N	-S'	S'	R'-	-	-	-
kai	se	hm	ye	ma	-n	len	tum	it	ne	a	ch chhe	ho	-	-	-
P	P	R	R	D	-	D	-	R	R	D	D	P	-	-	-
it	ne	a	ch chhe	ho	-	tum	-	it	ne	a	ch chhe	ho	-	-	-
P	-D	-	N	-	R'S'	-D	-P	PD	-D	-	M*	-	-	-	-
lo	-go	-	ne	-	hme	-ye	-b	ta	-ya	-	hai	-	-	-	-
M*	-	P	D	-D	D	-P	-R	RD	-D	-	P	-	-	-	-
pya	-	r	to	-bs	ik	-pl	-ki	chha	-ya	-	hai	-	-	-	-
S'	-R'	-	G'	-	-R'	R'	S'	S'	-R'	-	G'	-	R'	R'	R'
ja	-o	-	na	-	-h	me	bh	ka	-o	-	na	-	o	ba	ba
S'	R'R'	-	D	-	D	S'	S'	R'	-	S'	-	N	-	D	-
ja	-o	-	na	-	ja	ne	bhi	do	-	na	-	na	-	na	-
P	-	-	R	P	-D	-	N	S'	-S'	-	N	-	-	-	-
tum	-	-	se	kyu	-do	-	s	ti	-kr	-	len	-	-	-	-
M*	-	-	R	M*	-P	-	P	D	-D	-	P	-	-	-	-
hm	-	-	ye	kyu	-g	-	l	ti	-k	-r	len	-	-	-	-

Udit Narayan 51 Songs' Sargam

P	-	-	R	P	-D	-	N	S'	-S'	-	N	-	-	-	-
hm	-	-	se	tum	-do	-	s	ti	-k	-r	lo	-	-	-	-
															R'
															vo
R'	R'R'	R'	R'	R'	R'R'	R'	R'	R'	R'R'	R'	R'	G'	-S'	S'	S'
dil	bhiki	si	ka	dil	haibh	la	jis	dil	meki	si	ka	pya	r n	ho	ik
S'	-S'	S'	R'S'	S'	S'	S'	S'	S'	S'	S'	S'	R'	NN	N	-
ro	zto	vo	din	aa	ye	ga	jis	din	tum	bhi	hm	se	yek	ho	-
P	-	-	R	P	-D	-	N	S'	-S'	-	N	-	-	-	R'
hm	-	-	se	tum	-do	-	s	ti	-k	-r	lo	-	-	-	ye
R'	R'R'	R'	R'	R'	R'R'	R'	R'	R'	R'R'	R'	R'	G'	-S'	S'	S'
fa	sle	ye	du	ri	kb	tk	ab	aa	bhi	ja	o	ban	hon	me	hm
S'	-S'	S'	R'	S'	S'	S'	S'	S'	S'	S'	S'	R'	N	N	-
ra	htu	mha	ri	tk	te	hain	kb	se	in	pya	rki	ra	hon	me	-
P	-	-	R	P	-D	-	N	S'	-S'	-	N	-	-	P	M*
hm	-	-	se	tum	-do	-	s	ti	-k	-r	lo	-	-	i	n
P	-	D	-	N	-	P	M*	P	-	D	-	N	-	P	-
ba	-	to	-	me	-	kho	-	ja	-	un	-	gi	-	main	-
D	S'	S'	-	N	-	P	-	N	-	D	-	P	-	P	M*
kya	-	se	-	kya	-	ho	-	ja	-	un	-	gi	-	a	b
P	P	D	-	N	-	P	M*	P	-	D	-	N	-	P	D
l	g	ta	-	hai	-	di	l	kho	-	na	-	hai	-	jo	-
D	S'	S'	-	N	-	P	-	N	-	D	-	P	-	-	-
ho	-	na	-	hai	-	vo	-	ho	-	na	-	hai	-	-	-
S'	-R'	=	G'	-	-R'	-	-S'	S'	-R'	-	G'	-	R'	R'	R'
aa	-o	-	na	-	-ha	-th	mi	la	-o	-	na	-	o	be	bi
S'	R'R'	-	D	-	D	-S'	S'	R'	-	S'	-	N	-	D	-
aa	-o	-	na	-	ba	-t	su	no	-	han	-	han	-	han	-
P	-	-	R	P	-D	-	N	S'	-S'	-	N	-	-	-	-
hm	-	-	ne	ye	-do	-	s	ti	-k	-r	li	-	-	-	-
M*	-	-	R	M*	-P	-	P	D	-D	-	P	-	-	-	-
hm	-	-	ne	ye	-g	-	l	ti	-k	-r	li	-	-	-	-

P	-	-	R	P	-D	-	<u>N</u>	S'	-S'	-	<u>N</u>	-	-	-	-
hm	-	-	se	tum	-do	-	s	ti	-k	-r	lo	-	-	-	-
M*	-	-	R	M*	-P	-	P	D	-D	-	P	-	-	-	-
ye	-	-	hn	si	-g	-	l	ti	-k	-r	lo	-	-	-	-
S'	-R'	<u>-</u>	<u>G'</u>	-	-R'	-	-S'	S'	-R'	-	<u>G'</u>	-	R'	R'	R'
aa	-o	-	na	-	-ha	-th	mi	la	-o	-	na	-	o	be	bi
S'	R'R'	-	D	-	D	-S'	S'	R'	-	S'	-	<u>N</u>	-	D	-
aa	-o	-	na	-	ba	-t	su	no	-	han	-	han	-	han	-
P	-	-	R	P	-D	-	<u>N</u>	S'	-S'	-	<u>N</u>	-	-	-	-
hm	-	-	se	tum	-do	-	s	ti	-k	-r	lo	-	-	-	-
M*	-	-	R	M*	-P	-	P	D	-D	-	P	-	-	-	-
ye	-	-	hn	si	-g	-	l	ti	-k	-r	lo	-	-	-	-

20. HAMKO HAMI SE CHURA LO

Film: Mohabbatein (2001)	Music: Jatin Lalit
Lyrics: Anand Bakshi	Singer: Udit Narayan, Lata
Taal: Kaharwa	Chord: P<u>N</u>R' MDS' S=C

hamako hameen se chura lo, dil mein kaheen tum chhupa lo
ham akele kho na jaen, door tumase ho na jaen
paas aao gale se laga lo

ye dil dhadaka do, julphen bikhara do,
sharma ke apana aanchal lahara do
ham julphen to bikhara den, din mein raat na jo jae
ham aanchal to lahara den, par barasaat na ho jae
hone do barasaaten, karanee hain kuchh baaten,
paas aao gale se laga lo

tumape marate hain, ham mar jaayenge,
ye sab kahate hain, ham kar jaayenge
chutakee bhar sindoor se tum ab ye maang zara bhar do
kal kya ho kisane dekha, sab kuchh aaj abhee kar do
ho na ho sab raazee, dil raazee rab raazee,
paas aao gale se laga lo

HAMKO HAMI SE CHURA LO

dhage	nti	nke	dhin	dhage	nti	nke	dhin	dhage	nti	nke	dhin	dhage	nti	nke	dhin
12	34	56	78	12	34	56	78	12	34	56	78	12	34	56	78

prelude:

R' S'N—D—N—   R'S'R' S'N PND
aa----------------   aa----------------

DNS'--- NS'R'-G'P'M*'---
aa---------------------

R'S'R'--- S'N--- DDN----   MP---
aa---------------------   un hu---

P	-	R'	-S'	R'	-S'	-	N	N	-S'	-	D	D	N	S'	-
hm	-	ko	-h	mi	-se	-	chu	ra	-lo	-	-	hu................			
M	-	S'	-N	S'	-N	-	D	D	NN	-	P	-	-	N	D
dil	-	me	-k	hin	tum	-	chhu	pa	-lo	-	-	-	-	hm	a
P	DP	-	S'R'	S'	-	D	P	M	PM	-	S'R'	S'N	S'	N	-D
ke	-le	-	aa-	-	-	kho	n	ja	-ye	-	aa-	--	-	du	-r
P	DS'	-	D	P	-	D	P	M	PM	-	-	-	-	R	-
tum	-se	-	-	-	-	ho	n	ja	-yen	-	-	-	-	pa	-s
R	-N	-	N	N	-S'	-	R'	D	-P	-	PD	S'	ND	PD	M-
aa	-o	-	g	le	-se	-	l	ga	-lo	-	for repeat above.				

interlude:

GN DP—PS'ND PDPMPDNS'
G'R'NS' S'-R' G'M'G'R' G'R'NS'--- S'R'G'R'NS'
S'--- R' G'M'G'R' R'S'D—

R-M-R MPDN- NDPMP-
aa-----------------------

R-M-R MPDN- S'NDPD
aa----------------------

flute: P N R' G' R' S' S'-N- N-D- P-D PMP-
synthe: P N R' G' R' S'—R' G' M' M'G'R'—

PDN D- P- S'NS'N-D- NDPMP—
aa------------------------lalala----

N	-	D	-	P	-	M	-	P	-	-	-	-	-	-	-
ye	-	dil	-	dh	d	ka	-	do	-	-	-	-	-	-	-
D	-	P	-	M	M	G	-	P	M	-	-	-	-	-	-
zul	-	fen	-	bi	kh	ra	-	do	-	-	-	-	-	-	-

P	-	M	-	G	-	R	R	G	-	-	-	-	-	-	-
sh	r	ma	-	ke	-	a	p	na	-	-	-	-	-	-	-
N	-	D	-	P	P	M	D	D	P	-	-	-	-	D	N
aan	-	chl	-	l	h	ra	-	do	-	-	-	-	-	hm	zul
S'	-R'	S'S'	N	S'	-	D	N	S'	S'G'	R'	S'	S'	-	P	D
fen	-to	bikh	ra	den	-	din	me	ra	tn	ho	ja	ye	-	hm	aan
N	-S'	N	D	N	-	P	D	N	S'R'	S'	N	N	-	R'	G'
chl	-to	lh	ra	len	-	pr	br	sa	t,n	ho	ja	ye	-	ho	ne
M'	-	-	-	-	-	S'	G'	G'M'	R'	-	-	-	-	G'R'	S'
do	-	-	-	-	-	br	sa	te-	-	-	-	-	-	kr	ni
N	R'S'	-	-	-	-	DD	P	M	P	-	-	-	-	R	-
hai	-	-	-	-	-	kuchh	ba	te	-	-	-	-	-	pa	-s
R	-N	-	N	N	-S'	-	R'	D	-P	-	-	-	-	-	-
aa	-o	-	g	le	-se	-	l	ga	-lo	-	-	-	-	-	-

interlude:

N—DN DPM PP   N—DN DPM P MMP—
N—DN DPM PP

MN MP- MD- RP-
aa------------------

DND PPM MPPD-- NS'D-
aa-------------------------

DND PPM MMP—
aa------------------

PDND-P- S'-N-N-D- PDPMP-
aa--------------------lalala-

N	-	D	-	P	-	M	-	P	-	-	-	-	-	-	-
tum	-	pe	-	m	r	te	-	hain	-	-	-	-	-	-	-
D	-	P	-	M	-	G	-	M	-	-	-	-	-	-	-
hm	-	m	r	ja	-	yen	-	ge	-	-	-	-	-	-	-
P	-	M	-	G	-	R	-	G	-	-	-	-	-	-	-
ye	-	s	b	k	h	te	-	hain	-	-	-	-	-	-	-
N	-	D	-	P	-	M	-	MP	-	-	-	-	-	D	N
hm	-	k	r	ja	-	yen	-	ge-	-	-	-	-	-	chut	ki

S'	S'R'	S'	NN	S'	-	D	N	S'	S'G'	R'	S'	S'	-	P	D
bhr	sin-	du	rse	tum	-	ab	ye	man	gz	ra	bhr	do	-	kl	kya
N	NS'	N	D	N	-	P	D	N	NR'	S'	N	N	-	R'	G'
ho	kis	ne	de	kha	-	sb	kuchh	aa	ja	bhi	kr	do	-	ho	na
M'	-	-	-	-	-	S'	G'	G'M'	R'	-	-	-	-	G'R'	S'
ho	-	-	-	-	-	sb	ra	zi	-	-	-	-	-	dil	ra
N	R'S'	-	-	-	-	DD	P	M	P	-	-	-	-	R	-
zi	-	-	-	-	-	rb	ra	zi	-	-	-	-	-	pa	-s
R	-N	-	N	N	-S'	-	R'	D	-P	-	-	-	-		
aa	-o	-	g	le	-se	-	l	ga	-lo	-	-	-	-		

21. JAADU TERI NAZAR

Film: Dar (1993)	Music: Shiv Hari
Lyrics: Anand Bakshi	Singer: Udit Narayan
Taal: Kaharwa	Chord: MDS' PNR' S=C

jaadoo teree nazar, khushaboo tera badan (2)
too haan kar ya na kar (2) too hai meree kiran (2)
jaadoo teree nazar ...

(mere khvaabon kee tasveer hai too
bekhabar meree taqadeer hai too) - 2
too kisee aur kee ho na jaana
kuchh bhee kar jaoonga main deevaana
too haan kar ya ...

(faasale aur kam ho rahen hain
door se paas ham ho rahen hain) - 2
maang loonga main tujhe aasamaan se
chheen loonga tujhe is jahaan se
too haan kar ya ...

JAADU TERI NAZAR

dhage 12	nti 34	nke 56	dhin 78	dhage 12	nti 34	nke 56	dhin 78	dhage 12	nti 34	nke 56	dhin 78	dhage 12	nti 34	nke 56	dhin 78
															P
															ja
R'	-	-	-	-	S'	R'S'	N̲	D	-	-	-	-	-	-	M
du	-	-	-	-	te	-ri	n	zr	-	-	-	-	-	-	khush
S'	-	-	-	-	N̲	S'N̲	D	P	-	-	-	-	-	-	P
bu	-	-	-	-	te	-ra	b	dn	-	-	-	-	-	-	ja
R'S'	R'	-	-	-	M'	-R'	S'	D	-	-	-	-	-	-	M
du-	-	-	-	-	te	-ri	n	zr	-	-	-	-	-	-	khush
S'	-	-	-	-	N̲	S'N̲	D	P	-	-	-	-	-	-	M
bu	-	-	-	-	te	-ra	b	dn	-	-	-	-	-	-	tu
N̲	-D	-	-	-	M	D	-P	-	-	-	-	-	-	-	M
han	-kr	-	-	-	ya	na	-kr	-	-	-	-	-	-	-	tu
N̲	-D	-	M	D	-P	-	PP	G̲'	-	-M'	-G̲'	R'	-	-	PP
han	-kr	-	ya	na	-kr	-	tuhai	me	-	-ri	-ki	ran	-	-	tuhai
G̲'	-	-M'	-G̲'	R'	-	-	-	-							
me	-	-ri	-ki	ran	-	-	-	-							

interlude:

M'G̲'M'G̲' R'—S'N̲- R'- PP PP D N̲S'-
M'G̲'M'G̲' R'—S'N̲- R'- G̲'R' S'N̲ S' R'R'
M' R'S' N̲---

dhage 12	nti 34	nke 56	dhin 78	dhage 12	nti 34	nke 56	dhin 78	dhage 12	nti 34	nke 56	dhin 78	dhage 12	nti 34	nke 56	dhin 78
														-N̲	-S'
														-me	-re
N̲	-	-M	-P	M	-	-P	-M	G	-P	-	-	-	-	-P	-P
kha	-	-bo	-ki	Ts	-	-vii	-r	hai	-tu	-	-	-	-	-be	-kh
G̲'	-	-M'	-G̲'	R'	-	-S'	-N̲	S'	-N̲	-	-	-	-	-R'	-M'
br	-	-me	-ri	Tq	-	-di	-r	hai	-tu	-	-	-	-	-tu	-ki
G̲'	-	-R'	-S'	R'	-	-S'	N̲	S'	-R'	-	-	-	-	-R'	-R'
si	-	-au	-r	ki	-	-ho	-n	ja	-na	-	-	-	-	kuchh	-bhi
S'	-	-S'	-S'	N̲	-	-D	-P	D	-P	-	DP	G	-	-	M
kr	-	-ja	-un	ga	-	-main	-di	va	-na	-	-	-	-	-	tu
N̲	-D	-	-	-	M	D	-P	-	-	-	-	-	-	-	M
han	-kr	-	-	-	ya	na	-kr	-	-	-	-	-	-	-	tu

N	-D	-	M	D	-P	-	PP	G'	-	-M'	-G'	R'	-	-	PP
han	-kr	-	ya	na	-kr	-	tuhai	me	-	-ri	-ki	ran	-	-	tuhai
G'	-	-M'	-G'	R'	-	-	-	-							
me	-	-ri	-ki	ran	-	-	-	-							

interlude:

M'G'M'G' R'—S'N- R'- PP PP D NS'-

M'G'M'G' R'—S'N- R'- G'R' S'N S' R'R'

M' R'S' N---

														-N	-S'
														-fa	-s
N	-	-M	-P	M	-	-P	-M	G	-P	-	-	-	-	-P	-P
le	-	-au	-r	km	-	-ho	-r	he	-hain	-	-	-	-	-du	-r
G'	-	-M'	-G'	R'	-	-S'	-N	S'	-N	-	-	-	-	-R'	-M'
se	-	-pa	-s	hm	-	-ho	-r	he	-hain	-	-	-	-	-man	-g
G'	-	-R'	-S'	R'	-S'	-	N	S'	-R'	-	-	-	-	-R'	-R'
lun	-	-ga	-tu	jhe	-aa	-	s	man	-se	-	-	-	-	-chhi	-n
S'	-	-S'	-S'	N	-	-D	-P	D	-P	-	DP	G	-	-	M
lun	-	-ga	-tu	jhe	-	-is	-j	han	-se	-	-	-	-	-	tu
N	-D	-	-	-	M	D	-P	-	-	-	-	-	-	-	M
han	-kr	-	-	-	ya	na	-kr	-	-	-	-	-	-	-	tu
N	-D	-	M	D	-P	-	PP	G'	-	-M'	-G'	R'	-	-	PP
han	-kr	-	ya	na	-kr	-	tuhai	me	-	-ri	-ki	ran	-	-	tuhai
G'	-	-M'	-G'	R'	-	-	-	-							
me	-	-ri	-ki	ran	-	-	-	-							

22. JEEVAN TUMNE DIYA HAI

Film: Big Brother (2007)	Music: Sandesh Shandilya
Lyrics: Sameer	Singer: Udit Narayan, Alka
Taal: Daadra	Chord: SGP MDS' S=D

jeevan tumane diya hai, sambhaaloge tum -2
aasha hamen hai, vishvaas hai,
har mushkil se, vidhaata nikaaloge tum
jeevan tumane diya, hai sambhaaloge tum

saaye mein ham aap hee ke pita,
satkarm kee raah par ham chale
saare jahaan kee bhalaee kare,
ham na kisee kee buraee kare
is duniya ke dukhon se bacha loge tum -2
aasha hamen hai vishvaas hai,
har mushkil se vidhaata nikaaloge tum
jeevan tumane diya hai sambhaaloge tum

har pal agar tumhaare saath hai,
phir hamako darane kee kya baat hai
kathanaiyon se na haarenge ham,
tumako hamesha pukaarenge ham
apane gale se hamen bhee laga loge tum -2
aasha hamen hai vishvaas hai,
har mushkil se vidhaata nikaaloge tum
jeevan tumane diya hai sambhaaloge tum

chhaaya kaheen to kaheen dhoop hai,
hai naam kitane kaee roop hai
har shay mein tum ho samae hue,
ham sab hain tumhaare banaaye hue
ham jo roothe kabhee to mana loge tum -2
aasha hamen hai vishvaas hai,
har mushkil se vidhaata nikaaloge tum
jeevan tumane diya hai sambhaaloge tum.

JEEVAN TUMNE DIYA HAI

dha 1	tin 2	tin 3	ta 4	dhin 5	dhin 6	dha 1	tin 2	tin 3	ta 4	dhin 5	dhin 6

prelude:
G R S .N .D .N G R S
un----------------------

G R S .N .D .N G R S
aa---------------------

dha 1	tin 2	tin 3	ta 4	dhin 5	dhin 6	dha 1	tin 2	tin 3	ta 4	dhin 5	dhin 6
										S jii	GM vn
P tum	M ne	-G -di	M ya	P hai	-R -sm	R bha	G lo	-R -ge	S tum	- -	- -

SRGM P M GM P R RG RS
aa--------------------------

dha 1	tin 2	tin 3	ta 4	dhin 5	dhin 6	dha 1	tin 2	tin 3	ta 4	dhin 5	dhin 6
P aa	N sha	-S' -h	R' me	S' hai	- -	PP vish	GM va-	PP -s	M hai	SR hr	GM mush
P kil	M se	-G -vi	M dha	P ta	-R -ni	R ka	G lo	-R -ge	S tum		

interlude:
flute: M S'---- R' S' N D
S' N D P M-- S' N D N D M D
synthe: P GMP M GMP R S
     P GMP M GMP R .NS

G R S .N .D .N G R S
aa---------------------

dha 1	tin 2	tin 3	ta 4	dhin 5	dhin 6	dha 1	tin 2	tin 3	ta 4	dhin 5	dhin 6
D hr	S' pl	NR' -tu	S' mha	S' ra	-D -a	N gr	P sa	-M -th	M hai	- -	- -
D fir	S' hm	NR' -ko	S' dar	S' ne	-D -ki	N kya	P ba	-M -t	M hai	- -	- -
DD k,thi	S' na	NR' -i	S' yon	S' se	-D -n	N ha	P ren	-M -ge	M hm	- -	- -
D tum	S' ko	-R' -h	S' me	S' sha	-D -pu	N ka	M ren	-R -ge	GS hm	SS ap	GM ne,g
P le	M se	-G -h	M me	P bhi	-R -l	R ga	G lo	-R -ge	S tum	- -	- -
P aa	N sha	-S' -h	R' me	S' hai	- -	PP vish	GM va-	PP -s	M hai	SR hr	GM mush

P	M	-G	M	P	-R	R	G	-R	S	S	GM
kil	se	-vi	dha	ta	-ni	ka	lo	-ge	tum	jii	vn

P	M	-G	M	P	-R	R	G	-R	S	-	-
tum	ne	-di	ya	hai	-sm	bha	lo	-ge	tum	-	-

interlude:

D --- PD<u>N</u>S' R' – <u>N</u>- P- <u>G</u>- P-
P <u>N</u> D-- <u>G</u>MPD

D ---- M P <u>N</u> S' R' <u>N</u> P M <u>G</u> P
aa----------------------------

<u>D</u>---- P M P – M M ---
aa--------------------

<u>D</u>	S'	<u>NR'</u>	S'	S'	<u>-D</u>	<u>N</u>	P	-M	M	-	-
chha	ya	-k	hin	to	-k	hin	dhu	-p	hai	-	-

<u>D</u>	S'	<u>NR'</u>	S'	S'	<u>-D</u>	<u>N</u>	P	-M	M	-	-
hai	na	-m	kit	ne	-ka	yi	ru	-p	hain	-	-

<u>DD</u>	S'	<u>NR'</u>	S'	S'	<u>-D</u>	<u>N</u>	P	-M	M	-	-
hr	shai	-me	tum	hi	-s	ma	ye	-hu	e	-	-

<u>D</u>	S'<u>N</u>	<u>-R'</u>	S'	S'	<u>-D</u>	<u>N</u>	M	<u>-R</u>	<u>GS</u>	S	<u>GM</u>
hm	sb	-tum	ha	re	-b	na	ye	-hu	e-	hm	jo-

P	M	-<u>G</u>	M	P	<u>-R</u>	R	G	<u>-R</u>	S	-	-
ru	the	-k	bhi	to	-m	na	lo	-ge	tum	-	-

P	<u>N</u>	-S'	<u>R'</u>	S'	-	PP	<u>GM</u>	PP	M	<u>SR</u>	<u>GM</u>
aa	sha	-h	me	hai	-	vish	va-	-s	hai	hr	mush

P	M	-<u>G</u>	M	P	<u>-R</u>	R	G	<u>-R</u>	S	S	<u>GM</u>
kil	se	-vi	dha	ta	-ni	ka	lo	-ge	tum	jii	vn

P	M	-<u>G</u>	M	P	<u>-R</u>	R	G	<u>-R</u>	S	-	-
tum	ne	-di	ya	hai	-sm	bha	lo	-ge	tum	-	-

S<u>R</u>GM P M <u>G</u> M P <u>R</u> <u>R</u>G <u>R</u>S
aa----------------------------

23. KAHO NA PYAR HAI

Film: Kaho na Pyar hai (2000) Lyrics: Ibrahim Ashq Taal: Kaharwa	Music: Rajesh Raushan Singer: Udit Narayan, Alka Chord: P<u>N</u>R' RMD S=C

dil mera har baar ye sunane ko bekaraar hai
kaho na pyaar hai, kaho na pyaar hai
haan, tum se pyaar hai, ke tum se pyaar hai
in pyaaree baaton mein anjaana ikaraar hai
kaho na pyaar hai, kaho na pyaar hai
kaha na pyaar hai, kaha na pyaar hai

pyaar jahaan mein hota nahin, phir bolo kya hota ?
duniya mein dil koee kabhee na dhadaka hota
dhadaka hai dil aa yaar mil ye pyaar ka izahaar hai
kaho na pyaar hai, kaho na pyaar hai
kaha na pyaar hai, kaha na pyaar hai

do premee, do paagal, kya karate hain bolo
mujh se kya poochhate ho, apane dil ko tatolo
maaloom hai, ham ko tumhe kis baat ka intajaar hai
kaho na pyaar hai, kaho na pyaar hai
kaha na pyaar hai, kaha na pyaar hai

milate nahee ham tum to, phir bolo kya hota ?
sach boloon phir apana, khvaab na poora hota
kahata hai man apana milan duniya mein yaadagaar hai
kaho na pyaar hai, kaho na pyaar hai
kaha na pyaar hai, kaha na pyaar hai

KAHO NA PYAR HAI

dhage	nti	nke	dhin	dhage	nti	nke	dhin	dhage	nti	nke	dhin	dhage	nti	nke	dhin
12	34	56	78	12	34	56	78	12	34	56	78	12	34	56	78
prelude:															
R'—<u>N</u>'- D' P'—				S'—D'- P' M'--		<u>N</u> D <u>N</u>									
aa-----------				aa-----------		aa-----									
														G'	R'
														di	l
S'	-	R'	-	-	-	<u>G</u>'	R'	S'	-	R'	R'	-	-	<u>G</u>'	R'
me	-	ra	-	-	-	h	r	ba	-	r	ye	-	-	su	n

S'	-	R'	-	-	R'	-	R'	R'	M'	G'	R'	S'	-	-	R'
ne	-	ko	-	-	be	-	q	ra	-	-	r	hai	-	-	-
D	-	-	D	D	-	N	-	S'	-	-	D	N	-	-	D
-	-	-	k	ho	-	na	-	pya	-	-	r	hai	-	-	-
P	-	-	D	D	-	N	-	S'	-	-	D	N	-	-	-
-	-	-	k	ho	-	na	-	pya	-	-	r	hai	-	-	-
-	-	-	D	D	-	N	-	S'	-	-	D	N	-	-	D
-	-	-	han	tum	-	se	-	pya	-	-	r	hai	-	-	-
P	-	-	D	D	-	N	-	S'	-	-	D	N	-	-	-
-	-	-	ke	tum	-	se	-	pya	-	-	r	hai	-	-	-
M'P'	M'	G'M'	G'	R'G'	R'	S'R'	S'	NS'	N	DN	D	N	S'	G'	R'
-	-	-	-	-	-	-	-	-	-	-	-	-	-	i	n
S'	-	R'	-	-	-	G'	R'	S'	-	R'	-	-	-	G'	R'
pya	-	ri	-	-	-	ba	-	to	-	me	-	-	-	an	-
S'	-	R'	-	-	-	R'	M'	G'	-	-	R'	S'	-	-	R'
ja	-	na	-	-	-	i	q	ra	-	-	r	hai	-	-	-
D	-	-	D	D	-	N	-	S'	-	-	D	N	-	-	D
-	-	-	k	ho	-	na	-	pya	-	-	r	hai	-	-	-
P	-	-	D	D	-	N	-	S'	-	-	D	N	-	-	-
-	-	-	k	ho	-	na	-	pya	-	-	r	hai	-	-	-
-	-	-	D	D	-	N	-	S'	-	-	D	N	-	-	D
-	-	-	k	ha	-	na	-	pya	-	-	r	hai	-	-	-
P	-	-	D	D	-	S'	G'	G'	S'	-	R'	S'	N	-	-
-	-	-	k	ha	-	na	-	pya	-	-	r	hai	-	-	-

interlude:
P- N—ND P- S' P- R'—S' N- S'NP -2

P- R'- S' N S'   P S' N D N
M- N S' N D P- M- D – P M P-

R'—M' R' N S'   S' R' S' P N--

R	M	P	M	P	-	-	M	M	P	D	P	D	-	-	-
pya	-	r	j	han	-	-	me	ho	-	ta	n	hin	-	-	-
M	D	D	N	S'	-	N	S'	R'	S'	N	-	-	-	G'R'G'	-
fi	r	bo	-	lo	-	kya	-	ho	-	ta	-	-	-	-	-

R'	M'	M'	R'	M'	-	-	-	R'	M'	M'	P'	G'	-	-	-
du	ni	ya	-	me	-	-	-	di	l	ko	-	ee	-	-	-

G'	G'	-	R'	S'	S'	S'	R'	S'	-	N	-	-	-	G'	R'
k	bhi	-	n	dh	d	ka	-	ho	-	ta	-	-	-	dh	d

S'	-	R'	R'	-	-	G'	-	S'	-	R'	R'	-	-	G'	R'
ka	-	hai	dil	-	-	aa	-	ya	-	r	mil	-	-	ye	-

S'	-	R'	R'	-	-	R'	M'	G'	-	-	R'	S'	-	-	R'
pya	-	r	ka	-	-	i	z	ha	-	-	r	hai	-	-	-

D	-	-	D	D	-	N	-	S'	-	-	D	N	-	-	D
-	-	-	k	ho	-	na	-	pya	-	-	r	hai	-	-	-

P	-	-	D	D	-	N	-	S'	-	-	D	N	-	-	D
-	-	-	k	ho	-	na	-	pya	-	-	r	hai	-	-	-

-	-	-	D	D	-	N	-	S'	-	-	D	N	-	-	D
-	-	-	k	ha	-	na	-	pya	-	-	r	hai	-	-	-

P	-	-	D	D	N	S'	G'	G'	S'	-	R'	S'	N	-	-
-	-	-	k	ha	-	na	-	pya	-	-	r	hai	-	-	-

interlude: R M D RMD   R M D   RMD R M D   RMD
R'- R'R' G'- R'-   R'R'R' G'- R'-
S' S'R' R'- S' S'-
P PD NN- S' R' S' NN D D S' N D P -2

R	M	P	M	P	-	-	-	M	P	D	P	D	-	-	-
do	-	pre	-	mi	-	-	-	do	-	pa	-	gl	-	-	-

M	D	D	N	S'	-	N	S'	R'	S'	S'	N	-	-	-	-
kya	-	k	r	te	-	hain	-	bo	-	lo	-	-	-	-	-

M P R' S'R'S' NS'N   PD P   M--
rari ra rari ra rari ra   rari ra ra—

R'	M'	M'	R'	M'	-	-	-	R'	M'	M'	P'	G'	-	-	-
mu	jh	se	-	kya	-	-	-	pu	-	chh	te	ho	-	-	-

G'	G'	R'	-	S'	-	S'	R'	S'	-	N	-	-	-	G'	R'
a	p	ne	-	di	l	ko	t	to	-	lo	-	-	-	ma	-

S'	-	R'	R'	-	-	G'	R'	S'	-	R'	R'	-	-	G'	R'
lu	-	m	hai	-	-	h	m	ko	-	tu	mhe	-	-	ki	s

S'	-	R'	R'	-	-	R'	R'	R'	M'	G'	R'	S'	-	-	R'
ba	-	t	ka	-	-	in	t	za	-	-	r	hai	-	-	-

D	-	-	D	D	-	N	-	S'	-	-	D	N	-	-	D
-	-	-	k	ho	-	na	-	pya	-	-	r	hai	-	-	-

P	-	-	D	D	-	N	-	S'	-	-	D	N	-	-	-
-	-	-	k	ho	-	na	-	pya	-	-	r	hai	-	-	-
-	-	-	D	D	-	N	-	S'	-	-	D	N	-	-	D
-	-	-	k	ha	-	na	-	pya	-	-	r	hai	-	-	-
P	-	-	D	D	-	S'	G'	G'	S'	-	R'	S'	N	-	-
-	-	-	k	ha	-	na	-	pya	-	-	r	hai	-	-	-

interlude:
R' R'R' S' N-- N S' S' S' N P S' S' S' N P N - 2
R'---- N' D' P'   S' --- D' P' M'--

S' R' G'   G' R' S'   P' M'
ru ru ru   ru ru ru   ru ru

R	M	P	M	P	-	-	-	M	P	D	P	D	-	-	-
mi	l	te	n	hin	-	-	-	h	m	tu	m	to	-	-	-
M	D	D	N	S'	-	N	S'	R'	S'	N	-	-	-	-	-
fi	r	bo	-	lo	-	kya	-	ho	-	ta	-	-	-	-	-
R'	M'	M'	R'	M'	-	-	-	R'	M'	M'	P'	G'	-	-	-
s	ch	bo	-	lun	-	-	-	fi	r	a	p	na	-	-	-
G'	-	G'	R'	S'	-	S'	R'	S'	-	N	-	-	-	G'	R'
kha	-	b	n	pu	-	ra	-	ho	-	ta	-	-	-	k	h
S'	-	R'	R'	-	-	G'	R'	S'	-	R'	R'	-	-	G'	R'
ta	-	hai	mn	-	-	a	p	na	-	mi	ln	-	-	du	ni
S'	-	R'	-	-	R'	-	R'	R'	M'	G'	R'	S'	-	-	R'
ya	-	me	-	-	ya	-	d	ga	-	-	r	hai	-	-	-
D	-	-	D	D	-	N	-	S'	-	-	D	N	-	-	D
-	-	-	k	ho	-	na	-	pya	-	-	r	hai	-	-	-
P	-	-	D	D	-	N	-	S'	-	-	D	N	-	-	-
-	-	-	k	ho	-	na	-	pya	-	-	r	hai	-	-	-
-	-	-	R'	D	-	N	-	S'	-	-	D	N	-	-	D
-	-	-	k	ha	-	na	-	pya	-	-	r	hai	-	-	-
P	-	-	D	D	N	S'	G'	G'	S'	-	R'	S'	N	-	-
-	-	-	ke	tu	m	se	-	pya	-	-	r	hai	-	-	-

24. KITNA PYARA TUJHE RAB NE

Film: Raja Hindustani (1996)	Music: Nadeem Shrawan
Lyrics: Sameer	Singer: Udit Narayan, Alka
Taal: Kaharwa	Chord: P̲N̲R' S=C

kitana pyaara tujhe rab ne banaaya jee kare dekhata rahoon
kitana sona tujhe rab ne banaaya jee kare dekhata rahoon

too hai paagal, too hai jokar too hai dilabar jaanee
sabase pyaara mera yaara raaja hindustaanee,
kitana pyaara tujhe rab...

ambar se aaee hai pariyon kee raanee
dekh jise hotee hai sabako hairaanee
sundar sa mukhada hai phoolon ke jaisa
hoga na duniya mein koee aisa
kitana seedha, kitana sachcha mera raaja kitana achchha
mujhako to achchhee lagatee hai teree har naadaanee
sabase pyaara mera yaara raaja hindustaanee, o kitana pyaara tujhe rab...

koyal ke jaisee hai teree ye bolee
moorat ke jaisee hai soorat ye bholee
baagon mein jao na dil mera ghabarae
pairon mein kaanta koee haay na chubh jae
main deevaanee ho na jaoon
teree baaton mein kho na jaoon
udata baadal bahata paanee bole rut mastaanee
sabase pyaara mera yaara raaja hindustaanee,
kitana pyaara tujhe rab...

Vinod Kumar

KITNA PYARA TUJHE RAB NE

dha ge	nti	nke	dhin	dha ge	nti	nke	dhin	dha ge	nti	nke	dhin	dha ge	nti	nke	dhin
1 2	3 4	5 6	7 8	1 2	3 4	5 6	7 8	1 2	3 4	5 6	7 8	1 2	3 4	5 6	7 8

prelude:
N D P P P P R G P D P N D P
hu--------------------------

P D N S' S' N D N D P
hu--------------------------

P D N S' S' N D N D P
jii – k re   de kh ta- r hu

														NN	N
														kit	na
P	P	-P	P	-	RG	-P	-D	P	N	-	D	P	P	DN	S'
pya	ra	-tu	jhe	-	rb	-ne	-b	na	ya	-	-	-	jii	-k	-re
S'	-N	N	-D	P	N	NN	N	P	P	-P	P	-	RG	-P	-D
de	-kh	ta	-r	hu	o	kit	na	so	na	-tu	jhe	-	rb	-ne	-b
P	N	-	D	P	P	DN	S'	S'	-N	N	-D	P	-	-	-
na	ya	-	-	-	jii	-k	-re	de	-kh	ta	-r	hu	-	-	-
P	D	N	R'	R'	R'	R'	R'	D	N	D	P	P	D	-	-
tu	hai	pa	gl	tu	hai	jo	kr	tu	hai	dil	br	ja	ni	-	-
D	N	D	N	D	N	D	N	R'	S'	N	D	P	P		
sb	se	pya	ra	me	ra	ya	ra	ra	ja	hin	dus	ta	ni		

interlude:
R' R'G' R' N P—D N R'G' G'- R'N D P-
P PD P G P DN R' R' R'G' N D- P – R'-

R' G' R' G'R' G'R' N R' G'R'
aa--------------------

S' R' S' R'S' R'S' D G D P-
aa------------------------

R'S'N x4 S'NDx 4 D N
R G P D N S' R' S' D N P-

N	N	D	-	N	N	D	-	N	N	D	P	D	-	-	-
am	br	se	-	aa	yi	hai	-	pri	yon	ki	ra	ni	-	-	-
D	DD	P	-	D	D	P	-	G	GD	D	P	P	-	-	-
de	khji	se	-	ho	ti	hai	-	sb	ko-	hai	ra	ni	-	-	-

music: PD<u>N</u>R'- <u>G'G'</u>R'S'- <u>NN</u>DP-G-P   <u>NN</u>D-P-   (ho....) <u>N</u>---

<u>N</u>	<u>N</u>	D	-	<u>N</u>	<u>N</u>	D	-	<u>N</u>	<u>N</u>	D	P	D	-	-	-
sun	dr	sa	-	mukh	da	hai	-	fu	lo	ke	jai	sa	-	-	-

D	DD	P	-	D	D	P	-	G	G	D	D	P	-	PP	D
ho	ga	na	-	duni	ya	me	-	ko	ee	-	ae	sa	-	kit	na

R'	-G'	-	-	-	-	<u>N</u>D	P	D	<u>N</u>	-	-	-	-	D	P
si	-dha	-	-	-	-	kit	na	s	ch cha	-	-	-	-	me	ra

D	-D	-	-	PG	R	<u>NN</u>	<u>N</u>	D	P	-	-	-	-	-	-
ra	-ja	-	-	-	-	kit	na	a	ch chha	-	-	-	-	-	-

PP	D	<u>N</u>	R'	G'	R'R'	R'	R'	D	<u>N</u>	D	P	P	D	-	-
mujh	ko	to	a	chch hi	lg	ti	hai	te	ri	hr	na	da	ni	-	-

D	<u>N</u>	D	<u>N</u>	D	<u>N</u>	D	<u>N</u>	R'	S'	<u>N</u>	D	P	P
sb	se	pya	ra	me	ra	ya	ra	ra	ja	hin	dus	ta	ni

interlude:
RG RG R <u>N</u>-- D<u>N</u>D-P-
RG RG R <u>N</u>---
RG RG R D-- PDP- G-
RG RG R D—
S' R'<u>G'</u> R'S' <u>N</u>D DP D- P-
aa------------------

<u>N</u>R' <u>N</u>R' D- P- D- <u>N</u>R'-
ho--------------------

<u>N</u>R' <u>N</u>R' D- P- D-
ho---------------

flute: <u>N</u>R' <u>N</u>R' D- P- D- <u>N</u>R'-
       <u>N</u>R' <u>N</u>R' D- P- D-

S' R' S' <u>G'</u> G'   <u>N</u>S' <u>N</u> R' R'   D—<u>N</u>S'- <u>N</u>DP-
ho----------   ho---------   music

<u>N</u>	<u>N</u>	D	-	<u>N</u>	<u>N</u>	D	-	<u>N</u>	<u>N</u>	D	P	D	-	-	-
ko	yl	ke	-	jai	si	hai	-	te	ri	ye	bo	li	-	-	-

D	DD	P	-	D	D	P	-	G	GD	D	P	P	-	-	-
mu	rt	ke	-	jai	si	hai	-	su	rt	ye	bho	li	-	-	-

music: PD<u>N</u>R'- <u>G'G'</u>R'S'- <u>NN</u>DP-G-P   <u>NN</u>D-P-   (ho....) <u>N</u>---

<u>N</u>	<u>N</u>	D	-	<u>N</u>	<u>N</u>	D	-	<u>N</u>	<u>N</u>	D	P	D	-	-	-
ba	go	me	-	ja	o	na	-	dil	mera	ghb	ra	ye	-	-	-

D	DD	P	-	D	D	P	-	G	G	D	D	P	-	P	D
pai	ro	me	-	kan	tako	ee	-	ha	yena	chubh	ja	ye	-	main	di
R'	-G'	-	-	-	-	N	P	D	N	-	-	-	-	D	P
va	-ni	-	-	-	-	ho	na	ja	-un	-	-	-	-	te	ri
PD	-D	-	D	P	G	N	N	D	P	-	-	-	-	-	-
ba-	-to	-	me	-	-	kho	na	ja	-un	-	-	-	-	-	-
PP	D	N	R'	R'	R'	R'	R'	D	N	D	P	P	D	-	-
ud	ta	ba	dl	bh	ta	pa	ni	bo	le	rut	ms	ta	ni	-	-
D	N	D	N	D	N	D	N	R'	S'	N	D	P	P		
sb	se	pya	ra	me	ra	ya	ra	ra	ja	hin	dus	ta	ni		

25. KUCHH TUM BOLO KUCHH HAM BOLEN

Film: Dil to paagal hai (1997)	Music: Uttam Singh
Lyrics: Anand Bakshi	Singer: Udit Narayan
Taal: Kaharwa	Chord: PNR' S=C

kab tak chup baithen ab to kuchh hai bolana
kuchh tum bolo kuchh ham bolen o dholana
mar jaana tha ye bhed nahin tha kholana
o dholana, o dholana

do chaar kadam pe tum the, do chaar kadam pe ham the -2
do chaar kadam ye lekin sau meelon se kya kam the
phir usape kadam kadam pe dil ka dolana
haay dolana, ho dholana

lo jeet gae tum hamase, ham haar gae is dilase -2
aaya hai aaj labon pe, ye pyaar badee mushkil se
is pyaar mein hamako paagal na kar chhodana
na chhodana, ho dholana

KUCHH TUM BOLO KUCHH HAM BOLEN

dhage 12	nti 34	nke 56	dhin 78	dhage 12	nti 34	nke 56	dhin 78	dhage 12	nti 34	nke 56	dhin 78	dhage 12	nti 34	nke 56	dhin 78

prelude:

P N R' M*' R'   N R' G' M*' G' R' N P   -2
aa--------   aa------aa-------

N R' N P   P----- M* R P
aa------   aa---- aa----

(P N D P G P D   P N D P G D P-
N R'S' N D N S'   N R'S' N D S' N-
P N D P G P D   P N D P G D P-) 2

															P
															kb
D	N	D	P	D	N	D	P	GP	-P	D	-	DN	S'N	D	P
tk	chup	bai	the	ab	to	kuchh	hai	bo-	-l	na	-	-	-	-	kuchh
D	N	D	P	D	N	D	P	GP	-P	P	-	DP	DP	-	R'
tum	bo	lo	kuchh	hm	bo	len	o	dho	-l	na	-	-	-	-	mr
N	N	R'	R'	G'	-R'	S'	N	D	-P	N	-	-	-	-	R'
ja	na	tha	ye	bhe	d,n	hin	tha	kho	-l	na	-	-	-	-	o
N	-D	D	-	-	-	S'	N	D	-P	P	-	-	-	-	-
dho	-l	na	-	-	-	-	o	dho	-l	na	-	-	-	-	-

interlude:
P N D P G P D   P N D P G D P-
N R'S' N D N S'   N R'S' N D S' N-
P N D P G P D   P N D P G D P-

D N S'R'G'M*'P'M*'G'   P D N S'R'G'M*'G'R'- 2

P M* G   D M* P-
aa----   aa----- -2

P N D P G P D   P N D P G D P- 2

															G
															do
P	P	P	D	D	D	-	G	P	P	P	D	P	P	-	
cha	r,k	dm	pe	tum	the	-	do	cha	r,k	dm	pe	hm	the	-	

P M* G   D M* P-
un--------------

																P
																do
P	M*	D	P	M*	G	D	D	D	P	N	D	P	P	-	P	P
cha	r,k	dm	pe	tum	the	-	do	cha	r,k	dm	pe	hm	the	-	do	do
P	-M*	D	P	M*	G	D	D	D	P	N	D	P	P	-	R'	R'
cha	r,k	dm	ye	le	kin	-	sau	mi	lo	se	kya	km	the	-	fir	fir
N	N	R'R'	-R'	G'	R'	S'	N	D	-P	N	-	-	-	-	R'	R'
us	pe	kdm	-k	dm	pe	dil	ka	do	-l	na	-	-	-	-	hay	hay
N	-D	D	-	-	-	S'	S'	D	-P	P	-	-	-	-	P	P
do	-l	na	-	-	-	-	o	dho	-l	na	-	-	-	-	kb	kb
D	N	D	P	D	N	D	P	GP	-P	D	-	DN	S'N	D		
tk	chup	bai	the	ab	to	kuchh	hai	bo-	-l	na	-	-	-	-		

interlude:
P R' R̲' G' R' N P N R̲' R' P G' R' G' M*' G' R' N D- -2
R' S' N D P G P-R   RGM*PDNR'-DN-
D N S' R' G' S' G'- G' S' G'-
G' R' S' N D – P-   G NDN- DPD-
G NDN DP GP-   G DPD PM*G-

P ND P G P D   P ND P G D P- -2

															G
															lo
P	PP	P	N	D	D	-	G	P	P	P	D	P	P	-	G
jii	t,g	ye	tum	hm	se	-	hm	ha	r,g	ye	is	dil	se	-	lo

P M* G   D M* P-
un----------------

																P
																lo
P	PM*	D	P	M*	G	D	D	D	DP	N	D	P	P	-	P	P
jii	t,g	ye	tum	hm	se	-	hm	ha	r,g	ye	is	dil	se	-	aa	aa
P	M*	D	PP	M*	G	-	D	D	DP	N	D	P	P	-	R'	R'
ya	hai	aa	j,l	bo	pe	-	ye	pya	r,b	di	mush	kil	se	-	is	is
N	NN	R'R'	-R'	R'	G'	R'	S'N	D	-P	N	-	-	-	-	R'	R'
pya	r,me	hm	ko	pa	gl	na	kr	chho	-d	na	-	-	-	-	na	na
N	-D	D	-	-	-	S'	S'	D	-P	P	-	-	-	-	P	P
chho	-d	na	-	-	-	-	o	dho	-l	na	-	-	-	-	kb	kb

D	N	D	P	D	N	D	P	GP	-P	D	-	DN	S'N	D	P
tk	chup	bai	the	ab	to	kuchh	hai	bo-	-l	na	-	lala	lala	la	kuchh
D	N	D	P	D	N	D	P	GP	-P	P	-	DP	DP	-	R'
tum	bo	lo	kuchh	hm	bo	len	o	dho	-l	na	-	-	-	-	Mr
N	N	R'	R'	G'	-R'	S'	N	D	-P	N	-	-	-	-	R'
ja	na	tha	ye	bhe	d,n	hin	tha	kho	-l	na	-	-	-	-	o
N	-D	D	-	-	-	S'	N	D	-P	P	-	-	-	-	
dho	-l	na	-	-	-	-	o	dho	-l	na	-	-	-	-	

26. KOI MIL GAYA

Film: Kuchh kuchh hota hai (1998)	Music: Jatin Lalit
Lyrics: Sameer	Singer: Udit Narayan, Alka
Taal: Kaharwa	Chord: P̲NR' N̲R'M' S=C

mujhako kya hua hai, kyon main kho gaya hoon
paagal tha main pahale, ya ab ho gaya hoon
bahakee hai nigaahen, aur bikhare hain baal
tumane banaaya hai kya apana ye haal
koee mil gaya koee mil gaya
mera dil gaya mera dil gaya
kya bataoon yaaron main to hil gaya
koee mil gaya..

jaane kya ho gaya hai mujhe deevaana log kahane lage
ye deevaanagee hai kya hamen bhee to ho pata
tumako kya ho gaya are kal tak mujhako sab hosh tha
dil mein khushiyon ka josh tha phir ye bechainee hai kyon
phir ye betaabee hai kyon kya koee kho gaya
koee mil gaya..

baadal banakar kaun aa gaya kaun hai jo dil pe yoon chha gaya
chahun kii bataun main phir bhii kah na paun main
naam uska hai kya
o naam na lo par kuchh to kaho halka sa koee ishaara to do
meree aankhon mein hai vo meree saanson mein hai vo
aur kahoon tumase kya
koee mil gaya..

Vinod Kumar

KOI MIL GAYA

dhage	nti	nke	dhin	dhage	nti	nke	dhin	dhage	nti	nke	dhin	dhage	nti	nke	dhin
12	34	56	78	12	34	56	78	12	34	56	78	12	34	56	78

prelude: trumpet is mostly used for music in this song.

```
S' R' G' R' S'R' S'    N S' R' M' N
S' R' G' P' M' G' S' R' S'    S' R' S' N-P-  N S' R' S' N
S' R' G' R' S'R' S'    N S' N

NS' R'S' NN    S'R' G'R' S'S'    S'R' S'N PP
koee mil gya   koee mil  gya   koee mil  gya

N R' R' N S' S'    N R' R' N G' G'
M' P' D' P' M' G' M'
S' R' G'—R' G' M' -  G'- M'- R'  R' G' M' R'
G' N S'—G' G' M'-  M' G' R' R'  R' R' R' -
```

dhage	nti	nke	dhin	dhage	nti	nke	dhin	dhage	nti	nke	dhin	dhage	nti	nke	dhin
R'	M'	-	-	-	-	N	N	S'	G'	-	-	-	-	-	R'
mujh	-ko	-	-	-	-	kya	hu	aa	-hai	-	-	-	-	-	are
R'	M'	-	-	-	-	N	N	S'	P	-	-	-	-	-	-
kyu	-main	-	-	-	-	kho	g	ya	-hu	-	-	-	-	-	-
R'	M'	-	-	-	-	N	N	S'	G'	-	-	-	-	-	-
pa	-g	-l	-	-	-	tha	main	ph	-le	-	-	-	-	-	-
R'	-	M'	M'	-	-	N	N	S'	P	-	-	-	-	-	-
ya	-	a	b	-	-	ho	g	ya	-hu	-	-	-	-	-	-
S'	S'	S'	R'	G'	G'	G'	R'	S'	S'	S'	R'	S'	-	-	-
bh	ki	hain	ni	ga	hen	au	r	bi	kh	re	hain	ba	-l	-	-
S'	S'	S'	R'	G'	M'	M'	M'	M'	G'	G'	R'	R'	-	N	S'
tu	m	ne	b	na	ya	hai	kya	a	p	na	ye	ha	-l	ko	ee
R'	S'	N	N	-	-	N	S'	R'	S'	N	N	-	-	S'	R'
mi	l	g	ya	-	-	ko	ee	mi	l	g	ya	-	-	me	ra
G'	R'	S'	S'	-	-	S'	R'	G'	R'	S'	S'	-	-	N	S'
di	l	g	ya	-	-	me	ra	di	l	g	ya	-	-	kya	b
R'	S'	N	N	-	-	N	S'	R'	S'	N	N	-	-	S'	R'
ta	un	ya	ro	-	-	kya	b	ta	un	ya	ro	-	-	main	to
G'	R'	S'	S'	-	-	S'	R'	G'	R'	S'	S'	-	-	S'	R'
hi	l	g	ya	-	-	main	to	hi	l	g	ya	-	-	ko	ee
S'	N	P	P	-	-	-	-	-	-	-	-	G'	G'	R'	S'
mi	l	g	ya	-	-	-	-	-	-	-	-	mi	l	hi	g

R'	<u>N</u>	-	-	P'	P'	P'	M'	-	-	<u>G'</u>	-	G'	G'	R'	S'
ya	-	-	-	mi	l	g	ya	-	-	ae	-	mi	l	hi	g
M'	<u>N</u>	-	-	P'	P'	P'	M'	-	-						
ya	-	-	-	mi	l	g	ya	-	-						

interlude:
(P <u>D</u> <u>D</u> <u>N</u> <u>N</u> <u>N</u> <u>N</u> <u>N</u> <u>N</u> <u>N</u> <u>N</u> <u>N</u> <u>N</u> G'-
P <u>D</u> <u>D</u> <u>N</u> <u>N</u> R' <u>N</u> <u>N</u> <u>N</u> S' <u>N</u> <u>D</u>)– 2

M <u>D</u> R' S' <u>G'</u> R' S' R' S' M <u>D</u> S' <u>N</u> <u>N</u> <u>D</u> <u>D</u> <u>N</u>
he he----------------- ha ha ---------------- -2

R'<u>G'</u>M' <u>G'</u> R' S' <u>G'</u> M'-
R'<u>G'</u>M' <u>G'</u> R' <u>G'</u> S'-

S'<u>N</u> S' R' <u>G'</u> P'- S'<u>N</u> S' R' <u>G'</u> P'-
<u>G'</u> P'---- P' <u>N'</u> P' <u>G'</u> M'—
R'—R'—R' R' R' –

M'		<u>G'</u>	-	R'	R'	-	R'	S'	R'	-	<u>G'</u>	M'	-	-	-
ja	-	ne	-	kya	-ho	-	g	ya	-hai	-	mu	jhe	-	-	-
M'	-	<u>G'</u>	-	R'	R'	-	R'	S'	R'	-	<u>G'</u>	M'	-	-	-
di	-	va	-	na	-lo	-	g	kh	-ne	-	l	ge	-	-	-
<u>G'</u>	R'	R'	<u>N</u>	D	P	P	-	<u>G'</u>	R'	R'	<u>N</u>	D	P	P	-
ye	di	va	n	gi	hai	kya	-	h	me	bhi	to	ho	p	ta	-
-	S'	-	S'	S'	M'	-	<u>G'</u>	<u>G'</u>	M'	-	-	-	-	M'	M'
-	tum	-	ko	kya	-ho	-	g	ya	-	-	-	-	-	a	re
M'	<u>G'</u>	<u>G'</u>	R'	R'	R'	R'	-	S'	R'	-	<u>G'</u>	M'	-	-	-
k	l	t	k	mu	jh	ko	-	sb	-ho	-	sh	tha	-	-	-
M'	<u>G'</u>	<u>G'</u>	-	R'	R'	R'	-	S'	R'	-	<u>G'</u>	M'	-	-	-
di	l	me	-	khu	shi	yon	-	ka	-jo	-	sh	tha	-	-	-
<u>G'</u>	R'	R'	<u>N</u>	D	P	P	-	<u>G'</u>	R'	R'	<u>N</u>	D	P	P	-
fir	ye	be	chai	ni	hai	kyu	-	fir	ye	be	ta	bi	hai	kyu	-
-	S'	-	S'	S'	M'	-	<u>G'</u>	<u>G'</u>	M'	-	-	-	-	<u>N</u>	S'
-	kya	-	ko	ee	kho	-	g	ya	-	-	-	-	-	ko	ee
R'	S'	<u>N</u>	<u>N</u>	-	-	<u>N</u>	S'	R'	S'	<u>N</u>	<u>N</u>	-			
mi	l	g	ya	-	-	ko	ee	mi	l	g	ya	-			

interlude:
N D---- N R'--- -2
P' M'D' -- P' M' G' M'P'—M'-
R' S' R' M'

M-- N D------ M D D D N-
du du----------------------

N G'R' N G'R' N G'R'

M-- N D------ M D D D N-
du du--------------------

G' M' N S'--- R' R' M'---
M' G' R' R'   R' R'—

M'		G'	R'	R'	-	R'	R'	S'	R'	-	G'	M'	-	-	-
ba	-	d	l	bn	-	k	r	kau	n,aa	-	g	ya	-	-	-

M'	-	G'	G'	R'	R'	-	R'	S'	R'	-	G'	M'	-	-	-
kau	-	n	hai	jo	-dil	-	pe	yun	-chha	-	g	ya	-	-	-

G'	R'	R'	N	D	P	P	-	G'	R'	R'	N	D	P	P	-
cha	hu	ke	b	ta	un	main	-	fir	bhi	kah	na	pa	un	main	-

-	S'	-	S'	S'	R'	-	G'	G'	M'	-	-	-	-	R'	-
-	na	-	m	us	-ka	-	hai	kya	-	-	-	-	-	aa	-

M'	-	G'	G'	R'	-	R'	-	S'	R'	-	G'	M'	-	-	-
na	-	m	n	lo	-	p	r	kuchh	-to	-	k	ho	-	-	-

M'	-	G'	-	R'	R'	R'	R'	S'	R'	-	G'	M'	-	-	-
h	l	ka	-	sa	ko	ee	i	sha	-ra	-	to	do	-	-	-

G'	R'	R'	N	D	P	P	-	G'	R'	R'	N	D	P	P	-
me	ri	aan	kho	me	hai	vo	-	me	ri	san	so	me	hai	vo	-

-	S'	-	S'	S'	M'	-	G'	M'	-	G'	-	R'	-	N	S'
-	au	r	k	hu	-tum	-	se	kya	-	-	-	-	-	ko	ee

R'	S'	N	N	-	-	N	S'	R'	S'	N	N	-	-	S'	R'
mi	l	g	ya	-	-	ko	ee	mi	l	g	ya	-	-	me	ra

G'	R'	S'	S'	-	-	S'	R'	G'	R'	S'	S'	-	-	N	S'
di	l	g	ya	-	-	me	ra	di	l	g	ya	-	-	kya	b

R'	S'	N	N	-	-	N	S'	R'	S'	N	N	-	-	S'	R'
ta	un	ya	ro	-	-	kya	b	ta	un	ya	ro	-	-	main	to

G'	R'	S'	S'	-	-	S'	R'	G'	R'	S'	S'	-	-	S'	R'
hi	l	g	ya	-	-	main	to	hi	l	g	ya	-	-	ko	ee
S'	N	P	P	-	-	-	-	-	-	-	-	G'	G'	R'	S'
mi	l	g	ya	-	-	-	-	-	-	-	-	mi	l	hi	g
R'	N	-	-	P'	P'	P'	M'	-	-	G'	-	G'	G'	R'	S'
ya	-	-	-	mi	l	g	ya	-	-	ae	-	mi	l	hi	g
M'	N	-	-	P'	P'	P'	M'	-	-						
ya	-	-	-	mi	l	g	ya	-	-						

27. KYONKI ITNA PYAR TUMSE

Film: Kyonki (2005)	Music: Himesh Reshamiya
Lyrics: Sameer	Singer: Udit Narayan, Alka
Taal: Kaharwa	Chord: PNR' S=.B

kyon ki itana pyaar tumase karate hain ham
kya jaan loge hamaaree sanam
kyon ki itana pyaar...
hamaare dil kee tum, thodee see kadar kar lo
ham tumape marate hain, thodee see fikar kar lo
fikar kar lo
kyon ki itana pyaar...

toone o jaana deevaana kiya hai
deevaana kiya is kadar
chaahat mein teree bhulaaya jahaan ko
na dil ko kisee kee khabar
ragon mein mohabbat ka, ehasaas zara bhar lo
ham tumape marate hain, thodee see fikar kar lo
kyon ki itana pyaar...

tumase hain saansen, tumheen se hain dhadakan
tumheen se hain deevaanagee
rab ne hamen dee hai jaan-e-tamanna
tumhaare lie zindagee
vaada sang jeene ka, tum jaan-e-jigar kar lo
ham tumape marate hain ,thodee see fikar kar lo
kyon ki itana pyaar...

Vinod Kumar

KYONKI ITNA PYAR TUMSE

dha 1	ge 2	n 3	ti 4	n 5	ke 6	dhi 7	n 8	dha 1	ge 2	n 3	ti 4	n 5	ke 6	dhi 7	n 8
prelude: PD N̲ R' N̲ D P DN̲D--													P	-	D
													kyu	-	ki
N̲	N̲	R'	-	-	N̲	-	D	P	-	D	-	-	-	P	D
i	t	na	-	-	pya	-	r	tu	m	se	-	-	-	k	r
N̲	-	-	R'	-	N̲	-	D	D	-	-	-	-			
te	-	-	-	-	hain	-	-	hm	-	-	-	-			
music: mauth organ: R'-G' R'-G' R' R' R̲' R' R̲' N̲ D P N̲ D -														R'	-
														kya	-
G'	-	R'	-	G'	-	R'	-	R̲'	-	R'	-	-	-	-	R'
jan	-	-	-	lo	-	-	-	ge	-	-	-	-	-	-	h
N̲	-	D	-	G	-	-	N̲	D	-	-	-				
ma	-	-	-	ri	-	-	s	nm	-	-	-				

prelude: P R' S' R' N̲ R' -2   P S' N̲ R' N̲ -2 N̲ S' R' R' P---

G' R' N̲ R' G' ---- M' R' N̲ R' -- 2

aa---------------------

dha 1	ge 2	n 3	ti 4	n 5	ke 6	dhi 7	n 8	dha 1	ge 2	n 3	ti 4	n 5	ke 6	dhi 7	n 8
													P	-	D
													kyu	-	ki
N̲	-	R'	-	-	N̲	-	D	P	-	D	-	-	-	P	D
i	t	na	-	-	pya	-	r	tu	m	se	-	-	-	k	r
N̲	-	-	R'	-	N̲	-	D	D	-	-	-	-	-	R'	-
te	-	-	-	-	hain	-	-	hm	-	-	-	-	-	kya	-
G'	-	R'	-	G'	-	R'	-	R̲'	-	R'	-	-	-	-	R'
jan	-	-	-	lo	-	-	-	ge	-	-	-	-	-	-	h
R'	-	R'N̲	-	P	-	-	N̲	D	-	-	-	-			
ma	-	-	-	ri	-	-	s	nm	-	-	-	-			

interlude:

G' R'N̲ R' G' ---- M' R'N̲ R' -- 2

aa---------------------

D P- D – N̲ R', R' R' G' R' G' R' D D N̲-

P-D G' R' G' R' D D N̲- D N̲ D G- D N̲ D P-

violin: PD N̲ D N̲ S' N̲ S'R'–

dhin	-na	-	tin	tin	-na	-	dhin	dhin	-na	-	tin	tin	-na	-	dhin
G'	-R'	-	P	D	-N	-	G'	R'	-G'	-	P	D	-N	-	G'
tu	-ne	-	o	ja	-na	-	di	va	-na	-	ki	ya	-hai	-	di
R'	-G'	-	P	P	-D	-	S'	N	-	-	-	-	-	-	D
va	-na	-	ki	ya	-is	-	q	dr	-	-	-	-	-	-	di
D	-N	-	D	G	-N	-	D	P	-	-	-	-	-	-	-
va	-na	-	ki	ya	-is	-	q	dr	-	-	-	-	-	-	-
G'	- R'	-	P	D	-N	-	G'	R'	-G'	-	P	D	-N	-	G'
cha	-ht	-	me	te	-ri	-	bhu	la	-ya	-	j	han	-ko	-	n
R'	-G'	-	P	P	-D	-	S'	N	-	-	-	-	-	-	N
dil	-ko	-	ki	si	-ki	-	kh	br	-	-	-	-	-	-	n
D	-N	-	D	P	-G	-	N	D	P	-	-	-	-	-	-
dil	-ko	-	ki	si	-ki	-	kh	br	-	-	-	-	-	-	-

play taal here again as- dha ge n ti n ke dhi n

dhin	-na	-	tin	tin	-na	-	dhin	dhin	-na	-	tin	tin	-na	-	dhin
															R'
															ra
G'	-	R'	R'	G'	-	R'	R'	R'	N	-	-	-	-	R'	R'
gon	-	me	mo	ho	-	b	t	ka	-	-	-	-	-	e	h
G'	-	R'	R'	G'	-	R'	R'	R'	R'	-	-	-	-	R'	-
sa	-	s	z	ra	-	bh	r	lo	-	-	-	-	-	h	m
R'	-	R'	M'	G'	-	R'	-	S'	N	S'	N	-	-	R'	-
tu	m	pe	-	m	r	te	-	hain	-	-	-	-	-	tho	-
G'	-	R'	R'	G'	-	R'	R'	R'	-	R'	-	-	-	-	-
di	-	si	fi	k	r	k	r	lo	-	-	-	-	-	-	-
-	-	M'	G'	-	R'	-	S'	N	D	P	G	N	-	-	-
-	-	fi	k	r	k	-	r	lo	-	-	-	-	-	-	-
-	-	-	-	-	-	-	-	-	-	-	-	-	P	-	D
-	-	-	-	-	-	-	-	-	-	-	-	-	kyu	-	ki

interlude:
R' R'M' G' R' -2
R' R'M' G' R' S'N P D N R' S' N –
R' R'M' G' R' -2
R' R'M' G' R' S'N P D R' S' N –
violin: P D N R' G' R' N R' G'R'G'-
M' R' M' R' M' R' N G' R'-

dhin	-na	-	tin	tin	-na	-	dhin	dhin	-na	-	tin	tin	-na	-	dhin
G'	-R'	-	P	D	-N	-	G'	R'	-G'	-	P	D	-N	-	G'
tum	-se	-	hain	saan	-se	-	tu	mhi	-se	-	hai	dhd	-k	-n	tu

R'	-G'	-	P	P	-D	-	S'	N	-	-	-	-	-	-	D
mhi	-se	-	hai	di	-va	-	n	gi	-	-	-	-	-	-	tu
D	-N	-	D	P	-G	-	N	D	P	-	-	-	-	-	-
mhi	-se	-	hai	di	-va	-	n	gi	-	-	-	-	-	-	-
G'	-R'	-	P	D	-N	-	G'	R'	-G'	-	P	D	-N	-	G'
rb	-ne	-	h	me	-di	-	hai	ja	-ne	-	t	mn	-na	-	tu
R'	-G'	-	P	P	-D	-	S'	N	-	-	-	-	-	-	N
mha	-re	-	li	e	-zin	-	d	gi	-	-	-	-	-	-	tu
D	-N	-	D	P	-G	-	N	D	P	-	-	-	-	R'	
mha	-re	-	li	e	-zin	-	d	gi	-	-	-	-	-	va	-

yhan Taal fir dha ge n ti n ke dhi n bjaen

G'	-	R'	R'	G'	-	R'	-	N	-	-	-	-	-	R'	R'
da	-	sn	g	jii	-	ne	-	ka	-	-	-	-	-	tu	m
G'	-	R'	R'	G'	-	R'	R'	R'	R'	-	-	-	-	R'	-
ja	-	ne	ji	g	r	k	r	lo	-	-	-	-	-	h	m
G'	-	R'	-	G'	-	R'	-	R'	N	-	-	-	-	R'	-
tu	m	pe	-	m	r	te	-	hain	-	-	-	-	-	tho	-
G'	-	R'	R'	G'	-	R'	R'	R'	-	R'	-	-	-	-	-
di	-	si	fi	k	r	k	r	lo	-	-	-	-	-	-	-
-	-	M'	G'	-	R'	-	S'	N	D	P	G	N	-	-	-
-	-	fi	k	r	k	-	r	lo	-	-	-	-	-	-	-
-	-	-	-	-	-	-	-	-	-	-	-	-	P	-	D
-	-	-	-	-	-	-	-	-	-	-	-	-	kyu	-	ki
N	N	R'	-	-	N	-	D	P	-	D	-	-	-	P	D
i	t	na	-	-	pya	-	r	tu	m	se	-	-	-	k	r
N	-	-	R'	-	N	-	D	D	-	-	-	-	-	R'	-
te	-	-	-	-	hain	-	-	hm	-	-	-	-	-	kya	-
G'	-	R'	-	G'	-	R'	-	R'	-	R'	-	-	-	-	R'
jan	-	-	-	lo	-	-	-	ge	-	-	-	-	-	-	h
N	-	D	-	G	-	-	N	D	-	-	-	-			
ma	-	-	-	ri	-	-	s	nm	-	-	-	-			

28. MUJHE NEEND NA AAYE

Film: dil (1990)	Music: Anand Milind
Lyrics: Sameer	Singer: Udit Narayan, Anuradha
Taal: Kaharwa	Chord: SGP RPN S=E

u: mujhe neend na aae, mujhe chain na aae,
   koee jae zara dhoondh ke lae
   na jaane kahaan dil kho gaya, na jaane kahaan dil kho gaya
a: mujhe neend na aae, mujhe chain na aae,
   koee jae zara dhoondh ke lae
   na jaane kahaan dil kho gaya, na jaane kahaan dil kho gaya

a: haalat kya hai kaise tujhe bataoon main,
   karavat badal-badal ke raat bitaoon main
u: (poochho zara poochho kya haal hai, haal mera behaal hai) - 2
   koee samajh na pae kya rog satae, koee jae zara dhoondh ke lae
   na jaane kahaan ...

u: jaan se bhee pyaara mujhako mera dil hai
   usake bina ek pal bhee jeena mushkil hai
a: (tauba meree tauba kya dard hai, dard bada be-dard hai) - 2
   kabhee mujhako hansae, kabhee mujhako rulae,
   koee jae zara dhoondh ke lae
   na jaane kahaan ...

Vinod Kumar

MUJHE NEEND NA AAYE

dha	ge	n	ti	n	ke	dhi	n	dha	ge	n	ti	n	ke	dhi	n
1	2	3	4	5	6	7	8	1	2	3	4	5	6	7	8

prelude:
S' N P- P N S' N P-
P N P N P R' P R' S'   D M P
aa aa aa aa aa aa aa aa aa   aa aa aa

PN   NS'S'   N   NS'
mujhe   nin-d   n   aaye -3

NN   NPP   M MP
mujhe   nin-d n aaye -3

P – D P M— R .N S--

														P	N
														mu	jhe
N	S'	S'	S'	N	S'	-	-	-	-	-	-	-	-	-	-
nin	-	d	n	aa	ye	-	-	-	-	-	-	-	-	-	-
N	-	-	-	P	-	-	-	-	-	-	-	-	-	P	N
ho	-	-	-	o	-	-	-	-	-	-	-	-	-	mu	jhe
N	S'	S'	S'	S'	-	N	P	P	N	N	N	N	-	P	M
nin	-	d	n	aa	ye	mu	jhe	chai	-	n	n	aa	ye	ko	ee
M	P	P	M	M	R	R	S	S	R	-	M	R	S	S	.N
ja	ye	z	ra	dhun	-	dh	ke	la	ye	-	n	ja	ne	k	han
.N	S	S	S	R	-	-	-	-	-	-	M	R	S	S	.N
di	l	kho	g	ya	-	-	-	-	-	-	n	ja	ne	k	han
.N	S	S	S	S	-	-	-	-	-	-	M	R	S	S	.N
di	l	kho	g	ya	-	-	-	-	-	-	n	ja	ne	k	han
.N	S	S	S	R	-	M	-	P	-	-	M	R	S	S	.N
di	l	kho	g	ya	-	-	-	-	-	-	n	ja	ne	k	han
.N	S	S	S	S	-	-	-	-	-	-					
di	l	kho	g	ya	-	-	-	-	-	-					

interlude:
guitar: P P N G' R' R' R' N S' S' N P
         P P N R' S' S' S' N P S' S'
flute: S' S' S' S' N S' N-
       N N N N P N P –
       S' S' N P M M R .N S

```
S' ---- NP  M—R .N S
aa---------------------
S'    -    S'   N  | S'   -    S'   N  | S'   -    S'   -  | N   P   -   P
ha    -    l    t  | kya  -    hai  -  | kai  -    se   -  | tu  mhe  -   b

M     -    -    N  | -    -    N    -  | -    -    -    -  | -   -    -   -
ta    -    -    un | -    -    main -  | -    -    -    -  | -   -    -   -

N     -    N    P  | N    N    -    P  | N    -    N    -  | P   -    M   M
k     r    v    t  | b    d    l    b  | d    l    ke   -  | ra  -    t   bi

R     -    -    P  | -    -    P    -  | -    -    -    -  | -   -    -   -
ta    -    -    un | -    -    main -  | -    -    -    -  | -   -    -   -
```

music: G' R'S' R' S'N S' NP MPNS' uPryukt dohrane hetu.

```
S   G    G    G  | M    P    M    G  | G    M    M    R  | -   -    -   -
pu  chho z    ra | pu   chho kya  -  | ha   -    l    hai| -   -    -   -

S   G    G    G  | M    P    M    G  | M    -    M    N  | -   -    P   N
ha  -    l    me | ra   -    be   -  | ha   -    l    hai| -   -    ko  ee

N   S'   S'   S' | S'   -    N    P  | P    N    N    N  | N   -    P   M
s   m    jh   n  | pa   ye   kya  -  | ro   -    g    s  | ta  y    ko  ee

M   P    P    M  | M    -    R    S  | S    R    -    M  | R   S    S   .N
ja  ye   z    ra | dhun -    dh   ke | la   ye   -    n  | ja  ne   k   han

.N  S    S    S  | R    -    -    -  | -    -    -    M  | R   S    S   .N
di  l    kho  g  | ya   -    -    -  | -    -    -    n  | ja  ne   k   han

.N  S    S    S  | S    -    -    -  | -    -    -    M  | R   S    S   .N
di  l    kho  g  | ya   -    -    -  | -    -    -    n  | ja  ne   k   han

.N  S    S    S  | R    -    M    -  | P    -    -    M  | R   S    S   .N
di  l    kho  g  | ya   -    -    -  | -    -    -    n  | ja  ne   k   han

.N  S    S    S  | S    -    -    -  | -    -    -
di  l    kho  g  | ya   -    -    -  | -    -    -
```

interlude: S' S'N S' S'N S' NPN S' S'N S' S'N S'

P N S'----- R'S' R'S' N P N

aa---------- aa------   aa-----

S' R'S' N P R' S'

aa-------   aa------

flute: PP N S'- PP N S'-

      PP N M- N M- P-

      PP N S' PP N S'

      PP N S' R' G' M'-

guitar: P P P MG M M GM G R S -2

S'	-	S'	N	S'	-	S'	N	S'	-	S'	N	N	P	P	-
ja	-	n	se	bhi	-	pya	-	ra	-	mu	jh	ko	-	me	-

M	-	-	N	-	-	N	-	-	-	-	-	-	-	-	-
ra	-	-	dil	-	-	hai	-	-	-	-	-	-	-	-	-

N	-	N	P	N	-	N	P	N	-	N	-	P	M	M	-
u	s	ke	bi	na	-	i	k	pl	-	bhi	-	jii	-	na	-

R	R	-	P	-	-	P	-	-	-	-	-	-	-	-	-
mu	sh	-	ki	l	-	hai	-	-	-	-	-	-	-	-	-

music: G' R'S' R' S'N S' NP MPNS'   uPryukt dohrane hetu.

S	G	G	G	M	P	M	G	G	M	M	R	-	-	-	-
tau	ba	me	ri	tau	ba	kya	-	d	r	d	hai	-	-	-	-

S	G	G	G	M	P	M	G	M	-	M	N	-	-	P	N
d	r	d	b	da	-	be	-	d	r	d	hai	-	-	k	bhi

N	S'	S'	S'	S'	-	N	P	P	N	N	N	N	-	P	M
mu	jh	ko	hn	sa	ye	k	bhi	mu	jh	ko	ru	la	ye	ko	ee

M	P	P	M	M	-	R	S	S	R	-	M	R	S	S	.N
ja	ye	z	ra	dhun	-	dh	ke	la	ye	-	n	ja	ne	k	han

.N	S	S	S	R	-	-	-	-	-	-	M	R	S	S	.N
di	l	kho	g	ya	-	-	-	-	-	-	n	ja	ne	k	han

.N	S	S	S	S	-	-	-	-	-	-	M	R	S	S	.N
di	l	kho	g	ya	-	-	-	-	-	-	n	ja	ne	k	han

.N	S	S	S	R	-	M	-	P	-	-	M	R	S	S	.N
di	l	kho	g	ya	-	-	-	-	-	-	n	ja	ne	k	han

.N	S	S	S	S	-	-	-	-	-	-					
di	l	kho	g	ya	-	-	-	-	-	-					

29. MERA MAN KYUN TUMHE CHAHE

Film: Man (1999)	Music: Sanjeev Rathaur, Darshan Rathaur
Lyrics: Sameer	Singer: Udit Narayan, Alka
Taal: Kaharwa	Chord: MDS' S=D#

mera man kyon tumhen chaahe mera man
na jaane jud gaya kaise ye bandhan

mera man kyon tumhen chaahe mera man
na jaane jud gaya kaise ye bandhan
kaisee ye deevaanagee, kaisa ye deevaanaapan
mera man kyon tumhen chaahe mera man

main deevaanee ban gayee tumane aisa kya kiya
meree neenden lootee lee chain bhee mera liya
mera dil meree jaan ho, tum abhee naadaan ho
ishq se anajaan ho
mera man kyon tumhen chaahe mera man

pyaar kahate hain kise, hota hai ye dard kya
aaj pahalee baar ye mainne jaana dilaruba
jaagee jaagee so gaee kis jahaan mein kho gayee
kya se kya main ho gayee

mera man kyon tumhen chaahe mera man
na jaane jud gaya kaise ye bandhan
kaisee ye deevaanagee, kaisa ye deevaanaapan
mera man kyon tumhen chaahe mera man
mera man, ho mera man

Vinod Kumar

MERA MAN KYUN TUMHE CHAHE

dha 1	ge 2	n 3	ti 4	n 5	ke 6	dhi 7	n 8	dha 1	ge 2	n 3	ti 4	n 5	ke 6	dhi 7	n 8

prelude: M' G' R' S'

D D <u>N</u> S'R' S' <u>N</u>   G' R' S' D   P P D <u>N</u>S' <u>N</u> D   M' G' R' S'

he --------------   music   aa ha ha----------   music

D D <u>N</u> S'R' S' <u>N</u>   G' R' S' D

la la la --------   music

P P D <u>N</u>S' <u>N</u>S' <u>N</u> D

la la la --------------

1 dha	2 ge	3 n	4 ti	5 n	6 ke	7 dhi	8 n	1 dha	2 ge	3 n	4 ti	5 n	6 ke	7 dhi	8 n
												S	-	M	-
												me	-	ra	-
D	P	M	D	-	-	-	-	-	-	-	-	D	-	P	M
mn	-	-	-	-	-	-	-	-	-	-	-	kyu	-	tu	mhe
R	-	P		-	-	-	-	-	-	-	-	D	M	P	-
cha	-	he	-	-	-	-	-	-	-	-	-	me	-	ra	-
M	-	-	-	-	-	-	-	-	-	-	-	S	-	M	-
mn	-	-	-	-	-	-	-	-	-	-	-	na	-	ja	-
D	P	M	D	-	-	-	-	-	-	-	-	D	-	P	M
ne	-	-	-	-	-	-	-	-	-	-	-	ju	d	g	ya
R	-	P		-	-	-	-	-	-	-	-	D	M	P	-
kai	-	se	-	-	-	-	-	-	-	-	-	ye	-	bn	-
M	-	-	-	-	-	-	-	S'	-	S'	-	S'	-	S'	D
dhn	-	-	-	-	-	-	-	kai	-	si	-	ye	-	di	-
-	R'	-	S'	S'	-	-	-	-	P	-	P	P	-	P	-
-	va	-	n	gi	-	-	-	-	kai	-	sa	ye	-	di	-
-	D	-	P	M	-	S	R	-	-	-	-	S	-	M	-
-	va	-	na	pn	-	-	-	-	-	-	-	me	-	ra	-
D	P	M	D	-	-	-	-	-	-	-	-	D	-	P	M
mn	-	-	-	-	-	-	-	-	-	-	-	kyu	-	tu	mhe
R	-	P		-	-	-	-	-	-	-	-	D	M	P	-
cha	-	he	-	-	-	-	-	-	-	-	-	me	-	ra	-
M	-	-	-	-	-	-	-	-	-	-	-				
mn	-	-	-	-	-	-	-	-	-	-	-				

interlude:

M' G' R' S' --- D D S'- <u>N</u> – G' R' S' D

D D P M MPP M R MPP M R M- R M- R M- S' D-

R'	-	S'	D	-	S'	-	R'	-	-	S'	D	-	-	-
main	-	di	va	-	ni	-	bn	-	-	g	yi	-	-	-
-	P	-	P	D	-	R	-	M	-	-	M	M	-	-	-
-	tum	-	ne	ae	-	sa	-	kya	-	-	ki	ya	-	-	-
-	R'	-	S'	D	-	S'	-	R'	-	-	S'	D	M	P	-
-	me	-	ri	nin	-	den	-	lu	-	-	t	li	-	-	-
-	P	-	P	S'	-	P	-	M	-	-	M	M	-	-	-
-	chai	-	n	bhi	-	me	-	ra	-	-	li	ya	-	-	-
-	<u>N</u>	-	<u>N</u>	<u>N</u>	-	<u>N</u>	<u>N</u>	-	R'	-	S'	S'	D	-	-
-	me	-	ra	dil	-	me	ri	-	ja	-	n	ho	-	-	-
-	<u>N</u>	-	<u>N</u>	<u>N</u>	-	<u>N</u>	-	-	R'	-	S'	S'	D	-	-
-	tum	-	a	bhi	-	na	-	-	da	-	n	ho	-	-	-
-	P	-	P	P	-	P	-	-	D	-	P	M	R	S	R
-	i	sh	q	se	-	an	-	-	ja	-	n	ho	-	-	-
-	-	-	-	-	-	-	-	-	-	-	-	S	-	M	-
-	-	-	-	-	-	-	-	-	-	-	-	me	-	ra	-
D	P	M	D	-	-	-	-	-	-	-	-	D	-	P	M
mn	-	-	-	-	-	-	-	-	-	-	-	kyu	-	tu	mhe
R	-	P	-	-	-	-	-	-	-	-	-	D	M	P	-
cha	-	he	-	-	-	-	-	-	-	-	-	me	-	ra	-
M	-	-	-	-	-	-	-	-	-	-	-	S	-	M	-
mn	-	-	-	-	-	-	-	-	-	-	-	na	-	ja	-
D	P	M	D	-	-	-	-	-	-	-	-	D	-	P	M
ne	-	-	-	-	-	-	-	-	-	-	-	ju	d	g	ya
R	-	P	-	-	-	-	-	-	-	-	-	D	M	P	-
kai	-	se	-	-	-	-	-	-	-	-	-	ye	-	bn	-
M	-	-	-	-	-	-	-								
dhn	-	-	-	-	-	-	-								

interlude:

M' G' R' S' --- D D S'- <u>N</u> – G' R' S' D

D D P M MPP M R MPP M R M- R M- R M- S' D-

R'	-	S'		D	-	S'	-	R'	-	-	S'	D	-	-	-
pya	-	r		k	h	te	-	hai	-	-	ki	se	-	-	-
-	P	-	P	D	-	R	-	M	-	-	M	M	-	-	-
-	ho	-	ta	hai	-	ye	-	dr	-	-	d	kya	-	-	-
-	R'	-	S'	D	-	S'	-	R'	-	-	S'	D	M	P	-
-	aa	-	j	p	h	li	-	ba	-	-	r	ye	-	-	-
-	P	-	P	D	-	R	-	M	-	-	M	M	-	-	-
-	main	-	ne	ja	-	na	-	dil	-	-	ru	ba	-	-	-
-	N	-	N	N	-	N	-	-	R'	-	S'	S'	D	-	-
-	ja	-	gi	ja	-	gi	-	-	so	-	g	yi	-	-	-
-	N	-	N	N	-	N	-	-	R'	-	S'	S'	D	-	-
-	kis	-	j	han	-	me	-	-	kho	-	g	yi	-	-	-
-	P	-	P	P	-	P	-	-	D	-	P	M	R	S	R
-	kya	-	se	kya	-	main	-	-	ho	-	g	yi	-	-	-
-	-	-	-	-	-	-	-	-	-	-	-	S	-	M	-
-	-	-	-	-	-	-	-	-	-	-	-	me	-	ra	-
D	P	M	D	-	-	-	-	-	-	-	-	D	-	P	M
mn	-	-	-	-	-	-	-	-	-	-	-	kyu	-	tu	mhe
R	-	P	-	-	-	-	-	-	-	-	-	D	M	P	-
cha	-	he	-	-	-	-	-	-	-	-	-	me	-	ra	-
M	-	-	-	-	-	-	-	-	-	-	-	S	-	M	-
mn	-	-	-	-	-	-	-	-	-	-	-	na	-	ja	-
D	P	M	D	-	-	-	-	-	-	-	-	D	-	P	M
ne	-	-	-	-	-	-	-	-	-	-	-	ju	d	g	ya
R	-	P	-	-	-	-	-	-	-	-	-	D	M	P	-
kai	-	se	-	-	-	-	-	-	-	-	-	ye	-	bn	-
M	-	-	-	-	-	-	-								
dhn	-	-	-	-	-	-	-								

30. MERI SANSON ME BASA HAI

Film: Aur Pyar ho gaya (1997)	Music: Nusarat Fateh Ali
Lyrics: Javed Akhtar	Singer: Udit Narayan
Taal: Kaharwa	Chord: GPS' PNR' S=C

meree saanson mein basa hai tera hee ek naam
teree yaad hamasafar subaho shaam -2
too mere din mein raaton mein khaamoshee mein baaton mein
baadal ke haathon mein bhejoon tujhako ye payaam
teree yaad hamasafar subaho shaam -2
meree saanson mein basa hai tera hee ek naam
teree yaad hamasafar subaho shaam -2

(aankhon mein, tasveer hai jaise, too meree, taqadeer hai jaise
us dil se, is dil tak aatee, dhadakan kee zanjeer hai jaise) -2
khaabon khaabon too mile na jaane kya hain silasile
palakon par ye pyaar ke na jaane kitane gul khile
tere khvaab sajaate rahana ab hai mera kaam
teree yaad hamasafar subaho shaam -2

ho ho…
(phoolon par, shabanam kee nameen hai, rangon kee,
mahafil see jamee hain
mausam bhee, manzar bhee may bhee, kahate hain,
bas teree kamee hai) -2
baagon mein ham jo milen to gaayen saaree koyalen
mahake saara ye samaan havaen mahakee see chalen
teree khushaboo se bhar jaen kaliyon ke ye jaam
teree yaad hamasafar subaho shaam -2
meree saanson mein basa hai tera hee ek naam
teree yaad hamasafar subaho shaam -2

Vinod Kumar

MERI SANSON ME BASA HAI

dhin	-	na	dhin	-	dhin	na	-	tin	-	na	tin	-	tin	na	-
1	2	3	4	5	6	7	8	1	2	3	4	5	6	7	8

prelude:
flute: G' R' D M P- GMP S' P S' P S'-P GMP MG- RG- 2
sitar: G'G' S'R'R' S'-P   G'G' S'R'R' S'-   G'G' S'R'R' S'-P
synthe: S' M' G'- R' S' S' D P D – D N D N- D – P-

														P	P
														me	ri
S'	-	P	S'	-	P	P	-	P	-	-	-	G	M	P	-
san	-	so	me	-	b	sa	-	hai	-	-	-	te	ra	hi	-
N	N	D	-	-	-	-	-	P	-	-	-	-	-	G	M
i	k	na	-	-	-	-	-	-	-	-	m	-	-	te	ri
P	-	-	P	S'	-	-	S'	N	D	P	N	-	D	D	P
ya	-	-	d	hm	-	-	s	fr	-	-	-	-	su	b	ho
P	-	-	-	P	N	P	D	M	P	G	-	-	-	G	M
sha	-	-	-	-	-	-	-	-	-	-	m	-	-	te	ri
P	-	-	P	S'	-	-	S'	N	D	P	N	-	D	D	P
ya	-	-	d	hm	-	-	s	fr	-	-	-	-	su	b	ho
P	-	-	-	-	-	-	-	-	-	-	-	-	-	-	-
sha	-	-	-	-	m	-	-	-	-	-	-	-	-	-	-
P	-	P	S'	D	-	D	-	M	-	D	P	-	-	-	-
tu	-	me	re	di	n	me	-	ra	-	to	me	-	-	-	-
P	-	P	S'	D	-	D	-	M	-	D	P	-	-	-	-
kha	-	mo	-	shi	-	me	-	ba	-	to	me	-	-	-	-
P	-	P	G'	G'	-	G'	-	R'	G'	G'	-	S'	-	D	-
ba	-	d	l	ke	-	ha	-	tho	-	me	-	bhe	-	ju	-
R'	R'	R'	S'	-	S'	P	-	-	M	P	G	-	-	G	M
tu	jh	ko	ye	-	p	ya	-	-	-	-	-	m	-	te	ri
P	-	-	P	S'	-	-	S'	N	D	P	N	-	D	D	P
ya	-	-	d	hm	-	-	s	fr	-	-	-	-	su	b	ho
P	-	-	-	P	N	P	D	M	P	G	-	-	-	G	M
sha	-	-	-	-	-	-	-	-	-	-	m	-	-	te	ri

P	-	-	P	D	-	-	D	S'	-	R'	-	-	N	D	P
ya	-	-	d	hm	-	-	s	fr	-	-	-	-	su	b	ho

P	-	-	-	-	-	-	-	-	-	-	-	-	-	-	
sha	-	-	-	-	m	-	-	-	-	-	-	-	-		

interlude:

rubab: S R S P G R S R S G S .D
       S R S P G R S R
       S R S P G R S R S G S .D
       S R S P G R S R .D S S

violin: SS RR PP SRM MM S RG R-
       SS RR PP SRM G- RS G- R .D S-

synthe: G P S' N S' D P
       N D P- M- D P M – R- G-

S'	-	P	-	S'	-	P	-	-	-	-	-	-	-	P	P
aan	-	kho	-	me	-	-	-	-	-	-	-	-	-	t	s

P	D	N	S'	D	P	D	M	-	-	-	-	-	-	-	-
vii	-	r	hai	jai	-	se	-	-	-	-	-	-	-	-	-

M	G	G	R	D	-	-	-	-	-	-	-	-	-	D	R'
tu	-	me	-	ri	-	-	-	-	-	-	-	-	-	t	k

S'	-	S'	S'	S'	-	S'	-	-	-	-	-	-	-	P	-
di	-	r	hai	jai	-	se	-	-	-	-	-	-	-	-	-

S'	-	P	-	S'	-	P	-	-	-	-	-	-	-	P	P
u	s	di	l	se	-	-	-	-	-	-	-	-	-	i	s

P	D	N	S'	D	P	D	M	-	-	-	-	-	-	-	-
di	l	t	k	aa	-	ti	-	-	-	-	-	-	-	-	-

M	G	G	R	D	-	-	-	-	-	-	-	-	-	D	R'
dh	d	k	n	ki	-	-	-	-	-	-	-	-	-	jn	-

S'	-	S'	S'	S'	-	S'	-	-	-	-	-	-	-	P	-
jii	-	r	hai	jai	-	se	-	-	-	-	-	-	-	-	-

G'	-	S'	-	S'	-	D	-	M	-	D	P	-	G'	G'	G'
kha	-	bo	-	kha	-	bo	-	tu	-	mi	le	-	n	ja	ne

G'	-	S'	-	M	-	D	P	-	-	-	-	-	-	-	-
kya	-	hai	-	si	l	si	le	-	-	-	-	-	-	-	-

G'	G'	S'	-	S'	S'	D	-	M	-	D	P	-	G'	G'	G'
p	l	kon	-	p	r	ye	-	pya	-	r	ke	-	n	ja	ne

G'	S'	S'	-	M	-	D	P	-	-	-	-	-	-	-	-
ki	t	ne	-	gu	l	khi	le	-	-	-	-	-	-	-	-

P	-	P	-	G'	-	G'	G'	R'	G'	G'	-	S'	S'	D	-
te	-	re	-	kha	-	b	s	ja	-	te	-	r	h	na	-

R'	R'	R'	S'	-	S'	P	-	-	-	M	P	G	-	G	M
a	b	hai	me	-	ra	ka	-	-	-	-	-	-	m	te	ri

P	-	-	P	S'	-	-	S'	N	D	P	$\underline{N}$	-	D	D	P
ya	-	-	d	hm	-	-	s	fr	-	-	-	-	su	b	ho

P	-	-	-	P	$\underline{N}$	P	D	M	P	G	-	-	-	G	M
sha	-	-	-	-	-	-	-	-	-	-	m	-	-	te	ri

P	-	-	P	D	-	-	D	S'	-	R'	-	-	N	D	P
ya	-	-	d	hm	-	-	s	fr	-	-	-	-	su	b	ho

P	-	-	-	-	-	-	-	-	-	-	-	-	-		
sha	-	-	-	-	m	-	-	-	-	-	-	-	-		

interlude:
S' R' P' M'M' P'-
ho ho ho hoho ho

S' R' M' P'--- R' S' D P-
ho ho ho ho —--ho ho ho ho

 R' S' P D M' G' R' S'
o ho ho ho ho ho ho ho

rubab: PP G'G'G' R'G' R'S' D- MM DD S' DD P- 2
flute: PMG P- D- M- P- R G- P R G-
       S'S'S'S' S'- N-P P- D-
       DP PM MP D- P- D- S'-
       PMG P- D- M- P- R G- P R G-

S'	-	P	-	S'	-	P	-	-	-	-	-	-	-	P	P
fu	-	lo	-	pr	-	-	-	-	-	-	-	-	-	sh	b

P	D	$\underline{N}$	S'	D	P	D	M	-	-	-	-	-	-	-	-
n	m	ki	n	mi	-	hai	-	-	-	-	-	-	-	-	-

M	G	G	R	D	-	-	-	-	-	-	-	-	-	D	R'
rn	-	go	-	ki	-	-	-	-	-	-	-	-	-	m	h

S'	-	S'	S'	S'	-	S'	-	-	-	-	-	-	-	P	-
fi	l	si	j	mi	-	hai	-	-	-	-	-	-	-	-	-

S'	-	P	-	S'	-	P	-	-	-	-	-	-	-	P	-
mau	-	sm	-	bhi	-	-	-	-	-	-	-	-	-	mn	-

P	D	N	S'	D	P	D	M	-	-	-	-	-	-	-	-
z	r	bhi	-	m	y	bhi	-	-	-	-	-	-	-	-	-
M	G	G	R	D	-	-	-	-	-	-	-	-	-	D	R'
k	h	te	-	hain	-	-	-	-	-	-	-	-	-	b	s
S'	-	S'	S'	S'	-	S'	-	-	-	-	-	-	-	P	-
te	-	ri	k	mi	-	hai	-	-	-	-	-	-	-	-	-
G'	-	S'	-	S'	-	D	-	M	-	D	P	-	G'	G'	G'
ba	-	go	-	me	-	hm	-	jo	-	mi	le	-	to	ga	yen
G'	-	S'	-	M	-	D	P	-	-	-	-	-	-	-	-
sa	-	ri	-	ko	-	y	len	-	-	-	-	-	-	-	-
G'	G'	S'	-	S'	-	D	-	M	-	D	P	-	G'	G'	G'
m	h	ke	-	sa	-	ra	-	ye	-	s	ma	-	h	va	yen
G'	S'	S'	-	M	-	D	P	-	-	-	-	-	-	-	-
m	h	ki	-	si	-	ch	len	-	-	-	-	-	-	-	-
P	-	P	-	G'	G'	G'	-	R'	-	G'	G'	S'	-	D	-
te	-	ri	-	khu	sh	bu	-	se	-	bh	r	ja	-	yen	-
R'	R'	R'	S'	-	S'	P	-	-	-	M	P	G	-	G	M
k	li	yon	ke	-	ye	ja	-	-	-	-	-	-	m	te	ri
P	-	-	P	S'	-	-	S'	N	D	P	N	-	D	D	P
ya	-	-	d	hm	-	-	s	fr	-	-	-	-	su	b	ho
P	-	-	-	P	N	P	D	M	P	G	-	-	-	G	M
sha	-	-	-	-	-	-	-	-	-	-	m	-	-	te	ri
P	-	-	P	D	-	-	D	S'	-	R'	-	-	N	D	P
ya	-	-	d	hm	-	-	s	fr	-	-	-	-	su	b	ho
P	-	-	-	-	-	-	-	-	-	-	-	-	-		
sha	-	-	-	-	m	-	-	-	-	-	-	-	-		

31. MEHNDI LAGAA KE RAKHNA

Film: Dil vaale dulhaniya le jaayeinge (1995)	Music: Jatin Lalit
Lyrics: Anand Bakshi	Singer: Udit Narayan, Lata
Taal: Kaharwa	Chord: RMD P<u>N</u>R' S=C#

ye kudiyan nashe diyaan pudiyaan ye munde gali de gnde
nashe diyaan pudiyaan, gali de gnde

mehandee laga ke rakhana, dolee saja ke rakhana -2
lene tujhe o goree, aaenge tere sajana
sehara saja ke rakhana, chehara chhupa ke rakhana
ye dil kee baat apane, dil mein daba ke rakhana

ud-ud ke teree zulfen, karatee hain kya ishaare
dil thaam ke khade hain, aashiq sabhee kanvaare
chhup jaen saaree kudiyaan, ghar mein sharam ke maare
gaanvon mein aa gae hain, paagal shahar ke saare
nazaren jhuka ke rakhana, daaman bacha ke rakhana
lene tujhe o goree...

main ik javaan ladaka, tu ik haseen ladakee
ye dil machal gaya to, mera qusoor kya hai
rakhana tha dil pe qaaboo, ye husn to hai jaadoo
jaadoo ye chal gaya to, mera qusoor kya hai
rasta hamaara takana, daravaaza khulla rakhana
lene tujhe o goree, aaenge tere sajana
kuchh aur ab na kahana, kuchh aur ab na karana
ye dil kee baat apane...

MEHNDI LAGAA KE RAKHNA

dha	ge	n	ti	n	ke	dhi	n	dha	ge	n	ti	n	ke	dhi	n
1	2	3	4	5	6	7	8	1	2	3	4	5	6	7	8

prelude:

```
R' MPP    ND PP   MPP
ye kudiyan nshe diyan pudiyan

R' MP     ND P    MP
ye munde  gali de gunde

P MPP     ND  PP  MPP
ye kudiyan nshe diyan pudiyan

P  MP     ND P    MP
ye munde  gali de gunde

ND   PP   MPP      S'D G' R'R'
nshe diyan pudiyan gali de gunde

P------ NDNP    PDNR' -4
o-------------    music

PDNS'------ R' NDP    PDNR' -3
o--------------------    music
```

														R me	R h
N	-	N	D	-	P	N	N	D	-	-	-	-	-	R	-
di	-	l	ga	-	ke	r	kh	na	-	-	-	-	-	do	-
D	-	D	P	-	M*	D	D	P	-	-	-	-	-	R	R
li	-	s	ja	-	ke	r	kh	na	-	-	-	-	-	me	h
N	-	N	D	-	P	N	N	N	S'	D	-	-	-	R	-
di	-	l	ga	-	ke	r	kh	na	-	-	-	-	-	do	-
D	-	D	P	-	M*	D	D	P	-	-	-	-	-	P	-
li	-	s	ja	-	ke	r	kh	na	-	-	-	-	-	le	-
R'	-	R'	R'	-	R'	G'	R'	S'	-	-	-	-	-	D	N
ne	-	tu	jhe	-	o	go	-	ri	-	-	-	-	-	aa	-
S'	R'	S'	N	-	D	P	P	P	-	-	D	M	-	R	R
yen	-	ge	te	-	re	s	j	na	-	-	-	-	-	me	h
N	-	N	D	-	P	N	N	D	-	-	-	-	-	R	-
di	-	l	ga	-	ke	r	kh	na	-	-	-	-	-	do	-

D   -   D   P | -   M* D   D | P   -   -   - | -   -
li -   s   ja | -   ke r   kh| na -   -   - | -   -
D ---P---   D--- P----
aa--- ho--- o --- ho----

R'--------G' R' S' N S'
ho--------------------

S'NDP   M--- D---   DNR'N   D-P-
aa-----------------   aa------ aa---

| R   R
| se h

N   -   N   D | -   P   N   N | D   -   -   - | -   -   R   R
ra -   s   ja | -   ke r   kh| na -   -   - | -   -   che h

D   -   D   P | -   M* D   D | P   -   -   - | -   -   R   R
ra -   chhu pa| -   ke r   kh| na -   -   - | -   -   se h

N   -   N   D | -   P   N   N | N   S' D   - | -   -   R   R
ra -   s   ja | -   ke r   kh| na -   -   - | -   -   che h

D   -   D   P | -   M* D   D | P   -   -   - | -   -   P   -
ra -   chhu pa| -   ke r   kh| na -   -   - | -   -   ye -

R' -   R' R' | -   R' G' R'| S' -   -   - | -   -   D   N
dil -   ki ba | -   t   a   p | ne -   -   - | -   -   di l

S' R' S' N | -   D   P   P | P   -   -   D | M   -   R   R
me -   d   ba | -   ke r   kh| na -   -   - | -   -   se h

N   -   N   D | -   P   N   N | D   -   -   - | -   -   R   R
ra -   s   ja | -   ke r   kh| na -   -   - | -   -   che h

D   -   D   P | -   M* D   D | P   -   -   - | -   -   R   R
ra -   chhu pa| -   ke r   kh| na -   -   - | -   -   me h

N   -   N   D | -   P   N   N | N   S' D   - | -   -   R   -
di -   l   ga | -   ke r   kh| na -   -   - | -   -   do -

D   -   D   P | -   M* D   D | P   -   -   - | -   R'
li -   s   ja | -   ke r   kh| na -   -   - | -   -
music: R P P P D D P P N DP N DP PP -2
R' R' R'
oye hoe hoe

P D N S'   R'- S' N R'- S' N R'R'S'-
S' S' N D S'- N- D P R' S' N- DS'ND P—
P D N S' R'- S' N R'- S' N R'R'S'-
S' S' N D S'- N- D P R' S' N- PDNS'R' -

Isolated (top right): N | D over u | d

	1	2	3	4	5	6	7	8	9	10	11	12	13	14	15	16
notes	P	-	P	P	-	P	P	-	R'	-	-	-	-	-	N	D
lyr	u	d	ke	te	-	ri	zu	l	fen	-	-	-	-	-	k	r
notes	P	-	P	P	-	P	P	-	R'	-	-	-	-	-	R'	R'
lyr	ti	-	hain	kya	-	i	sha	-	re	-	-	-	-	-	di	l
notes	G'	M'	G'	R'	-	S'	N	-	S'	-	-	-	-	-	D	-
lyr	tha	-	m	ke	-	kh	de	-	hain	-	-	-	-	-	aa	-
notes	N	-	R'	N	-	D	N	D	P	-	-	-	-	-	N	D
lyr	shi	k	s	bhi	-	kun	va	-	re	-	-	-	-	-	chhu	p
notes	P	-	P	P	-	P	P	-	R'	-	-	-	-	-	N	D
lyr	ja	-	yen	sa	-	ri	ku	di	yan	-	-	-	-	-	gh	r
notes	P	-	P	P	-	P	P	-	R'	-	-	-	-	-	R'	-
lyr	me	-	sh	rm	-	ke	ma	-	re	-	-	-	-	-	ga	-
notes	G'	M'	G'	R'	-	S'	N	-	S'	-	-	-	-	-	D	-
lyr	von	-	me	aa	-	g	ye	-	hain	-	-	-	-	-	pa	-
notes	N	-	R'	N	-	D	N	D	P	-	-	-	-	-	R	R
lyr	gl	-	sh	hr	-	ke	sa	-	re	-	-	-	-	-	n	z
notes	N	-	N	D	-	P	N	N	D	-	-	-	-	-	R	-
lyr	ren	-	jhu	ka	-	ke	r	kh	na	-	-	-	-	-	da	-
notes	D	-	D	P	-	M*	D	D	P	-	-	-	-	-	R	R
lyr	mn	-	b	cha	-	ke	r	kh	na	-	-	-	-	-	n	z
notes	N	-	N	D	-	P	N	N	N	S'	D	-	-	-	R	-
lyr	ren	-	jhu	ka	-	ke	r	kh	na	-	-	-	-	-	da	-
notes	D	-	D	P	-	M*	D	D	P	-	-	-	-	-	P	-
lyr	mn	-	b	cha	-	ke	r	kh	na	-	-	-	-	-	le	-
notes	R'	-	R'	R'	-	R'	G'	R'	S'	-	-	-	-	-	D	N
lyr	ne	-	tu	jhe	-	o	go	-	ri	-	-	-	-	-	aa	-
notes	S'	R'	S'	N	-	D	P	P	P	-	-	D	M	-	R	R
lyr	yen	-	ge	te	-	re	s	j	na	-	-	-	-	-	me	h

N	-	N	D	-	P	N	N	D	-	-	-	-	-	R	-
di	-	l	ga	-	ke	r	kh	na	-	-	-	-	-	do	-

D	-	D	P	-	M*	D	D	P	-	-	-	-	-	R	R
li	-	s	ja	-	ke	r	kh	na	-	-	-	-	-	se	h

N	-	N	D	-	P	N	N	N	S'	D	-	-	-	R	R
ra	-	s	ja	-	ke	r	kh	na	-	-	-	-	-	che	h

D	-	D	P	-	M*	D	D	P	-	-	-	-	R'		
ra	-	chhu	pa	-	ke	r	kh	na	-	-	-	-	-		

music:
DD-PM* DD-PM* DDDD DDDD - DN S'S'S'S' NN DD PPPP-2
R'R' R'G'G' S' S'R'R' N NS'S' ND N—DP— 2

D-PM* D-PM* D - DN S'--- N- D- P- 2
o----   o----o o------- o--------

														N	D
														main	-

P	-	P	P	-	P	P	P	R'	-	-	-	-	-	N	D
i	k	j	va	-	n	l	d	ka	-	-	-	-	-	tu	-

P	-	P	P	-	P	P	P	R'	-	-	-	-	-	R'	-
i	k	h	si	-	n	l	d	ki	-	-	-	-	-	ye	-

G'	M'	G'	R'	-	S'	N	-	S'	-	-	-	-	-	D	-
di	l	m	ch	l	g	ya	-	to	-	-	-	-	-	me	-

N	-	R'	N	-	D	N	D	P	-	-	-	-	-	N	D
ra	-	k	su	-	r	kya	-	hai	-	-	-	-	-	r	kh

P	-	P	P	-	P	P	-	R'	-	-	-	-	-	N	D
na	-	tha	dil	-	pe	ka	-	bu	-	-	-	-	-	ye	-

P	-	P	P	-	P	P	-	R'	-	-	-	-	-	R'	-
hu	s	n	to	-	hai	ja	-	du	-	-	-	-	-	ja	-

G'	M'	G'	R'	-	S'	N	-	S'	-	-	-	-	-	D	-
du	-	ye	ch	l	g	ya	-	to	-	-	-	-	-	me	-

N	-	R'	N	-	D	N	D	P	-	-	-	-	-	R	-
ra	-	k	su	-	r	kya	-	hai	-	-	-	-	-	r	s

N	-	N	D	-	P	N	N	D	-	-	-	-	-	R	-
ta	-	h	ma	-	ra	t	k	na	-	-	-	-	-	d	r

D	-	D	P	-	M*	D	D	P	-	-	-	-	-	R	R
va	-	za	khu	l	la	r	kh	na	-	-	-	-	-	r	s
N̲	-	N̲	D	-	P	N̲	N̲	N̲	S'	D	-	-	-	R	-
ta	-	h	ma	-	ra	t	k	na	-	-	-	-	-	d	r
D	-	D	P	-	M*	D	D	P	-	-	-	-	-	P	-
va	-	za	khu	l	la	r	kh	na	-	-	-	-	-	le	-
R'	-	R'	R'	-	R'	G̲'	-	S'	R'	G'	R'	S'	-	D	N̲
ne	-	tu	jhe	-	o	go	-	ri	-	-	-	-	-	aa	-
S'	R'	S'	N̲	-	D	P	P	P	-	-	D	M	-	R	R
yen	-	ge	te	-	re	s	j	na	-	-	-	-	-	ku	chh
N̲	-	N̲	D	-	P	N̲	N̲	D	-	-	-	-	-	R	R
au	-	r	a	b	n	k	h	na	-	-	-	-	-	ku	chh
D	-	D	P	P	M*	D	D	P	-	-	-	-	-	R	R
au	-	r	a	b	n	k	r	na	-	-	-	-	-	ku	chh
N̲	-	N̲	D	-	P	N̲	N̲	N̲	S'	D -	-	-	-	R	R
au	-	r	a	b	n	k	h	na	-	-	-	-	-	ku	chh
D	-	D	P	P	M*	D	D	P	-	-	-	-	-	P	-
au	-	r	a	b	n	k	r	na	-	-	-	-	-	ye	-
R'	-	R'	R'	-	R'	G̲'	R'	S'	-	-	-	-	-	D	N̲
dil	-	ki	ba	-	t	a	p	ne	-	-	-	-	-	di	l
S'	R'	S'	N̲	-	D	P	P	P	-	-	D	M	-	R	R
me	-	d	ba	-	ke	r	kh	na	-	-	-	-	-	me	h
N̲	-	N̲	D	-	P	N̲	N̲	D	-	-	-	-	-	R	-
di	-	l	ga	-	ke	r	kh	na	-	-	-	-	-	do	-
D	-	D	P	-	M*	D	D	P	-	-	-	-	-	R	R
li	-	s	ja	-	ke	r	kh	na	-	-	-	-	-	se	h
N̲	-	N̲	D	-	P	N̲	N̲	N̲	S'	D	-	-	-	R	R
ra	-	s	ja	-	ke	r	kh	na	-	-	-	-	-	che	h
D	-	D	P	-	M*	D	D	P	-	-	-	-	R'		
ra	-	chhu	pa	-	ke	r	kh	na	-	-	-	-			

```
DP      PDP   PDP   PDP   PM    MPM   MPM   MPM
shava   oye   oye   oye   shava oye   oye   oye
music:
R'—S'D  R'—S'D  P D N̲ S' R'---
R'—S'D  R'—S'D  P D N̲ D P---
```

```
DP        PDP   PDP  PDP   PM     MPM   MPM   MPM
(shava    oye   oye  oye   shava  oye   oye   oye) x4

D  P
shava
```

32. MAIN NIKLA GADDI LE KE

Film: Gadar (2001)	Music: Uttam Singh
Lyrics: Anand Bakshi	Singer: Udit Narayan
Taal: Kaharwa	Chord: M<u>D</u>S' S=C#

o ho aa ha ha ha
main nikala o gaddee le ke o raste par o sadak mein
ek mod aaya, main utthe dil chhod aaya -2
rab jaane kab guzara amrtasar o kab jaane
laahaur aaya, main utthe dil chhod aaya
ek mod aaya, main utthe dil chhod aaya

us mod pe vo mutiyaar milee, jat yamala paagal ho gaya
usakee zulphon kee chhaanv mein, main bistar daal ke so gaya
o jab jaaga, main bhaaga, sab phaatak, sab signal
main tod aaya, main utthe dil chhod aaya
ek mod aaya, main utthe dil chhod aaya

bas ek nazar usako dekha, dil mein usakee tasveer lagee
kya naam tha usaka rab jaane, mujhako raanjhe kee heer lagee
o mainne dekha ek sapana, sang usake naam apana,
main jod aaya, main utthe dil chhod aaya
ek mod aaya, main utthe dil chhod aaya

sharama ke vo yoon simat gayee, jaise vo neend se jaag gayee
mainne kaha gal sun o kudiye, vo dar ke peechhe bhaag gayee
vo samajhee o ghar usake, choree se, o chupake se,
koee chor aaya, main utthe dil chhod aaya
ek mod aaya, main utthe dil chhod aaya

MAIN NIKLA GADDI LE KE

dha	ge	n	ti	n	ke	dhi	n	dha	ge	n	ti	n	ke	dhi	n
1	2	3	4	5	6	7	8	1	2	3	4	5	6	7	8

prelude:

S'	R'S'S'	S'	S'S'	R'	S'										
main	nikla	o	gddi	le	ke										

S'	N	D	N	D	N	S'	S' M								
o	ho	ho	ho	ho	ho	ho	ho ho								

S'	N	D	N	D	N	S'	S' M								
aa	ha	ha	ha	ha	ha	ha	ha ha								

														S'	-
														main	-

R'	S'	S'	-	-	S'	S'	S'	R'	-	S'	-	-	S'	S'	S'
ni	k	la	-	-	o	g	ddi	le	-	ke	-	-	o	r	s

R'	-	S'	-	-	-	S'	S'	R'	S'	S'	-	-	-	D	M
te	-	p	r	-	-	o	s	d	k	me	-	-	-	i	k

M	D	-	D	N	S'	-	-	N	-	-	N	D	N	D	P
mo	-	-	d	aa	-	-	-	ya	-	-	main	o	tthe	di	l

D	-	-	D	P	-	-	-	M	-	-	-	-	-	S'	S'
chho	-	-	d	aa	-	-	-	ya	-	-	-	-	-	r	b

R'	-	S'	-	-	-	S'	S'	R'	S'	S'	-	-	-	S'	S'M
ja	-	ne	-	-	-	k	b	gu	z	ra	-	-	-	a	m

R'	S'	S'	-	-	S'	S'	S'	R'	-	S'	-	-	-	D	-
ri	t	s	r	-	o	k	b	ja	-	ne	-	-	-	la	-

M	D	-	D	N	S'	-	-	N	-	-	N	D	N	D	P
hau	-	-	r	aa	-	-	-	ya	-	-	main	o	tthe	di	l

D	-	-	D	P	-	-	-	M	-	-	-	-	-		
chho	-	-	d	aa	-	-	-	ya	-	-	-	-	-		

interlude:

D D P P D P M M D N N D D N D P -2

M D N S'--- N D N D N S' S' M -2

														D	D
														u	s

D	-	N	D	D	-	N	S'	S'	-	D	M	M	-	D	D
mo	-	d	pe	vo	-	mu	ti	ya	-	r	mi	li	-	j	t

D	D	N	-	D	-	N	S'	S'	-	-	M	M	-	D	D
y	m	la	-	pa	-	g	l	ho	-	-	g	ya	-	u	s
D	-	N	S'	N	-	D	-	N	-	N	-	N	-	N	-
ki	-	ju	l	fo	-	ki	-	chha	-	on	-	me	-	main	-
N	-	S'	R'	S'	-	N	N	S'	-	-	S'	S'	S'	S'	S'
bi	s	t	r	da	-	l	ke	so	-	-	g	ya	o	j	b
R'	-	S'	-	-	S'	S'	-	R'	-	S'	-	-	S'	S'	S'
ja	-	ga	-	-	o	main	-	bha	-	ga	-	-	o	s	b
R'	-	S'	S'	-	S'	S'	S'	R'	S'	S'	-	-	-	S'	-
fa	-	t	k	-	o	s	b	si	g	n	l	-	-	main	-
M	D	-	D	N	S'	-	-	N	-	-	N	D	N	D	P
to	-	-	d	aa	-	-	-	ya	-	-	main	o	tthe	di	l
D	-	-	D	P	-	-	-	M	-	-	-	-	D	D	M
chho	-	-	d	aa	-	-	-	ya	-	-	-	-	ho	i	k
M	D	-	D	N	S'	-	-	N	-	-	N	D	N	D	P
mo	-	-	d	aa	-	-	-	ya	-	-	main	o	tthe	di	l
D	-	-	D	P	-	-	-	S'	-	-	-	-	-		
chho	-	-	d	aa	-	-	-	ya	-	-	-	-			

interlude: MMMM P D P   MMMM P D P   GGGG M P MM -2

														D	D
														b	s
D	-	N	D	D	D	N	S'	S'	-	D	-	M	-	D	D
e	-	k	n	z	r	u	s	ko	-	de	-	kha	-	di	l
D	-	N	D	D	-	N	S'	S'	-	D	M	M	-	D	-
me	-	u	s	ki	-	t	s	vii	-	r	l	gi	-	kya	-
D	-	N	S'	N	N	D	-	N	N	N	-	N	-	N	N
na	-	m	tha	u	s	ka	-	r	b	ja	-	ne	-	mu	jh
N	-	S'	R'	S'	-	N	-	S'	-	S'	S'	S'	S'	S'	S'
ko	-	ran	-	jhe	-	ki	-	hi	-	r	l	gi	au	main	ne
R'	-	S'		-	-	S'	S'	R'	S'	S'	-	-	-	S'	S'
de	-	kha	-	-	-	i	k	s	p	na	-	-	-	sn	g
R'	S'	S'		-	-	S'	-	R'	S'	S'	-	-	-	S'	-
u	s	ke	-	-	-	na	-m	a	p	na	-	-	-	main	-

M	D	-	D	N	S'	-	-	N	-	-	N	D	N	D	P
jo	-	-	d	aa	-	-	-	ya	-	-	main	o	tthe	di	I
D	-	-	D	P	-	-	-	M	-	-	-	-	-	D	M
chho	-	-	d	aa	-	-	-	ya	-	-	-	-	-	i	k
M	D	-	D	N	S'	-	-	N	-	-	N	D	N	D	P
mo	-	-	d	aa	-	-	-	ya	-	-	main	o	tthe	di	I
D	-	-	D	P	-	-	-	M	-	-	-	-	-		
chho	-	-	d	aa	-	-	-	ya	-	-	-	-	-		

interlude: R'S'ND DN- G' R'

S'—N R' R' S'   R'S'ND DN- G' R'
ho-----------   music

S'—D N S'—D   MPD PD ND
ho--------------   o-----------

MPD PD ND   MPD PD NS'
lll   ll lla   ho----------------

MPD PD NS'
lll   ll lla

G'------R' S' R'   G'------R' S' R'
aa----aa ha ha   o ----ho ho ho

N S' G' R' S' N D--
aa------------------

D M MD-- D S'—N-- N DN DP D-D P- M -
ik mod----

										D	-	-	-	D	D
										o	-	-	-	sh	r
D	-	N	-	D	-	S'	-	S'	D	D	P	M	-	D	-
ma	-	ke	-	vo	-	yun	-	si	m	t	g	yi	-	jai	-
D	-	N	-	D	-	N	S'	S'	-	-D	P	M	-	D	-
se	-	vo	-	nin	-	d	se	ja	-	-g	g	yi	-	main	-
D	-	N	S'	N	-	D	-	N	-	N	N	N	-	N	-
ne	-	k	ha	g	l	su	n	o	-	ku	di	ye	-	vo	-
N	N	S'	R'	S'	-	N	-	S'	-	-	S'	S'	-	S'	-
d	r	ke	-	pi	-	chhe	-	bha	-	-g	g	yi	-	vo	-

Vinod Kumar

R'	S'	S'	-	-	S'	S'	S'	R'	S'	S'	-	-	-	S'	-
s	m	jhi	-	-	o	gh	r	u	s	ke	-	-	-	cho	-
R'	S'	S'	-	-	S'	S'	S'	R'	S'	S'	-	-	-	S'	-
ri	-	se	-	-	o	chu	p	ke	-	se	-	-	-	ko	ee
M	D	-	D	N	S'	-	-	N	-	-	N	D	N	D	P
cho	-	-	r	aa	-	-	-	ya	-	-	main	o	tthe	di	l
D	-	-	D	P	-	-	-	M	-	-	-	-	-	D	M
chho	-	-	d	aa	-	-	-	ya	-	-	-	-	-	i	k
M	D	-	D	N	S'	-	-	N	-	-	N	D	N	D	P
mo	-	-	d	aa	-	-	-	ya	-	-	main	o	tthe	di	l
D	-	-	D	P	-	-	-	M	-	-	-	-	-		
chho	-	-	d	aa	-	-	-	ya	-	-	-	-	-		

33. MAIN PARDESI HUN

Film: Jaagran ki Raat (2004)	Music: -
Lyrics: Saral Kavi	Singer: Udit Narayan, Anuradha
Taal: Kaharwa	Chord: PNR' GPN S=C

ho main paradesee hoon pahalee baar aaya hoon
darshan karane maiya ke darabaar aaya hoon
pahalee baar aaya hoon -2
main paradeshee hoon pahalee baar aaya hoon

ai laal chunariya vaalee betee
ye to batao maan ke bhavan jaane ka raasta kidhar se hai
idhar se hai ya udhar se

sun re bhakt paradeshee itanee jaldee hai kaisee
are jara ghoom lo phir lo raunak dekho katara kee

jao tum vah jao pahale parchee katao
dhyaan maiya ka dharo ik jaikaara lagao
chale bhakton kee tolee sang tum mil jao

tamhe raasta dikha doon mere peechhe chale aao
ye hai darshanee dayodhee darshan pahala hai ye
karo yaatra shuroo to jay maata dee kah

yahaan talak to laayee betee aage bhee le jao na
main paradesee hoon pahalee baar aaya hoon
darshan karane maiya ke darabaar aaya hoon

itana sheetal jal ye kaun sa sthaan hai betee

ye hai baanaganga paanee amrt samaan
hota tan man paavan karo yahaan snaan
maatha mandir mein teko karo aage prasthaan
charan paaduka vo jaane mahima jahaan

maiya jag kalyaanee maaf karana meree bhool
mainne maathe se lagaee teree charanon kee dhool
are yahaan talak to laayee betee aage bhee le jao na
main paradesee hoon pahalee baar aaya hoon
darshan karane maiya ke darabaar aaya hoon

paudee paudee chadhada ja bhagata
 jay maata dee karada ja bhagata
ye ham kahaan aa pahunche, ye kaun see jagah hai betee

ye hai aadi kumaaree mahima hai isakee bhaaree
garbhajoon vo gupha hai katha hai jisakee nyaaree
bhairo jatee ik jogee maans madira haaree
lene maan kee pareeksha baat usane vichaaree
maas aur madhu maange mati usakee thee maaree
huee antardhyaan maata aaya peechhe duraachaaree
nau maheene isee mein rahee maiya avataaree
ise gupha garbhajoon jaane duniya ye saaree

aur gupha se nikalakar maata vaishno raanee
oopar paavan gupha mein pindee roop me prakat huee

dhany dhany meree maata dhany teree shakti
milatee paapon se mukti karake teree bhakti
are yahaan talak to laayee betee aage bhee le jao na
main paradesee hoon pahalee baar aaya hoon
darshan karane maiya ke darabaar aaya hoon

oh meree maiya itanee kathin chadhaee,
ye kaun sa sthaan hai betee

Vinod Kumar

dekho ooncha vo pahaad aur gaharee khaee
jara chadhana sambhal ke haathee matthe kee chadhaee
tedhe medhe raste hai par darana na bhaee
dekho saamane vo dekho saanjhee chhat kee dikhaee

paradesee yahaan kuchh kha lo pee lo,
bas thodee yaatra aur baakee hai

aisa lagata hai mujhako mukaam aa gaya
maata vaishno ka nikat hee dhaam aa gaya
are yahaan talak to laayee betee aage bhee le jao na
main paradesee hoon pahalee baar aaya hoon
darshan karane maiya ke darabaar aaya hoon

vaah, kya sundar nazaara hai
aakhir ham maan ke bhavan pahunch hee gae na
ye paavan gupha kidhar hai beta

dekho saamane gupha hai maiya raanee ka duaara
maata vaishno ne yahaan roop pindiyon ka dhaara
charan ganga mein naha lo thaalee pooja kee saja lo
leke laal laal chunaree apane sar pe bandhava lo
jaake sindooree gupha mein maan ke darshan pa lo
bin maange hee yahaan se man ichchha phal pa lo

gupha se baahar aakar kanjake bithaate hai
unako halava pooree aur dakshina dekar aasheervaad paaten hai
aur lautate samay baaba bhairo darshan karane se yaatra sampoorn maanee jaatee hai

aaj tumane "saral" pe upakaar kar diya
daaman khushiyon se aanand se bhar diya
bhej bulaava agale baras bhee paradesee ko bulao maan
har saal aaoonga jaise is baar aaya hoon
main paradesee, o maiya main paradesee, paradesee
main paradesee hoon pahalee baar aaya hoon
darshan karane maiya ke darabaar aaya hoon

MAIN PARDESI HUN

dha 1	ge 2	n 3	ti 4	n 5	ke 6	dhi 7	n 8	dha 1	ge 2	n 3	ti 4	n 5	ke 6	dhi 7	n 8
prelude: MP<u>D</u>S' P-P P-P P- P- M-															
MP<u>D</u>S' P-P P-P P- P- --															
												P	-	-	-
												ho	-	-	-
P	-	P	-	<u>D</u>	-	P	-	P	-	R	-	R	-	M	-
main	-	p	r	de	-	si	-	hu	-	-	-	p	h	li	-
<u>N</u>	-	-	-	<u>D</u>	-	<u>D</u>	-	P	-	-	-	-	-	-	-
ba	-	-	r	aa	-	ya	-	hu	-	-	-	-	-	-	-
P	-	P	-	<u>D</u>	-	P	-	P	-	P	-	R	-	M	-
d	r	sh	n	k	r	ne	-	main	-	ya	-	ke	-	d	r
<u>N</u>	-	-	-	-	<u>D</u>	<u>D</u>	-	P	-	-	-	S'	-	S'	-
ba	-	-	-	-r	aa	ya	-	hu	-	-	-	p	h	li	-
<u>N</u>	-	S'	R'	S'	-	S'	-	S'	-	-	-	<u>D</u>	-	<u>D</u>	-
ba	-	-	r	aa	-	ya	-	hu	-	-	-	p	h	li	-
<u>D</u>	-	S'	-	<u>N</u>	-	<u>N</u>	-	<u>D</u>	<u>N</u>	-	<u>D</u>	P	-	-	-
ba	-	-	r	aa	-	ya	-	hu	-	-	-	-	-	-	-
P	-	P	-	<u>D</u>	-	P	-	P	-	R	-	R	-	M	-
main	-	p	r	de	-	si	-	hu	-	-	-	p	h	li	-
<u>N</u>	-	-	-	<u>D</u>	-	<u>D</u>	-	P	-	-	-	-	-	-	-
ba	-	-	r	aa	-	ya	-	hu	-	-	-	-	-	-	-

music:
MP<u>D</u>S' P-P P-P P- P- M-
MP<u>D</u>S' P-P P-P P- P- --

MP<u>D</u>S' P-P P-P P- P- M-
aa----------------------

MP<u>D</u>S' P-P P-P P- P- --
aa----------------------

dha 1	ge 2	n 3	ti 4	n 5	ke 6	dhi 7	n 8	dha 1	ge 2	n 3	ti 4	n 5	ke 6	dhi 7	n 8
P	-	<u>N</u>	P	-	<u>N</u>	<u>N</u>	R'	S'	-	<u>N</u>	P	-	-	-	-
su	n	re	bh	k	t	p	r	de	-	si	-	-	-	-	-
P	P	P	<u>N</u>	<u>N</u>	-	P	<u>N</u>	<u>N</u>	R'	S'	-	<u>N</u>	P	<u>N</u>	<u>N</u>
i	t	ni	-	j	l	di	-	hai	-	kai	-	si	-	a	re

P z	N ra	- -	P ghu	- -	N m	N lo	R' -	S' fi	S' r	N lo	P -	- -	- -	N rau	P -
P n	N k	N de	P -	P kho	N -	N k	R' t	S' ra	- -	N ki	P -	- -	- -	N ja	N o
D tu	N m	D v	P han	P ja	- -	P o	- -	- -	- -	- -	- -	- -	- -	N ph	N le
D p	N r	D chi	P k	P ta	- -	P o	- -					- -	- -	N dhya	N n
D main	N ya	D ka	P dh	P ro	- -	G -	- -					- -	- -	N i	N k
D jy	N ka	D ra	P l	P ga	- -	P o	- -					- -	- -	N ch	N li
D bh	N g	D to	P ki	P to	P li	N sn	N g	D tu	N m	D mi	P l	P ja	P o	N tu	N mhe
D ra	N s	D ta	P di	P kha	P dun	N me	N re	D pi	N chhe	D ch	P le	P aa	P o	- -	- -
- -	- -	- -	- -	P ye	- -	N hai	- -	R' dr	- -	- -	R' sh	G' ni	- -	R' d	- -
R' yo	- -	R' dhi	- -	S' d	- r	R' sh	- n	S' p	N h	- -	R' la	- -	- -	R' hai	- -
R' ye	- -	- -	- -	P k	- -	N ro	- -	R' ya	- -	- -	R' t	G' ra	- -	R' shu	- -
R' ru	- -	R' tu	- m	R' jy	- -	- -	- -	N ma	- -	- -	S' ta	R' -	- -	R' di	- -
R' k	R' h	- -	- -	- -	- -	- -	- -	R' y	R' han	- -	R' t	G' lk	- -	R' to	- -
S' la	- -	S' yi	- -	S' be	- -	S' ti	- -	R' aa	- -	S' ge	- -	N bhi	- -	P le	- -
P ja	- -	D o	N -	N na	P -	- -	- -	P main	- -	P p	- r	D de	- -	P si	- -
P hu	- -	R -	- -	R p	- h	M li	- -	N ba	- -	- -	- r	D aa	- -	D ya	- -

P	-	-	-	-	-	-	-	P	-	P	-	D	-	P	-
hu	-	-	-	-	-	-	-	d	r	sh	n	k	r	ne	-

P	-	P	-	R	-	M	-	N	-	-	-	D	-	D	-
main	-	ya	-	ke	-	d	r	ba	-	-	-	-r	aa	ya	-

P	-	-	-
hu	-	-	-

interlude: MPDS' P-P P-P P- P- M-
MPDS' P-P P-P P- P- --

D	N	D	P	P	P	-	-	-	-	-	-	-	-	N	N
ye	hai	ba	n	gn	ga	-	-	-	-	-	-	-	-	pa	ni

D	N	D	P	P	-	P	-	-	-	-	-	-	-	N	N
a	mri	t	s	ma	-	n	-	-	-	-	-	-	-	ho	ta

D	N	D	P	P	-	P	P	-	-	-	-	-	-	N	N
t	n	m	n	pa	-	v	n	-	-	-	-	-	-	k	ro

D	N	D	P	P	-	P	-	-	-	-	-	-	-	N	N
y	han	i	s	na	-	n	-	-	-	-	-	-	-	m	ttha

D	N	D	P	P	P	N	N	D	N	D	P	P	-P	N	N
mn	di	r	me	te	ko	k	ro	aa	ge	pr	s	tha	-n	ch	rn

D	N	D	P	P	P	N	N	D	N	D	P	P	-P	-	-
pa	du	ka	vo	aa	yi	ja	ne	m	hi	ma	j	ha	-n	-	-

P	-	N	-
main	-	ya	-

R'	-	R'	-	-	G'	-	R'	R'	-	R'	-	-	S'	-	R'
j	-	g	-	-	k	-	l	ya	-	ni	-	-	ma	-	f

S'	N	S'	R'	R'	-	R'	-	R'	-	-	-	P	-	N	-
k	r	na	-	me	-	ri	-	bhu	-	-	l	main	-	ne	-

R'	-	R'	-	-	G'	-	R'	R'	-	R'	-	R'	-	R'	-
ma	-	the	-	-	pe	-	l	ga	-	yi	-	te	-	re	-

N	N	-	S'	R'	-	R'	-	R'	-	-	R'	-	-	R'	R'
ch	r	-	no	-	-	ki	-	dhu	-	-	l	-	-	a	re

R'	R'	-	G'	R'	-	S'	-	S'	-	S'	-	S'	-	S'	-
y	han	-	t	l	k	to	-	la	-	yi	-	be	-	ti	-

R'	-	S'	-	N	-	P	-	P	-	D	N	N	P	-	-
aa	-	ge	-	bhi	-	le	-	ja	-	o	-	na	-	-	-

P	-	P	-	D	-	P	-	P	-	R	-	R	-	M	-
main	-	p	r	de	-	si	-	hu	-	-	-	p	h	li	-
N	-	-	-	D	-	D	-	P	-	-	-	-	-	-	-
ba	-	-	r	aa	-	ya	-	hu	-	-	-	-	-	-	-
P	-	P	-	D	-	P	-	P	-	P	-	R	-	M	-
d	r	sh	n	k	r	ne	-	main	-	ya	-	ke	-	d	r
N	-	-	S'	-	D	D	-	P	-	-	-				
ba	-	-	-	-r	aa	ya	-	hu	-	-	-				

interlude: MPDS' P-P P-P P- P- M-
MPDS' P-P P-P P- P- --

MP	DN	PP	P	PPDM	M	PD	S'	P P		P	PPP
paudi	paudi	chdhda	ja	bhgta	jy	mata	di	krda		ja	bhgta

P	N	N	P	P	N	N	R'	S'	-	N	P	-	-	N	N
ye	-	hai	-	aa	-	dh	k	va	-	ri	-	-	-	m	hi
P	N	N	-	P	N	N	R'	S'	-	N	P	-	-	-	-
ma	-	hai	-	i	s	ki	-	bha	-	ri	-	-	-	-	-
P	N	N	P	-	N	N	R'	S'	-	N	P	-	-	-	-
g	r	bh	ju	-	n	vo	gu	fa	-	hai	-	-	-	-	-
P	N	-	N	P	N	N	R'	S'	-	N	P	-	-	N	N
k	tha	-	hai	i	s	ki	-	nya	-	ri	-	-	-	bhai	ro
D	N	D	P	P	-	P	-	-	-	-	-	-	-	N	N
j	ti	i	k	jo	-	gi	-	-	-	-	-	-	-	man	s
D	N	D	P	P	P	-	-	-	-	-	-	-	-	N	N
m	di	ra	-	ha	ri	-	-	-	-	-	-	-	-	le	ne
D	N	D	P	P	-	P	-	G	-	-	-	-	-	N	N
man	-	ki	p	ri	-	ksha	-	-	-	-	-	-	-	ba	t
D	N	D	P	P	P	-	-	-	-	-	-	-	-	N	N
u	s	ne	vi	cha	ri	-	-	-	-	-	-	-	-	man	s
D	N	D	P	P	P	N	N	D	N	D	P	P	P	N	N
au	r	m	dhu	man	ge	m	ti	u	s	ki	thi	ma	ri	hu	ee
D	N	D	P	P	P	N	N	D	N	D	P	P	P	N	-
an	tr	dhya	n	ma	ta	aa	ya	pi	chhe	du	ra	cha	ri	no	-
D	N	D	P	P	P	N	N	D	N	D	P	P	P	N	N
m	hi	ne	i	si	me	r	hi	main	ya	a	v	ta	ri	i	si

Udit Narayan 51 Songs' Sargam

D gu	N fa	D g	P rbh	P ju	P n	N ja	N ne	D du	N ni	D ya	P ye	P sa	P ri	- -	- -
												P dhn	- -	N y	- -
R' dh	- n	R' y	- -	G' me	- -	R' ri	- -	R' ma	- -	R' ta	- -	- -	S' dhn	- -	R' y
N te	- -	S' ri	R' -	- -	R' sh	- -	R' k	R' ti	- -	- -	- -	P mi	- I	N ti	- -
R' pa	- -	- -	G' pon	- -	- -	R' se	- -	R' mu	- k	R' ti	- -	S' k	- r	R' ke	- -
N te	- -	S' ri	R' -	- -	R' bh	- -	R' g	R' ti	- -	- -	- -	- -	- -	R' a	R' re
R' y	R' han	- -	G' t	R' I	- k	S' to	- -	S' la	- -	S' yi	- -	S' be	- -	S' ti	- -
R' aa	- -	S' ge	- -	N bhi	- -	P le	- -	P ja	- -	D o	N -	N na	P -	- -	- -
														N de	N kho
D un	N cha	D vo	P p	P ha	- -	- -	P d	- -	- -	- -	- -	- -	- -	N au	N r
D g	N h	D ri	P ye	P kha	- -	P yi	- -	- -	- -	- -	- -	- -	- -	N z	N ra
D ch	N dh	D na	P sn	P bh	- I	P ke	- -	G -	- -	- -	- -	- -	- -	N ha	N thi
D m	N tthe	D ki	P ch	P dha	P ee	- -	- -	- -	- -	- -	- -	- -	- -	N te	N dhe
D me	N dhe	D r	P s	P te	P hain	N p	N r	D ch	N dh	D na	P hai	P bha	P ee	N de	N kho
D sa	N m	D ne	P vo	P de	P kho	N san	N jhi	D chh	N t	D ki	P di	P kha	P yi	- -	- -
												P ae	- -	N sa	- -

Vinod Kumar

R'	R'	-	G'	-	-	R'	-	R'	R'	-	R'	-	-	-	R'
l	g	-	ta	-	-	hai	-	mu	jh	-	ko	-	-	-	mu
N		S'	R'	-	R'	-	R'	R'	-	-	-	P	-	N	-
ka	-	-	-	m	aa	-	g	ya	-	-	-	ma	-	ta	-
R'	-	-	R'	G'	-	R'	-	R'	-	R'	-	S'	-	R'	-
vai	-	-	sh	no	-	ka	-	ni	-	k	-	t	-	hi	-
N		S'	R'	-	R'	-	R'	R'	-	-	-	-	-	R'	R'
dha	-	-	-	m	aa	-	g	ya	-	-	-	-	-	a	re
R'	R'	-	G'	R'	-	R'	-	S'	-	S'	-	S'	-	S'	-
y	han	-	t	l	k	to	-	la	-	yi	-	be	-	ti	-
R'	-	S'	-	N	-	P	-	P	-	D	N	N	P	-	-
aa	-	ge	-	bhi	-	le	-	ja	-	o	-	na	-	-	-
														N	N
														de	kho
D	-N	D	P	P	P	-	-	-	-	-	-	-	-	N	N
sa	-m	ne	gu	fa	hai	-	-	-	-	-	-	-	-	main	ya
D	N	D	P	P	P	-	-	-	-	-	-	-	-	N	N
ra	ni	ka	du	va	ra	-	-	-	-	-	-	-	-	ma	ta
D	N	D	P	P	P	-	-	G	-	-	-	-	-	N	N
vai	sh	no	ne	y	han	-	-	-	-	-	-	-	-	ru	p
D	N	D	P	P	P	-	-	-	-	-	-	-	-	N	N
pin	di	yon	ka	dha	ra	-	-	-	-	-	-	-	-	ph	le
D	N	D	P	P	P	N	N	D	N	D	P	P	P	N	N
gn	ga	me	n	ha	lo	tha	li	pu	ja	ki	s	ja	lu	le	ke
D	N	D	P	P	P	N	N	D	N	D	P	P	P	-	-
la	l	la	l	chu	nni	ap	ne	s	r	pe	bn	dha	lo	-	-
						N	N	D	N	D	P	P	P	N	N
-	-	-	-	-	-	ja	ke	sun	d	r	gu	fa	me	man	ke
D	N	D	P	P	P	N	N	D	N	D	P	P	P	N	N
d	r	sh	n	pa	lo	bi	n	man	ge	hi	y	han	se	m	n
D	N	D	P	P	P	-	-								
i	chchha	f	l	pa	lo	-	-								

Udit Narayan 51 Songs' Sargam

												P	-	-	N
												aa	-	-	j
R'	-	-	G'	-	-	R'	-	R'	-	R'	-	-	-	S'	R'
tu	m	-	ne	-	-	s	-	r	l	pe	-	-	-	u	p
N	-	S'	R'	-	R'	-	R'	R'	-	-	-	P	-	N	-
ka	-	-	-	r	k	r	di	ya	-	-	-	da	-	m	n
R'	R'	-	G'	-	-	R'	-	-	-	R'	-	-	S'	-	R'
khu	shi	-	yon	-	-	se	-	-	-	aa	-	-	nn	-	d
N	-	S'	R'	-	R'	-	R'	R'	-	-	-	-	-	-	-
se	-	-	-	-	bh	r	di	ya	-	-	-	-	-	-	-
R'	-	R'	R'	G'	-	R'	-	S'	S'	S'	S'	S'	S'	S'	-
bhe	-	j	bu	la	-	va	-	a	g	le	b	r	s	bhi	-
R'	-	S'	-	N	-	N	P	P	-	D	N	N	-	P	-
p	r	de	-	si	-	ko	bu	la	-	o	-	ma	-	-	-
P	-	P	-	D	-	P	-	P	-	P	-	R	-	M	-
h	r	sa	-l	aa	-	un	-	ga	-	jai	-	se	-	i	s
N	-	-	-	D	-	D	-	P	-	-	-	-	-	-	-
ba	-	-	r	aa	-	ya	-	hu	-	-	-	-	-	-	-
P	-	P	-	D	-	P	-	-	-	-	N	D	N	D	-
main	-	p	r	de	-	si	-	-	-	-	o	main	-	ya	-
P	-	P	-	D	-	P	-	-	-	P	-	D	-	P	-
main	-	p	r	de	-	si	-	-	-	p	r	de	-	si	-
P	-	P	-	D	-	P	-	P	-	R	-	R	-	M	-
main	-	p	r	de	-	si	-	hu	-	-	-	p	h	li	-
N	-	-	-	D	-	D	-	P	-	-	-	-	-	-	-
ba	-	-	r	aa	-	ya	-	hu	-	-	-	-	-	-	-

34. NA JAANE MERE DIL KO KYA

Film: Dil vale dulhaniya le jaayeinge (1995)	Music: Jatin Lalit
Lyrics: Anand Bakshi	Singer: Udit Narayan, Lata
Taal: Kaharwa	Chord: PNR' S=C#

na jaane mere dil ko kya ho gaya, abhee to yaheen tha,
abhee kho gaya -2
ho gaya hai tujhako to pyaar sajana,
laakh kar le too inakaar sajana-2
diladaar sajana, hai ye pyaar sajana
aa aa aa aa

dekha na toone mud ke bhee peechhe,
kuchh der to main ruka tha
jab dil ne tujhako rokana chaaha,
door too ja chuka tha
hua kya, na jaana, ye dil kyoon, deevaana
ho gaya hai tujhako to pyaar sajana,
laakh kar le too inakaar sajana -2
diladaar sajana, hai ye pyaar sajana

ai vaqt ruk ja, tham ja, thahar ja,
vaapas zara daud peechhe
main chhod aayee, khud ko jahaan pe,
vo rah gaya mod peechhe
kahaan main, kahaan too, ye kaisa, hai jaadoo
are ho gaya hai tujhako to pyaar sajana,
laakh kar le too inakaar sajana -2
diladaar sajana, hai ye pyaar sajana

NA JAANE MERE DIL KO KYA

dhage 12	nti 34	nke 56	dhin 78	dhage 12	nti 34	nke 56	dhin 78	dhage 12	nti 34	nke 56	dhin 78	dhage 12	nti 34	nke 56	dhin 78
prelude: Chord: RP<u>N</u>															
P M P		P RP-M													
<u>N</u> D P D R-		M P--													
		R	P	-	D	-	P	P	-	-	-	-	D	-	P
		n	ja	-	ne	-	me	re	-	-	-	-	dil	-	ko
P	-	-	-	-	D	-	<u>N</u>	<u>N</u>	S'	-	D	-	-	-	-
kya	-	-	-	-	ho	-	g	ya	-	-	-	-	-	-	-
-	-	R	M*	-	D	-	P	M*	-	-	-	-	D	-	P
-	-	a	bhi	-	to	-	y	hin	-	-	-	-	tha	-	a
M*	-	-	-	-	D	-	P	P	-	-	-	-	-	-	-
bhi	-	-	-	-	kho	-	g	ya	-	-	-	-	-	-	-
		R	P	-	D	-	P	P	-	-	-	-	D	-	P
		n	ja	-	ne	-	me	re	-	-	-	-	dil	-	ko
P	-	-	-	-	D	-	<u>N</u>	<u>N</u>	S'	-	D	-	-	-	-
kya	-	-	-	-	ho	-	g	ya	-	-	-	-	-	-	-
-	-	R	M*	-	D	-	P	M*	-	-	-	-	D	-	P
-	-	a	bhi	-	to	-	y	hin	-	-	-	-	tha	-	a
M*	-	-	-	-	P	-	D	D	<u>N</u>	-	P	-	-	-	-
bhi	-	-	-	-	kho	-	g	ya	-	-	-	-	-	-	-
P	R'	S'	R'	<u>NN</u>	-S'	-	<u>N</u>	S'	-	D	D	D	-	-	-
ho	g	ya	hai	tujh	-ko	-	to	pya	-r	s	j	na	-	-	-
M	-S'	<u>N</u>	S'	D	D	<u>N</u>	D	<u>N</u>	-P	P	P	P	-	-	-
la	-kh	k	r	le	tu	i	n	ka	-r	s	j	na	-	-	-
P	R'	S'	R'	<u>NN</u>	-S'	-	<u>N</u>	S'	-	D	D	D<u>N</u>	S'	D	-
ho	g	ya	hai	tujh	-ko	-	to	pya	-r	s	j	na-	-	-	-
M	-S'	<u>N</u>	S'	D	D	<u>N</u>	D	<u>N</u>	-P	P	P	P	<u>N</u>	<u>N</u>	D
la	-kh	k	r	le	tu	i	n	ka	-r	s	j	na	-	dil	-
<u>N</u>	-	P	P	P	<u>N</u>	<u>N</u>	D	<u>N</u>	-	P	P	P	-	-	-
da	-r	s	j	na	-	hai	ye	pya	-r	s	j	na	-	-	-

R'---- S'R' <u>G</u>'M'<u>G</u>'R'<u>G</u>'   R'S'<u>ND</u>-- S' <u>N</u> D P---
aa---------------   aa------------------

P	R'	S'	R'	NN	-S'	-	N	S'	-	D	D	DN	S'	D	-
ho	g	ya	hai	tujh	-ko	-	to	pya	-r	s	j	na-	-	-	-

M	-S'	N	S'	D	D	N	D	N	-P	P	P	P	N	N	D
la	-kh	k	r	le	tu	i	n	ka	-r	s	j	na	-	dil	-

N	-	P	P	P	N	N	D	N	-	P	P	P	-	-	-
da	-r	s	j	na	-	hai	ye	pya	-r	s	j	na	-	-	-

interlude:
PM P D PM P P
PM P D PM PS' P
S' S' S' R' D N
S R' S R' N D PDS'
SR'S' N NS' N N D PD S'
G'R'S' NS'N   DP DN---

	N	-N	-D	N	-	N	-	-	DN	-S'	-R'	R'	-	D	-
	de	-kha	-n	tu	-	ne	-	-	mud	-ke	-bhi	pi	-	chhe	-

-	DD	-D	-D	D	-S'	-	N	D	-	P	-	P	-	MP	DN
-	kuchh	-de	-r	to	-main	-	ru	ka	-	tha	-	-	-	-	-

-	N	D	P	N	N	N	-	-	N	-S'	-R'	R'	-	D	-
-	jb	dil	ne	tu	jh	ko	-	-	ro	-k	-na	cha	-	ha	-

-	D	-	D	D	-R'	-	S'	R'	-	R'	-	R'S'	N	-	N
-	du	-	r	tu	-ja	-	chu	ka	-	tha	-	-	-	-	hu

R'	S'	R'-	-	S'	-	-	D	S'	-S'	-	N	-	-	-	N
aa	kya	-	-	-	-	-	n	ja	-na	-	-	-	-	-	ye

R'	-S'	G'	R'	S'	-	-	M	D	-D	P	-	-	-	-	-
dil	-kyu	-	-	-	-	-	di	va	-na	-	-	-	-	-	-

P	R'	S'	R'	NN	-S'	-	N	S'	-	D	D	D	-	-	-
ho	g	ya	hai	tujh	-ko	-	to	pya	-r	s	j	na	-	-	-

M	-S'	N	S'	D	D	N	D	N	-P	P	P	P	-	-	-
la	-kh	k	r	le	tu	i	n	ka	-r	s	j	na	-	-	-

P	R'	S'	R'	NN	-S'	-	N	S'	-	D	D	DN	S'	D	-
ho	g	ya	hai	tujh	-ko	-	to	pya	-r	s	j	na-	-	-	-

M	-S'	N	S'	D	D	N	D	N	-P	P	P	P	N	N	D
la	-kh	k	r	le	tu	i	n	ka	-r	s	j	na	-	dil	-

N	-	P	P	P	N	N	D	N	-	P	P	P	-	-	-
da	-r	s	j	na	-	hai	ye	pya	-r	s	j	na	-	-	-

interlude:
flute: R'G'R'S' R' S' D – DNS'G'R'—2
N P R' S' R' N S' G' R'
N P R' S' R' N S' N D
N P R' S' R' N S' G' R'
D N R' R' G'R' S'-
D D N S' – P N D P--

N	-N	-D	N	N	N	-	-	DN	-S'	-R'	R'	-	D	-
ae	v	kt	ru	k	ja	-	-	thm	-ja	-th	hr	-	ja	-
-	D	-D	-D	D	-S'	-	N	D	-	P	-	P	-	MP	DN
-	va	ps	z	ra	-dau	-	d	pi	-	chhe	-	-	-	-	-
-	N	-D	-P	N	-	N	-	-	NN	-S'	-R'	R'	-	D	-
-	main	-chho	-d	aa	-	yi	-	-	khud	ko	j	han	-	pe	-
-	D	D	D	D	-R'	-	S'	R'	-	R'	-	R'S'	N	-	N
-	vo	rh	g	ya	-mo	-	d	pi	-	chhe	-	-	-	-	k
R'	-S'	R' -	-	S'	-	-	D	S'	-S'	-	N	-	-	-	N
han	-main	-	-	-	-	-	k	han	-tu	-	-	-	-	-	ye
R'	-S'	G'	R'	S'	-	-	M	D	-D	P	-	-	-	-	P
kai	-sa	-	-	-	-	-	hai	ja	-du	-	-	-	-	-	are
P	R'	S'	R'	NN	-S'	-	N	S'	-	D	D	D	-	-	-
ho	g	ya	hai	tujh	-ko	-	to	pya	-r	s	j	na	-	-	-
M	-S'	N	S'	D	D	N	D	N	-P	P	P	P	-	-	-
la	-kh	k	r	le	tu	i	n	ka	-r	s	j	na	-	-	-
P	R'	S'	R'	NN	-S'	-	N	S'	-	D	D	DN	S'	D	-
ho	g	ya	hai	tujh	-ko	-	to	pya	-r	s	j	na-	-	-	-
M	-S'	N	S'	D	D	N	D	N	-P	P	P	P	N	N	D
la	-kh	k	r	le	tu	i	n	ka	-r	s	j	na	-	dil	-
N	-	P	P	P	N	N	D	N	-	P	P	P	-	-	-
da	-r	s	j	na	-	hai	ye	pya	-r	s	j	na	-	-	-

Vinod Kumar

35. O PAALANHAARE

Film: Lagaan (2001)	Music: A. R. Rahman
Lyrics: Javed Akhtar	Singer: Lata Mangeshkar, Udit Narayan.
Taal: Kaharwa	Saadhna Sargam
	Chord: SGP RMD MDS' S=D#

o paalanahaare, nirgun aur nyaare
o paalanahaare, nirgun aur nyaare,
tumhare bin hamara kauno naaheen
hamaree ulajhan, sulajhao bhagavan,
tumhare bin hamara kauno naaheen
tumhai hamaka ho sambhaale,
tumhai hamare rakhavaale
tumhare bin hamara kauno naaheen, -3

lata:
chanda mein tumheen to bhare ho chaandanee,
sooraj mein ujaala tumheen se
ye gagan hai magan, tumheen to die ho ise taare
bhagavan ye jeevan, tumhai na sanvaaroge to kya koee sanvaare
o paalanahaare nirgun aur nyaare,
tumhare bin hamara kauno naaheen -3

udit:
jo, suno to, kahen, prabhujee hamaree hai binatee
dukhee jan ko, dheeraj do haare nahin vo kabhee dukhase
tum nirbal ko raksha do rah paen nirbal sukh se
bhakti ko, shakti do, (bhakti ko, shakti do)
jag ke jo svaamee ho, itanee to araj suno
hain path mein andhiyaare, de do varadaan mein ujiyaare

(o paalanahaare nirgun aur nyaare
tumhare bin hamara kauno naaheen
hamaree ulajhan, sulajhao bhagavan,
tumhare bin hamara kauno naaheen) -3
o paalanahaare…   o paalanahaare…

O PAALANHAARE

dha	ge	n	ti	n	ke	dhi	n	dha	ge	n	ti	n	ke	dhi	n
1	2	3	4	5	6	7	8	1	2	3	4	5	6	7	8

```
R   GR PM    RG    R  MG--- RS
o   palnhare, nirgun au nyare

flute: R   GR PM    RG    R  MG--- S
       S R S .N  S S R    G- R R S
```

1	2	3	4	5	6	7	8	1	2	3	4	5	6	7	8
R	G	R	P	M	-	-	-	R	G	R	M	G	-	R	S
o	pa	ln	ha	re	-	-	-	nir	gun	au	nya	re	-	-	-
S	R	S	.N	S	S	R	-	G	-	R	R	S	-	-	-
tumh	re	bi	n	h	m	ra	-	kau	-	no	na	hin	-	-	-
R	G	R	P	M	-	-	-	R	G	R	M	G	-	R	S
hm	ri	ul	-	jhn	-	-	-	sul	jha	o	bhg	vn	-	-	-
S	R	S	.N	S	S	R	-	G	-	R	R	S	-	-	-
tumh	re	bi	n	h	m	ra	-	kau	-	no	na	hin	-	-	-
-	-	-	-	-	-	-	-	G	G	M	M	M	-	-	-
-	-	-	-	-	-	-	-	tum	hai	h	m	ka	-	-	-
R	M	G	-	G	-	S	-	G	G	M	M	D	-	M	-
ho	sn	bha	-	le	-	-	-	tum	hai	h	m	re	-	-	-
R	M	G	-	G	-	S	-	S	R	S	.N	S	S	R	-
r	kh	va	-	le	-	-	-	tumh	re	bi	n	h	m	ra	-
G	-	R	R	S	-	-	-	S	R	S	.N	S	S	R	-
kau	-	no	na	hin	-	-	-	tumh	re	bi	n	h	m	ra	-
G	-	R	R	S	-	-	-	S	R	S	.N	S	S	R	-
kau	-	no	na	hin	-	-	-	tumh	re	bi	n	h	m	ra	-
G	-	R	R	S	-	-	-								
kau	-	no	na	hin	-	-	-								

```
interlude: flute: M M P --- N- P- D-M-P-----D-M G S,
           M G M G - M G M G- S R S
```

1	2	3	4	5	6	7	8	1	2	3	4	5	6	7	8
M	M	P	-	-	-	-	-	P	D	N	S'	R'	N	P	P
chn	da	me	-	-	-	-	-	tum	hai	to	bh	re	ho	chan	d
D	P	M	-	-	-	-	S'	N	S'P	-	S'	N	S'P	-	P
ni	-	-	-	-	-	-	su	r	j,me	-	u	ja	-la	-	tum
M	-	P	-	-	G	M	P	G'	-	M'	G'	R'	S'	G	M
hin	-	se	-	-	-	-	-	-	-	-	-	-	-	ye	g

MP	D	S'	-	-	-	S'	R'	N	-	-	D	N	P	M	-
gn-	-	-	-	-	-	hai	m	gn	-	-	-	-	-	-	-
M	M	P	P	P	N	-D	P	M	-	P	-	-	-	G	M
tu	mhai	to	di	ye	ho	-i	se	ta	-	re	-	-	-	bh	g
MP	D	S'	-	-	-	S'	R'	N	-	-	D	N	P	M	-
vn	-	-	-	-	-	ye	jii	vn	-	-	-	-	-	-	-
M	M	P	P	P	P	P	N	D	D	P	P	M	-	G	R
tum	hai	na	sn	va	ro	ge	to	kya	ko	ee	sn	va	-	re	-
R	G	R	P	M	-	-	-	R	G	R	M	G	-	R	S
o	pa	ln	ha	re	-	-	-	nir	gun	au	nya	re	-	-	-
S	R	S	.N	S	R	S	.N	S	R	S	S	S	-	-	-
tumh	re	bi	n	h	m	ra	-	kau	-	no	na	hin	-	-	-
S	R	S	.N	S	S	R	-	G	-	R	R	S	-	-	-
tumh	re	bi	n	h	m	ra	-	kau	-	no	na	hin	-	-	-

interlude: S G R M G S R S S G R M G S R S   S P – D P M G G S
S P --- D P M G M P D N – P D M P M P G P M G
P G M G M D – M P G M R G S R .N S –

P	-	-	-	-	-	D	M	P	-	-	-	-	-	D	P
jo	-	-	-	-	-	su	no	to	-	-	-	-	-	k	hen
-	PD	N	DD	P	D	P	M	GM	GP	M	-	GM	GP	M	M
-	prbhu	jii	hm	ri	hai	bin	ti	dukhi	jn	ko	-	dhi	rj	do	ha
G	GP	M	MG	RR	G	-	G	GM	GP	M	-	G	GP	M	MM
ren	nhin	vo	kbhi	dukh	se	-	tum	nir	bl	ko	-	r	ksha	do	rh
M	MD	P	MG	RR	G	-	S	R	S	-	-	-	-	-	S
pa	yen-	nir	bl	sukh	se	-	bh	kti	ko	-	-	-	-	-	sh
R	S	-	-	-	-	-	S	R	S	-	-	-	-	-	S
kti	do	-	-	-	-	-	bh	kti	ko	-	-	-	-	-	sh
R	S	-	-	-	-	PP	D	PD	S'	-	-	-	-	NS'	R'
kti	do	-	-	-	-	jg	ke	jo-	-	-	-	-	-	swa	mi
N	-	-	-	D	P	MM	M	P	-	-	-	-	-	PD	NS'
ho	-	-	-	-	-	it	ni	to	-	-	-	-	-	ar	j,su
P	-	-	-	-	-	P	PD	PD	S'	-	-	-	-	NS'	R'
no	-	-	-	-	-	hr	pth	me-	-	-	-	-	-	andhi	ya

N	-	-	-	D	P	-	M	M	P	P	P	P	D	N	N
re	-	-	-	-	-	-	de	do	-	v	r	da	-	n	me
D	D	P	-	M	-	-	G	R	G	R	P	M	-	-	-
u	ji	ya	-	re	-	-	-	o	pa	ln	ha	re	-	-	-
R	G	R	M	G	-	-	RS	S	R	S	.N	S	R	S	.N
nir	gun	au	nya	re	-	-	-	tumh	re	bi	n	h	m	ra	-
S	R	S	S	S	-	-	-	R	G	R	P	M	-	-	-
kau	-	no	na	hin	-	-	-	hm	ri	ul	-	jhn	-	-	-
R	G	R	M	G	-	-	RS	S	R	S	.N	S	R	S	.N
sul	jha	o	bhg	vn	-	-	-	tumh	re	bi	n	h	m	ra	-
S	R	S	S	S	-	-	-								
kau	-	no	na	hin	-	-	-								

```
              S'     R'S'      G'G'  R'M'  M'G'  R'S'
udit:    o     paln      hare --------------

         S'------ NR'S'ND--- DPM- R  GP    M      GG-- ᴿS
Lata: o ------------------------     pa- ln    hare ------
```

36. PARDESI 2 JANA NAHIN

Film: Raja Hindustani (1996)	Music: Nadeem Shrawan
Lyrics: Sameer	Singer: Udit Narayan, Alka Yagnik
Taal: Kaharwa	Chord: RMD S=C#

a: paradesee paradesee jaana nahin, mujhe chhod ke
   paradesee mere yaara vaada nibhaana
   mujhe yaad rakhana kaheen bhool na jaana

u: paradesee paradesee jaana nahin, mujhe chhod ke
   paradesee mere yaara vaada nibhaana
   tum yaad rakhana kaheen bhool na jaana

a: mainne tumako chaaha tumase pyaar kiya
   sab kuchh tum pe yaar apana vaar diya
   ban gaee jogan mainne preet ka jog liya
   na socha na samajha dil ka rog liya
u: paradesee mere yaara laut ke aana, tum yaad rakhana kaheen bhool na jaana
a: paradesee paradesee jaana nahin, mujhe chhod ke
   tum yaad rakhana kaheen bhool na jaana

Vinod Kumar

PARDESI 2 JANA NAHIN

dha	ge	n	ti	n	ke	dhi	n	dha	ge	n	ti	n	ke	dhi	n
1	2	3	4	5	6	7	8	1	2	3	4	5	6	7	8

prelude:
M- M- M- M-
M M P D S' S' S' R' S' D D D D D -2
D-M D-M R R R D-M D-M M M M -2
Chord: MDS' - - - - -
D S' G' R' S' S' R' S' R' D D D D – 2
D-M D-M GM R- D-M D-M RG M- -2

D   S'   S'S'   DS'   D S'S'   R'S'   S'S'S'D
main ye nhin   khti ke pyar mt krna—

S'R'   S'DD   D DD   DDDS' DP   M M
kisi   musafir ka mgr aetbar mt krna

D- PM D- PM MP MR RM D-PP------ D DD P MM
hu---

D	-	-	-	P	-	M	-	D	-	-	-	P	-	M	-
pr	-	-	-	de	-	si	-	pr	-	-	-	de	-	si	-
M	P	-	M	R	-	-	-	M	P	-	M	R	-	-	-
ja	na	-	n	hin	-		-	-	-	-	-	-	-	-	-
-	-	R	M	-	D	-	P	P	-	-	-	-	-	-	-
-	-	mu	jhe	-	chho	-	d	ke	-	-	-	-	-	-	-
D	-	D	D	-	P	-	M	M	-	-	-	-	-	S'	-
-	-	mu	jhe	-	chho	-	d	ke	-	-	-	-	-	p	r
D	-	S'	-	S'	-	S'	-	S'	-	R'	-	-	-	-	-
de	-	si	-	me	-	re	-	ya	-	ra	-	-	-	-	-
-	-	S'	-	R'	S'	-	D	D	-	D	-	-	-	-	-
-	-	va	-	-	da	-	ni	bha	-	na	-	-	-	-	-
-	-	D	S'	-	S'	-	S'	S'	S'	R'	-	-	S'	R'	-
-	-	mu	jhe	-	ya	-	d	r	kh	na	-	-	k	hin	-
G'	-	-	-	R'	-	-	S'	D	-	-	-	P	-	M	
bhu	-	-	-	l	-	-	n	ja	-	-	-	na	-	-	

interlude:
S'S' S'S' S'S' D S' R' S'R' M'-G'
S'S' S'S' S'S' D S' R' S'R' R' S'
S' R'- S' R'- S'- D   D S' D S' D- P-
P D P D P-M-M M
D D M P P G M- P M DS'- D
D D M P P G M- P D D –M
DP DP M-M-P- MR M-

P	D	D	P	P	D	D	P	P	D	D	P	P	D	D	P
main	-	ne	-	tu	m	ko	-	cha	-	ha	-	tu	m	se	-
M	-	P	D	P	-	-	-	M	-	P	D	P	-	-	-
pya	-	r	ki	ya	-	-	-	-	-	-	-	-	-	-	-
N	-	N	-	N	-	N	-	S'	-	-	D	D	D	D	-
s	b	ku	chh	tu	m	pe	-	ya	-	-	r	a	p	na	-
P	-	D	D	D	M	-	-	-	-	-	-	-	-	-	-
va	-	r	di	ya	-	-	-	-	-	-	-	-	-	-	-
P	D	D	P	P	D	D	P	P	D	D	P	P	D	D	P
b	n	g	yi	jo	-	g	n	main	-	ne	-	pri	-	t	ka
M	-	P	D	P	-	-	-	M	-	P	D	P	-	-	-
jo	-	g	li	ya	-	-	-	-	-	-	-	-	-	-	-
N	-	N	-	N	-	N	-	N	S'	S'	-	D	D	D	-
na	-	so	-	cha	-	na	-	s	m	jha	-	di	l	ka	-
P	-	D	D	D	M	-	-	-	-	-	-	-	-	S'	-
ro	-	g	li	ya	-	-	-	-	-	-	-	-	-	p	r
D	-	S'	-	S'	-	S'	-	S'	-	R'	-	-	-	-	-
de	-	si	-	me	-	re	-	ya	-	ra	-	-	-	-	-
-	-	S'	-	R'	S'	-	D	D	-	D	-	-	-	-	-
-	-	lau	-	-	t	-	ke	aa	-	na	-	-	-	-	-
-	-	D	S'	-	S'	-	S'	S'	S'	R'	-	-	S'	R'	-
-	-	tu	m	-	ya	-	d	r	kh	na	-	-	k	hin	-
G'	-	-	-	R'	-	-	S'	D	-	-	-	P	-	M	-
bhu	-	-	-	l	-	-	n	ja	-	-	-	na	-	-	-

interlude:
M' M' M' R' S' D S' D G' R' D S'
D S' D G' R' D S'
D S'R' G'—S' D P D P S' D P M-
P D P R' S' D P M-M-M-

```
MD  S'  R'S'R'----------------------- G' R' G' R' R'
bhul n  ja-na

MD  S'  R'S'S'----------------------R'G'S'
bhul n  ja-na

R'S' M PP     D-PRM-    D-P- MRM--
bhul n jana   o---      music
```

P	D	D	P	P	D	D	P	P	D	D	P	P	D	D	P
h	r	p	l	me	-	ri	-	ya	-	d	tu	mhe	-	t	d
M	-	P	D	P	-	P	-	M	-	P	D	P	-	-	-
pa	-	ye	-	gi	-	td	-	pa	-	ye	-	gi	-	-	-
N	-	N	-	N	-	N	-	S'	-	-	D	D	-	D	-
main	-	ja	-	gun	-	ga	-	nin	-	d	tu	mhe	-	na	-
P	-	D	-	D	-	M	-	-	-	-	-	-	-	-	-
aa	-	ye	-	gi	-	-	-	-	-	-	-	-	-	-	-
P	D	D	P	P	D	D	P	P	D	D	P	P	D	D	P
chho	-	d	ke	ae	-	se	-	ha	-	l	me	jo	-	tu	m
M	-	P	D	P	-	P	-	M	-	P	D	P	-	-	-
ja	-	o	-	ge	-	tum	-	ja	-	o	-	ge	-	-	-
N	-	N	-	N	-	N	-	S'	-	-	D	D	D	D	D
s	ch	k	h	ta	-	hu	-	ja	-	n	b	hu	t	p	chh
P	-	D	-	D	-	M	-	-	-	-	-	-	-	S'	-
ta	-	o	-	ge	-	-	-	-	-	-	-	-	-	p	r
D	-	S'	-	S'	-	S'	-	S'	-	R'	-	-	-	-	-
de	-	si	-	me	-	re	-	ya	-	ra	-	-	-	-	-
-	-	S'	R'	-	S'	-	D	D	-	D	-	-	-	-	-
-	-	mu	jhe	-	na	-	ru	la	-	na	-	-	-	-	-
-	-	D	S'	-	S'	-	S'	S'	S'	R'	-	-	S'	R'	-
-	-	tu	m	-	ya	-	d	r	kh	na	-	-	k	hin	-
G'	-	-	-	R'	-	-	S'	D	-	-	-	P	-	M	-
bhu	-	-	-	l	-	-	n	ja	-	-	-	na	-	-	-
D	-	-	-	P	-	M	-	D	-	-	-	P	-	M	-
pr	-	-	-	de	-	si	-	pr	-	-	-	de	-	si	-

M	P	-	M	R	-	-	-	-	-	-	-	-	-	-	-
ja	na	-	n	hin	-	-	-	-	-	-	-	-	-	-	-
-	-	R	M	-	D̲	-	P	P	-	-	-	-	-	-	-
-	-	mu	jhe	-	chho	-	d	ke	-	-	-	-	-	-	-
D	-	D	D	-	P	-	M	M	-	-	-	-	-	-	-
-	-	mu	jhe	-	chho	-	d	ke	-	-	-	-	-	-	-

37. PAHLA NASHA PAHLA KHUMAR

Film: Jo Jeeta Vahi Sikandar (1992)	Music: Jatin Lalit
Lyrics: Majrooh Sultanpuri	Singer: Udit Narayan, Saadhna Sargam
Taal: Kaharwa	Chord: RMD S=C

chaahe tum kuchh na kaho, maine sun liya

ke saathee pyaar ka mujhe chun liya,

chun liya mainne sun liya

pahala nasha, pahala khumaar,

naya pyaar hai, naya intazaar

kar loon main kya apana haal, ai dil-e-bekaraar

mere dil-e-bekaraar, too hee bata,

pahala nasha, pahala khumaar

udata hee phiroon in havaon mein kaheen,

ya main jhool jaoon in ghataon mein kaheen

ek kar doon aasamaan aur zameen,

kaho yaaron kya karoon, kya nahin, pahala nasha,

usane baat kee kuchh aise dhang se,

sapane de gaya vo hazaaro rang ke

rah jaoon jaise main haar ke,

aur choome vo mujhe pyaar se,

pahala nasha, pahala khumaar

Vinod Kumar

PAHLA NASHA PAHLA KHUMAR

dha	ge	n	ti	n	ke	dhi	n	dha	ge	n	ti	n	ke	dhi	n
1	2	3	4	5	6	7	8	1	2	3	4	5	6	7	8

DD   P MM M PR   D<u>N</u>   D MM
chahe tum kuchh na kaho, maine sun liya

D PM   S'S' P D<u>N</u>   D   MM
ke sathi pyar ka mujhe chun liya

M   DDP PP M   D DP
chun liya- mainne sun liya-

DDS' S'S'   S'PD S'S'
phla nsha, phla khumar

DD S'S' S'—R'   DD PPP
nya pyar hai,   nya intzar

MM R G   M <u>NNN</u> D R G   M <u>N</u>DP-
kr   lun main kya apna hal, ae dil-e-bekrar

MR G   M <u>N</u>DD   MP   D MP
mere dil-e-bekrar, tu-   hi bta

DDS' S'S'R' S'PD S'S'
phla nsha,   phla khumar

M'G'M'--S' R'   <u>G</u>'R'   R' S'PP R' S'S'
udta -- hi firun in   hvaon me   khin

M'G' M'-S'   R'<u>G</u>'   R'R' R' S'PP   R' S'S'
ya-   main- - jhul   jaun in ghtaon me khin

S'S' S' R'   <u>G</u>'R'S' S' NS'
ek   kr dun aasman aur zmi

S'S' S'R'   <u>G</u>'   M'M'S'   S' NS'
kho yaro kya krun,   kya nhin

DDS' S'S'R' S'PD S'S'
phla nsha-,   phla khumar…

M'G'M'S' R'<u>G</u>' R'   S'D PP R'S' S'
usne   bat ki kuchh aese dhng se

M'G'M'S' R' G̲'R' S' DPP   R'S' S'
spne-   de gya vo hzaro rng ke

S'N̲ S'R' G̲'R' S'   S'N S'
rh   jaun jaise main har ke

S'N̲   S'R' G̲' M'M'S' N̲D S'N̲
aur chume vo mujhe- pyar se-

DDS' S'S'R' S'PD S'S'
phla nsha, phla khumar

38. PAPA KAHTE HAIN BADA NAAM

Film: Qayamat se Qayamat tak (1988)	Music: Anand Milind
Lyrics: Majrooh Sultanpuri	Singer: Udit Narayan
Taal: Kaharwa	Chord: PS'G' S=C

paapa kahate hain bada naam karega,
beta hamaara aisa kaam karega
magar ye to, koee na jaane,
ke meree manzil, hai kahaan

baithe hain milake, sab yaar apane,
sabake dilon mein, aramaan ye hai
vo zindagee mein, kal kya banega,
har ik najar ka, sapana ye hai
koee injeeniyar ka kaam karega,
bijanes mein koee apana naam karega
magar ye to ...

mera to sapana, hai ek chehara,
dekhe jo usako, jhoome bahaar
gaalon mein khilatee, kaliyon ka mausam,
aankhon mein jaadoo, hothon mein pyaar
banda ye khoobasoorat kaam karega,
dil kee duniya mein apana naam karega
magar ye to ...

Vinod Kumar

PAPA KAHTE HAIN BADA NAAM

dha	ge	n	ti	n	ke	dhi	n	dha	ge	n	ti	n	ke	dhi	n
1	2	3	4	5	6	7	8	1	2	3	4	5	6	7	8

prelude:
```
S  GD- P----D R- S- R-  .D S  G-G M-G-  2
(D—PD- DDD D—PD- PDN S'—ND-
M ---GM- M  M- GM- MGMP-) 2
P----- D-P D-P-    D----- D-P D-P-
M----- D-P D-P-    P----- D-P D-P-
S R  G P- M- G-
S  GD- P----D R- S- R-  .D S  G-G M-G-  2
```

dha	ge	n	ti	n	ke	dhi	n	dha	ge	n	ti	n	ke	dhi	n
1	2	3	4	5	6	7	8	1	2	3	4	5	6	7	8
		G'	-	G'	-	R'	-	S'	-	S'	-	P	-	D	-
		pa	-	pa	-	k	h	te	-	hain	-	b	-	da	-
S'	-	-	-	M'	-	G'	-	R'	-	-	-	-	-	-	-
na	-	-	m	k	-	re	-	ga	-	-	-	-	-	-	-
-	-	G'	-	G'	-	R'	-	S'	-	S'	-	P	-	D	-
-	-	be	-	ta	-	h	-	ma	-	ra	-	ae	-	sa	-
S'	-	-	-	M'	-	G'	-	R'	-	-	-	-	P	D	N
ka	-	-	m	k	-	re	-	ga	-	-	-	-	m	g	r
S'	-	-	S'	-	-	-	-	-	-	-	S'	-	S'	-	N
ye	-	-	to	-	-	-	-	-	-	-	ko	-	ee	-	n
D	-	-	D	-	-	-	-	-	-	-	D	-	D	-	P
ja	-	-	ne	-	-	-	-	-	-	-	ke	-	me	-	ri
M	-	-	M	-	-	-	-	-	-	-	G	-	-	M	-
mn	-	-	zi	-	l	-	-	-	-	-	hai	-	-	k	-
P	-	-	-	-	-	-	-	-	-	G'	-	G'	-	R'	-
han	-	-	-	-	-	-	-	-	-	pa	-	pa	-	k	h
S'	-	S'	-	P	-	D	-	S'	-	-	m	M'	-	G'	-
te	-	hain	-	b	-	da	-	na	-	-	m	k	-	re	-
R'	-	-	-	-	-	G'	R'	S'	-	-	-	-	-	-	-
ga	-	-	-	-	-	-	-	-	-	-	-	-	-	-	-

interlude:
```
P—G P- G P N D G  DDD  PD PS' N D P G – 2
SRGD—PMG  M- R-  SRGP—MGR  G- S- 2
P--- D--- S'NDP-
```

dha	ge	n	ti	n	ke	dhi	n	dha	ge	n	ti	n	ke	dhi	n
1	2	3	4	5	6	7	8	1	2	3	4	5	6	7	8
		P	-	P	-	P	-	P	D	-	P	-	-	-	-
		bai	-	the	-	hain	-	mi	l	-	ke	-	-	-	-

-	-	P	-	P	-	-	P	P	D	-	P	-	-	-	-
-	-	s	b	ya	-	-	r	a	p	-	ne	-	-	-	-
-	-	S'	-	S'	-	N	-	D	-	-	D	-	-	-	-
-	-	s	b	ke	-	di	-	lo	-	-	me	-	-	-	-
-	-	N	-	D	-	N	-	S'	-	P	-	D	-	P	-
-	-	a	r	man	-	ye	-	hai	-	-	-	-	-	-	-
-	-	P	-	P	-	P	-	P	D	-	P	-	-	-	-
-	-	vo	-	zin	-	d	-	gi	-	-	me	-	-	-	-
-	-	P	-	P	-	P	-	P	D	-	P	-	-	-	-
-	-	k	l	kya	-	b	-	ne	-	-	ga	-	-	-	-
-	-	S'	-	S'	-	N	-	D	-	-	D	-	-	-	-
-	-	h	r	i	k	n	-	zr	-	-	ka	-	-	-	-
-	-	N	N	D	-	N	-	S'	-	-	-	R'	-	-	-
-	-	s	p	na	-	ye	-	hai	-	-	-	-	-	-	-
G'	-	G'	-	G'	-	R'	-	S'	-	S'	-	P	-	D	-
-	-	ko	-	ee	-	in	-	jii	-	ni	-	y	r	ka	-
S'	-	-	-	M'	-	G'	-	R'	-	-	-	-	-	-	-
ka	-	-	m	k	-	re	-	ga	-	-	-	-	-	-	-
-	-	G'	-	G'	-	R'	-	S'	-	S'	-	P	-	D	-
-	-	bi	j	ne	s	me	-	ko	-	ee	-	a	p	na	-
S'	-	-	-	M'	-	G'	-	R'	-	-	-	-	P	D	N
na	-	-	m	k	-	re	-	ga	-	-	-	-	m	g	r
S'	-	-	S'	-	-	-	-	-	-	-	S'	-	S'	-	N
ye	-	-	to	-	-	-	-	-	-	-	ko	-	ee	-	n
D	-	-	D	-	-	-	-	-	-	-	D	-	D	-	P
ja	-	-	ne	-	-	-	-	-	-	-	ke	-	me	-	ri
M	-	-	M	-	-	-	-	-	-	-	G	-	-	M	-
mn	-	-	zi	-	l	-	-	-	-	-	hai	-	-	k	-
P	-	-	-	-	-	-	-	-	-	G'	-	G'	-	R'	-
han	-	-	-	-	-	-	-	-	-	pa	-	pa	-	k	h
S'	-	S'	-	P	-	D	-	S'	-	-	-	M'	-	G'	-
te	-	hain	-	b	-	da	-	na	-	-	m	k	-	re	-

1	2	3	4	5	6	7	8	9	10	11	12	13	14	15	16
R'	-	-	-	-	-	G'	R'	S'	-	-	-	-	-	-	-
ga	-	-	-	-	-	-	-	-	-	-	-	-	-	-	-

interlude:

S' G'D'- P'----D' R'- S'- R'- D S' G'-G' M'-G'- 2
(D—PD- DDD D—PD- PDN S'—ND-
M ---GM- M M- GM- MGMP-) 2

1	2	3	4	5	6	7	8	9	10	11	12	13	14	15	16
-	-	P	-	P	-	P	-	P	D	-	P	-	-	-	-
-	-	me	-	ra	-	to	-	s	p	-	na	-	-	-	-
-	-	P	-	P	-	P	-	P	D	-	P	-	-	-	-
-	-	hai	-	e	-	k	-	che	h	-	ra	-	-	-	-
-	-	S'	-	S'	-	N	-	D	-	-	D	-	-	-	-
-	-	de	-	khe	-	jo	-	u	s	-	ko	-	-	-	-
-	-	N	-	D	-	N	-	S'	-	P	-	D	-	P	-
-	-	jhu	-	me	-	b	-	ha	-	-	-	-	-	-	r
-	-	P	-	P	-	P	-	P	D	-	P	-	-	-	-
-	-	ga	-	lo	-	me	-	kr.	l	-	ti	-	-	-	-
-	-	P	-	P	-	P	-	P	D	-	P	-	-	-	-
-	-	k	li	yon	-	ka	-	mau	-	-	sm	-	-	-	-
-	-	S'	-	S'	-	N	-	D	-	-	D	-	-	-	-
-	-	aan	-	kho	-	me	-	ja	-	-	du	-	-	-	-
-	-	N	-	D	-	N	-	S'	-	-	-	R'	-	-	-
-	-	ho	-	ton	-	me	-	pya	-	-	-	-	-	-	-
G'	-	G'	-	G'	-	R'	-	S'	-	-	S'	P	-	D	-
-	r	bn	-	da	-	ye	-	khu	-	-	b	su	-	r	t
S'	-	-	-	M'	-	G'	-	R'	-	-	-	-	-	-	-
ka	-	-	m	k	-	re	-	ga	-	-	-	-	-	-	-
-	-	G'	-	G'	-	R'	-	S'	-	S'	-	P	-	D	-
-	-	di	l	ki	-	du	ni	ya	-	me	-	a	p	na	-
S'	-	-	-	M'	-	G'	-	R'	-	-	-	-	P	D	N
na	-	-	m	k	-	re	-	ga	-	-	-	-	me	ri	n
S'	-	-	S'	-	-	-	-	-	-	-	-	-	S'	-	N
z	r	-	se	-	-	-	-	-	-	-	-	-	kho	-	to
D	-	-	D	-	-	-	-	-	-	-	-	-	D	-	P
ya	-	-	ro	-	-	-	-	-	-	-	-	-	me	-	ri

M	-	-	M	-	-	-	-	-	-	-	G	-	-	M	-
mn	-	-	zi	-	l	-	-	-	-	-	hai	-	-	k	-
P	-	-	-	-	-	-	-	-	-	G'	-	G'	-	R'	-
han	-	-	-	-	-	-	-	-	-	pa	-	pa	-	k	h
S'	-	S'	-	P	-	D	-	S'	-	-	-	M'	-	G'	-
te	-	hain	-	b	-	da	-	na	-	-	m	k	-	re	-
R'	-	-	-	-	-	G'	R'	S'	-	-	-	-	-	-	-
ga	-	-	-	-	-	-	-	-	-	-	-	-	-	-	-

39. PHULON SA CHEHRA TERA

Film: Anadi (1993)	Music: Anand Milind
Lyrics: Sameer	Singer: Udit Narayan
Taal: Daadra	Chord: PS'G' MDR' S=C

phoolon sa chehara tera, kaliyon see muskaan hai
rang tera dekh ke, roop tera dekh ke, kudarat bhee hairaan hai

hiranee ke jaisee aankhen hain teree, bulabul ke jaisee teree chaal hai
maathe pe tere sooraj kee laalee, resham ke jaisa tera baal hai
chaand sitaaron mein, ek hazaaron mein, tera yahaan koee javaab nahin hai
shokh bahaaron mein, mahake nazaaron mein, baag mein bhee aisa gulaab nahin hai
khushiyon mein, too hai palee, har gam se anjaan hai
rang tera dekh ke, roop tera dekh ke, kudarat bhee hairaan hai
phoolon sa chehara tera...

saare jahaan mein phaila ujaala, dharatee pe aaee chamak chaandanee
hothon pe tere geeton kee maala, saanson mein teree khulee raaginee
baind bajaoonga, jhoom ke gaoonga, byaah tera hoga, baaraat sajegee
sajanee sajan honge, log magan honge, meree duaon se vo raat sajegee
lambee ho teree umar, ham sabaka aramaan hai
rang tera dekh ke, roop tera dekh ke, kudarat bhee hairaan hai
phoolon sa chehara tera...

Vinod Kumar

PHULON SA CHEHRA TERA

dha 1	ti 2	na 3	na 4	dhi 5	na 6	dha 1	ti 2	na 3	na 4	dhi 5	na 6
prelude:											
G GP P D- N- R' R' R' R' R' S' N											
D D D S' S' S' DNN- MP—											
R'	-	-	R'	-	-	R'	-	-	S'	D	-
chhm	-	-	chhm	-	-	chhm	-	-	chhm	chhm	-
-	-	R'	-	R'	-	R'	-	-	S'	D	-
-	-	chhm	-	chhm	-	chhm	-	-	chhm	chhm	-
-	-	S'	-	S'	-	S'	-	-	D	P	-
-	-	chhm	-	chhm	-	chhm	-	-	chhm	chhm	-
P	-	D	-	P	-	P	-	-	-	-	-
chhm	-	chhm	-	chhm	-	chhm	-	-	-	-	-
music: D S' R' G'- P D S' R' –											
R' R' R' D D R' R' R' D D P D M P--											
P	-	-	D	-	-	R'	-	-	-	-	-
fu	-	-	lo	-	-	sa	-	-	-	-	-
S'	-	R'	-	G'	-	R'	-	-	-	-	-
che	h	ra	-	te	-	ra	-	-	-	-	-
S'	-	R'	-	G'	-	R'	-	S'	-	D	-
k	li	yon	-	si	-	mu	s	ka	-	n	-
D	S'	-	-	-	-	-	-	-	-	-	-
hai	-	-	-	-	-	-	-	-	-	-	-
P	-	D	D	D	-	P	-	D	D	-	-
rn	-	g	te	ra	-	de	-	kh	ke	-	-
P	-	D	D	D	-	P	-	D	D	-	-
ru	-	p	te	ra	-	de	-	kh	ke	-	-
P	-	D	-	S'	-	N	-	D	-	P	-
ku	d	r	t	bhi	-	hai	-	ra	-	n	-
P	-	-	-	-	-	-	-	-	-	-	-
hai	-	-	-	-	-	-	-	-	-	-	-
interlude:											
NN NN P DN N P DN N G											
M PD D D NS'R' NS'N P-											

```
G'  G'  G'  R'  G'  N  R'
aa  aa  aa  aa  aa  aa aa

D   D   D   D   P   D  M  P
aa aa   aa aa aa aa   aa aa

P' G' R' x4 G' R' S' x4
PDN  G'R'N  NR'N  PD
D N D P M D P---
```

R'	-	R'	G'	S'	-	R'	-	-	R'	-	-
hi	r	ni	-	ke	-	jai	-	-	si	-	-

R'	-	R'	G'	S'	-	R'	-	-	R'	-	-
aan	-	khen	-	hain	-	te	-	-	ri	-	-

D	-	R'	-	S'	-	D	-	P	-	D	-
bu	l	bu	l	ke	-	jai	-	si	-	te	-

M	-	D	-	P	-	P	-	-	-	-	-
ri	-	cha	-	l	-	hai	-	-	-	-	-

music: R'- N D P   D- P M P   R'- N D P   M P D P-

R'	-	R'	G'	S'	-	R'	-	-	R'	-	-
ma	-	the	-	pe	-	te	-	-	re	-	-

R'	-	R'	G'	S'	-	R'	-	-	R'	-	-
su	-	r	j	ki	-	la	-	-	li	-	-

D	-	R'	-	S'	-	D	-	P	-	D	-
re	-	shm	-	ke	-	jai	-	sa	-	te	-

M	-	D	-	P	-	P	-	-	-	-	-
ra	-	ba	-	l	-	hai	-	-	-	-	-

M	-	M	P	D	-	P	-	D	-	-	-
chan	-	d	si	ta	-	ro	-	me	-	-	-

M	-	M	P	D	-	P	-	D	-	-	-
e	-	k	h	za	-	ro	-	me	-	-	-

M	M	-	P	D	-	P	-	D	-	D	-
te	ra	-	y	han	-	ko	-	ee	-	j	-

S'	-	S'	D	D	-	P	-	-	-	-	-
va	-	b	n	hin	-	hai	-	-	-	-	-

M	-	M	P	D	-	P	-	D	-	-	-
sho	-	kh	b	ha	-	ro	-	me	-	-	-

M	-	M	P	D	-	P	-	D	-	-	-
m	h	ke	n	za	-	ro	-	me	-	-	-
M	-	M	P	D	-	P	-	D	-	D	-
ba	-	g	me	bhi	-	ae	-	sa	-	gu	-
S'	-	S'	D	D	-	P	-	-	-	-	-
la	-	b	n	hin	-	hai	-	-	-	-	-
P	-	-	D	-	-	R'	-	-	-	-	-
khu	shi	-	yon	-	-	me	-	-	-	-	-
S'	-	R'	-	G'	-	R'	-	-	-	-	-
tu	-	hai	-	p	-	li	-	-	-	-	-
S'	-	R'	-	G'	-	R'	-	S'	-	D	-
h	r	gm	-	se	-	an	-	ja	-	n	-
D	S'	-	-	-	-	-	-	-	-	-	-
hai	-	-	-	-	-	-	-	-	-	-	-
P	-	D	D	D	-	P	-	D	D	-	-
rn	-	g	te	ra	-	de	-	kh	ke	-	-
P	-	D	D	D	-	P	-	D	D	-	-
ru	-	p	te	ra	-	de	-	kh	ke	-	-
P	-	D	-	S'	-	N	-	D	-	P	-
ku	d	r	t	bhi	-	hai	-	ra	-	n	-
P	-	-	-	-	-	-	-	-	-	-	-
hai	-	-	-	-	-	-	-	-	-	-	-

interlude:
N S' G'- G' R'- S' D -2
D N R' R' N- D - N N D M P--

R'	-	R'	G'	S'	-	R'	-	-	R'	-	-
sa	-	re	-	j	-	han	-	-	me	-	-
R'	-	R'	G'	S'	-	R'	-	-	R'	-	-
fai	-	la	-	u	-	ja	-	-	la	-	-
D	-	R'	-	S'	-	D	-	P	-	D	-
dh	r	ti	-	pe	-	aa	-	yi	-	ch	-
M	-	D	-	-	P	P	-	-	-	-	-
m	k	chan	-	-	d	ni	-	-	-	-	-

music: R'- N D P   D- P M P   R'- N D P   M P D P-

R'	-	R'	G'	S'	-	R'	-	-	R'	-	-
ho	-	ton	-	pe	-	te	-	-	re	-	-
R'	-	R'	G'	S'	-	R'	-	-	R'	-	-
gi	-	to	-	ki	-	ma	-	-	la	-	-
D	-	R'	-	S'	-	D	-	P	-	D	-
san	-	so	-	me	-	te	-	ri	-	ghu	-
M	-	D	-	-	P	P	-	-	-	-	-
li	-	ra	-	-	gi	ni	-	-	-	-	-
M	-	M	P	D	-	P	-	D	-	-	-
bain	-	d	b	ja	-	un	-	ga	-	-	-
M	-	M	P	D	-	P	-	D	-	-	-
jhu	-	m	ke	ga	-	un	-	ga	-	-	-
M	-	M	P	D	-	P	-	D	-	D	-
bya	-	h	te	ra	-	ho	-	ga	-	ba	-
S'	-	S'	D	D	-	P	-	-	-	-	-
ra	-	t	s	je	-	gi	-	-	-	-	-
M	M	M	P	D	-	P	-	D	-	-	-
s	j	ni	s	j	n	hon	-	ge	-	-	-
M	-	M	P	D	-	P	-	D	-	-	-
lo	-	g	m	g	n	hon	-	ge	-	-	-
M	-	M	P	D	-	P	-	D	-	D	-
me	-	ri	du	aa	-	on	-	se	-	vo	-
S'	-	S'	D	D	-	P	-	-	-	-	-
ra	-	t	s	je	-	gi	-	-	-	-	-
P	-	-	D	-	-	R'	-	-	-	-	-
lm	-	-	bi	-	-	ho	-	-	-	-	-
S'	-	R'	-	G'	-	R'	-	-	-	-	-
te	-	ri	-	u	-	m	r	-	-	-	-
S'	-	R'	-	G'	-	R'	-	S'	-	D	-
h	m	s	b	ka	-	a	r	ma	-	n	-
D	S'	-	-	-	-	-	-	-	-	-	-
hai	-	-	-	-	-	-	-	-	-	-	-

P	-	D	D	D	-	P	-	D	D	-	-
rn	-	g	te	ra	-	de	-	kh	ke	-	-
P	-	D	D	D	-	P	-	D	D	-	-
ru	-	p	te	ra	-	de	-	kh	ke	-	-
P	-	D	-	S'	-	N	-	D	-	P	-
ku	d	r	t	bhi	-	hai	-	ra	-	n	-
P	-	-	-	-	-	-	-	-	-	-	-
hai	-	-	-	-	-	-	-	-	-	-	-

40. PYAR KI KASHTI ME

Film: Kaho na pyar hai (2000)	Music: Rajesh Raushan
Lyrics: Saavan Kumar	Singer: Udit Narayan, Alka
Taal: Kaharwa	Chord: MDS' S=C#

haeeya shee chu ru haiya hun haiya hun haiya hun
pyaar kee kashtee mein, laharon kee mastee mein
pavan ke shor shor mein chalen ham zor zor mein
gagan se door, gagan se door

vahaan kya pyaar milega, chaman ka phool khilega
jise dil dhoondh raha hai, kya vo diladaar milega
la la la la la la la la

vahaan sach honge sapane, banenge gair bhee apane
dil kee baaraat sajegee, milenge saajan apane
la la la la la la la la
mainne suna kya suna, jo kaha kya kaha, jaana hai bahut door
pyaar kee kashtee mein, laharon kee mastee mein.......

pyaar ko pyaar mile to, nazar kaheen lag na jae
mile jeevan mein ham tum, kaheen phir bichhad na jaen
la la la la la la la la
nazar kya lage vahaan par, hai pyaar hee pyaar jahaan par
na bichhaden milane vaale, jahaan hon sab dil vaale
la la la la la la la la
to chalo chale, haan chalen, yoon milake, haan milake, hoke khushee mein choor
pyaar kee kashtee mein, laharon kee mastee mein......
ho raama ho ho raama ho

Vinod Kumar

PYAR KI KASHTI ME

dha 1	ge 2	n 3	ti 4	n 5	ke 6	dhi 7	n 8	dha 1	ge 2	n 3	ti 4	n 5	ke 6	dhi 7	n 8

prelude:
M R M R M R M M R-
dhk chik ...

flute: D S'-- R' M'--

DD   D   DD PP   D
haiya   shi   churu haiya hu

PP   D PP D   D D D DN   N   S'---------R'
haiya hu haiya hu   pyar ki kshti me hen--------e

dha 1	ge 2	n 3	ti 4	n 5	ke 6	dhi 7	n 8	dha 1	ge 2	n 3	ti 4	n 5	ke 6	dhi 7	n 8
								D	-	D	D	-			
								pya	-	r	ki	-			
D	-	N̲	-	N̲	-	S'	-	D	-	D	-	D			
k	sh	ti	-	me	-	he	-	l	h	ro	-	ki			
D	-	N̲	-	N̲	-	S'	-	D	D	-	P	-			
m	s	ti	-	me	-	he	-	p	v	n	ke	-			
P	-	M	P	-	M	M	-	D	D	-	P	-			
sho	-	r	sho	-	r	me	-	ch	len	-	h	m			
P	-	M	P	-	M	M	-	D	D	-	N̲	-			
zo	-	r	zo	-	r	me	-	g	g	n	se	-			
S'	-	-	-	-	-	N̲	-	D	-	-					
du	-	-	-	-	-	u	-	u	-	r					
								R'	R'	-	D	-			
								v	han	-	kya	-			
N̲	-	N̲	S'	S'	-	S'	-	R'	R'	S'	D	-			
pya	-	r	mi	le	-	ga	-	ch	m	n	ka	-			
N̲	-	N̲	S'	S'	-	S'	-	M	P	-	N̲	-			
fu	-	l	khi	le	-	ga	-	ji	se	-	di	l			
D	-	D	P	P	-	P	-	G̲	M	-	D	-			
dhun	-	dh	r	ha	-	hai	-	kya	vo	-	di	l			
P	-	-	M	M	-	M	-	M	P	-	N̲	-			
da	-	r	mi	le	-	ga	-	l	l	-	l	-			

D	-	D	P	-	P	P	-	-	-	-	G	M	-	D	-
l	-	l	l	-	l	la	-	-	-	-	l	l	-	l	-

P	-	P	M	-	-	-	-	-	-	-	R'	R'	-	D	D
l	-	l	la	-	-	-	-	-	-	-	v	han	-	s	ch

N	-	N	S'	S'	S'	S'	-	-	-	-	R'	R'	-	D	-
hon	-	ge	-	s	p	ne	-	-	-	-	b	nen	-	ge	-

N	-	N	S'	S'	S'	S'	-	-	-	-	M	-	M	N	-
gai	-	r	bhi	a	p	ne	-	-	-	-	di	l	ki	ba	-

D	-	-	P	P	-	P	-	-	-	-	G	M	-	D	-
ra	-	t	s	je	-	gi	-	-	-	-	mi	len	-	ge	-

P	-	P	-	M	M	M	-	-	-	-	M	P	-	N	-
sa	-	j	n	a	p	ne	-	-	-	-	l	l	-	l	-

D	-	D	P	-	P	P	-	-	-	-	G	M	-	D	-
l	-	l	l	-	l	la	-	-	-	-	l	l	-	l	-

P	-	P	M	-	-	-	-	-	-	-					
l	-	l	la	-	-	-	-	-	-	-					

```
MM      PM M PM    M PM  M  PM
mainne suna kya suna   jo kaha kya kaha
```

```
 MM  MM  M  S'
jana  bhut hai dur
```

```
D D  D  DN  N   S'
pyar ki kshti  me  hen.......
```

music: guitar:
```
D D P M P P P M G  G M D D P P P P
N N D P D D P G  G M D P M M M M
```

											R'	-	S'	D	-
											pya	-	r	ko	-

N	-	N	S'	S'	-	S'	-	-	-	-	R'	R'	S'	D	-
pya	-	r	mi	le	-	to	-	-	-	-	n	z	r	k	hin

N	N	N	S'	S'	-	S'	-	-	-	-	M	M	-	N	-
l	g	na	-	ja	-	ye	-	-	-	-	mi	le	-	jii	-

D	-	D	-	P	-	P	-	-	-	-	G	M	-	D	-
vn	-	me	-	hm	-	tum	-	-	-	-	k	hin	-	fi	r

P	P	-	M	M	-	M	-	-	-	-	M	P	-	N	-
bi	chh	d	n	ja	-	yen	-	-	-	-	l	l	-	l	-

D	-	D	P	-	P	P	-	-	-	-	-	G̲	M	-	D	-
l	-	l	l	-	l	la	-	-	-	-	-	l	l	-	l	-

| P | - | P | M | - | - | - | - | - | - | - | - | R' | R' | S' | D | - |
| l | - | l | la | - | - | - | - | - | - | - | - | n | z | r | kya | - |

| N̲ | N̲ | - | S' | S' | - | S' | - | - | - | - | - | R' | R' | - | S' | D |
| l | ge | - | v | han | - | p | r | - | - | - | hai | pya | - | r | hi |

| N̲ | - | N̲ | S' | S' | - | S' | - | - | - | - | - | M | P | P | N̲ | - |
| pya | - | r | j | han | - | p | r | - | - | - | n | bi | chh | den | - |

| D | - | D | - | P | - | P | - | - | - | - | - | G̲ | M | - | D | - |
| mi | l | ne | - | va | - | le | - | - | - | - | j | han | - | s | b |

| P | - | M | - | M | - | M | - | - | - | - | - | M | P | - | N̲ | - |
| hon | - | di | l | va | - | le | - | - | - | - | l | l | - | l | - |

| D | - | D | P | - | P | P | - | - | - | - | - | G̲ | M | - | D | - |
| l | - | l | l | - | l | la | - | - | - | - | l | l | - | l | - |

| P | - | P | M | - | - | - | - | - | - | - | - | | | | | |
| l | - | l | la | - | - | - | - | - | - | - | | | | | | |

M MM PM   M   PM M P M   M P M   M M MM   M S'
to chlo chlen han chlen yun mil ke han mil ke   ho ke khushi me chur

D D D D N̲ N̲   S'
pyar ki kshti   me hen.......

MM   M MM   G̲P M G̲P   M G̲P   M
haiya shi churu haiya hu haiya hu   haiya hu

D DD   N̲--- P D P M
ho rama ho ----ho------

M MM   P---- N̲ D P M
ho rama ho---- o -------

D DD   N̲   S' S'R' M' R'R' G̲'   R'S' R' N̲R' S'
ho rama ho   ho rama ho rama ho   rama ho rama ho

MM   M MM   G̲P M G̲P M   G̲P   M
haiya shi churu haiya hu haiya hu   haiya hu

41. RAJA KO RANI SE PYAR

Film: Akele ham akele tum (1995) Lyrics: Majrooh Sultanpuri Taal: Kaharwa	Music: Anu Malik Singer: Udit Narayan, Alka, Kumar Shanu Chord: GPN PNR' RMD S=C

raaja ko raanee se pyaar ho gaya,
pahalee nazar mein pahala pyaar ho gaya
dil jigar donon ghaayal hue, teere nazar dil ke paar ho gaya

raahon se raahen, baahon se baahen, milake bhee milatee nahin
hota hai aksar aramaan kee kaliyaan, khil ke bhee khilatee nahin
phir bhee na jaane kyoon nahin maane -2
deevaana dil beqaraar ho gaya
raaja ko raanee se pyaar ho gaya...

raanee ko dekho, nazaren milee to aankhen churaane lagee
karatee bhee kya vo sar ko jhuka ke kangana ghumaane lagee
raaja ne aisa jaadoo chalaaya -2 na karate karate ikaraar ho gaya
raaja ko raanee se pyaar ho gaya...

RAJA KO RANI SE PYAR

dhage	nti	nke	dhin	dhage	nti	nke	dhin	dhage	nti	nke	dhin	dhage	nti	nke	dhin
12	34	56	78	12	34	56	78	12	34	56	78	12	34	56	78
	G	P	N	D	P	D	P	G	-	M	-G	R	-	-	-
	ra	ja	ko	ra	-	ni	se	pya	-r	ho	-g	ya	-	-	-
-	G	P	N	D	P	R'	N	S'	-	S'	-S'	S'	-	-	-
-	ph	li	n	zr	me	ph	la	pya	-r	ho	-g	ya	-	-	-
-	S'	-	R'	G'	-	R'	S'	N	-N	-	S'	R'	-	-	-
-	dil	-	ji	gr	-	do	no	gha	-yl	-	hu	e	-	-	-
-	M'	R'	S'	N	-	D	N	R'	-N	S'	-D	N	-P	D	-
-	ti	re	n	zr	-	dil	ke	pa	-r	ho	-g	ya	-	aa	-
P															
aa															
															R'	-
														ho	-

-	R'	-S'	-N	R'	-	R'	-	-	D	NS'	-N	D	-	P	-
-	ra	-hon	-se	ra	-	hen	-	-	ba	-hon	-se	ba	-	hen	-
-	S'	-S'	-S'	G'	-	R'	S'	R'	-	-	-	-	R'	-	-
-	mil	-ke	-bhi	mil	-	ti	n	hin	-	-	-	-	ho	-	-
-	R'	-S'	-N	R'	R'	R'	R'	-	DN	-S'	N	D	D	P	-
-	ho	-ta	-hai	a	k	s	r	-	ar	-man	-ki	k	li	yan	-
-	S'	-S'	-S'	G'	-	-R'	S'	R'	-	-	-	-	-	G'	-
-	khil	-ke	-bhi	khil	-	-ti	n	hin	-	-	-	-	-	ae	-
-	G'	-S'	-N	D	-	P	M	-	DN	-S'	G'	R'	-	R'	S'
-	fir	-bhi	-n	ja	-	ne	-	-	kyu	-n	hin	ma	-	ne	-
-	R'	S'	N	D	-	D	N	R'	-N	S'	D	N	-P	D	-
-	di	va	na	dil	-	be	k	ra	-r	ho	g	ya	-	-	-
P	G	P	N	D	P	D	P	G	-	M	-G	R	-	-	-
-	ra	ja	ko	ra	-	ni	se	pya	-r	ho	-g	ya	-	-	-
-	-	-	-	-	-	-	-	-	-	-	-	-	-	R'	-
-	-	-	-	-	-	-	-	-	-	-	-	-	-	ae	-
-	R'	-S'	-N	R'	-	R'	-	-	D	NS'	-N	D	-	P	-
-	ra	-ni	-ko	de	-	kho	-	-	nz	-ren	-mi	li	-	to	-
-	S'	-S'	-S'	G'	-	R'	S'	R'	-	-	-	-	-	R'	-
-	aan	-khen	-chu	ra	-	ne	l	gi	-	-	-	-	-	ho	-
-	R'	-S'	-N	R'	-	R'	-	-	DN	-S'	N	D	-	P	-
-	kr	-ti	-bhi	kya	-	vo	-	-	sr	-ko	-jhu	ka	-	ke	-
-	S'	-S'	-S'	G'	-	-R'	S'	R'	-	-	-	-	-	G'	-
-	kng	-na	-ghu	ma	-	-ne	-l	gi	-	-	-	-	-	ho	-
-	G'	-S'	-N	D	-	P	M	-	DN	-S'	G'	R'	-	R'	S'
-	ra	-ja	-ne	ae	-	sa	-	-	ja	-du	-ch	la	-	ya	-
-	R'	S'	N	D	D	D	N	R'	-N	S'	D	N	-P	D	-
-	na	kr	te	kr	te	i	k	ra	-r	ho	-g	ya	-	-	-
P	G	P	N	D	P	D	P	G	-	M	-G	R	-	-	-
-	ra	ja	ko	ra	-	ni	se	pya	-r	ho	-g	ya	-	-	-
-	G	P	N	D	P	R'	N	S'	-	S'	-S'	S'	-	-	-
-	ph	li	n	zr	me	ph	la	pya	-r	ho	-g	ya	-	-	-

42. RADHA KAISE NA JALE

Film: Lagaan (2001)	Music: A. R. Rahman
Lyrics: Javed Akhtar	Singer: Udit Narayan, Asha, Vaishali
Taal: Daadra	Chord: RMD PNR' MDS' S=C

madhuban mein jo kanhaiya kisee gopee se mile
kabhee muskaaye, kabhee chhede, kabhee baat kare
raadha kaise na jale, raadha kaise na jale
aag tanaman mein lage
raadha kaise na jale, raadha kaise na jale

madhuban mein bhale kaanha kisee gopee se mile
man mein to raadha ke hee prem ke hain phool khile
kis liye raadha jale, kis liye raadha jale
bina soche samajhe
kis liye raadha jale, kis liye raadha jale

o gopiyaan taare hain, chaand hai raadha
phir kyon hai usako bisavaas (vishvaas) aadha
kaanha jee ka jo sada idhar-udhar dhyaan rahe
raadha bechaaree phir ko apane pe kya maan rahe
gopiyaan aanee-jaanee hain, raadha to man kee raanee hai
saanjh sakhaare, jamuna kinaare,
raadha raadha hee kaanha pukaare
baahon ke haar jo daale koee kaanha ke gale
raadha kaise na jale...

na dir dir na dir dir na dir dir dinna ho
man mein hai raadhe ko kaanha jo basaaye
to kaanha kaahe ko use na batae
prem kee apanee alag, bolee alag, bhaasa (bhaasha) hai
baat nainon se ho, kaanha kee yahee aasa (aasha) hai
kaanha ke ye jo naina hain jinamen gopiyon ke chaina hain -2
milee najariya, huee baavariya goree goree see koee gujariya
kaanha ka pyaar kisee gopee ke man mein jo pale
kis liye raadha jale, raadha jale, raadha jale
kis liye raadha jale raadha kaise na jale
raadha kaise na jale...

Vinod Kumar

RADHA KAISE NA JALE

dha 1	dhi 2	na 3	dha 4	tun 5	na 6	dha 1	dhi 2	na 3	dha 4	tun 5	na 6
								P	P	D	-
								m	dhu	b	n
S'	-	S'	D	P	-	S'	-	S'	D	P	-
me	-	jo	kn	hai	-	ya	-	ki	si	go	-
R'	-	R'	D	P	-	-	-	P	P	D	-
pi	-	se	mi	le	-	-	-	k	bhi	mu	s
S'	-	S'	D	P	-	S'	S'	-	D	P	-
ka	-	ye	k	bhi	-	chhe	de	-	k	bhi	-
R'	-	R'	D	P	-	-	-	M	M	P	-
ba	-	t	k	re	-	-	-	ra	dha	kai	-
D	-	D	M	R	-	-	-	M	M	P	-
se	-	n	j	le	-	-	-	ra	dha	kai	-
D	-	D	D	D	-	-	-	M	M	P	-
se	-	n	j	le	-	-	-	aa	g	t	n
D	-	D	D	D	-	-	-	M	M	P	-
m	n	me	l	ge	-	-	-	ra	dha	kai	-
N	-	N	N	N	-	-	-	M	M	P	-
se	-	n	j	le	-	-	-	ra	dha	kai	-
D	-	D	D	D	-	-	-				
se	-	n	j	le	-	-	-				
								P	P	D	-
								m	dhu	b	n
S'	-	S'	D	P	-	S'	-	S'	D	P	-
me	-	bh	le	kan	-	ha	-	ki	si	go	-
R'	-	R'	D	P	-	-	-	P	P	D	-
pi	-	se	mi	le	-	-	-	mn	me	to	-
S'	S'	-	D	P	-	S'	-	S'	D	P	-
ra	dha	-	ke	hi	-	pre	-	m	ke	hain	-
R'	-	R'	D	P	-	-	-	M	M	P	-
fu	-	l	khi	le	-	-	-	kis	li	ye	-

D	D	-	M	R	-	-	-	M	M	P	-
ra	dha	-	j	le	-	-	-	kis	li	ye	-
D	D	-	D	DS'	-	-	-	M	M	P	-
ra	dha	-	j	le	-	-	-	bi	na	so	-
D	-	D	-	D	-	-	-	M	M	P	-
che	-	s	m	jhe	-	-	-	kis	li	ye	-
N	N	-	N	N	-	-	-	M	M	P	-
ra	dha	-	j	le	-	-	-	kis	li	ye	-
D	D	-	D	D	-	-	-				
ra	dha	-	j	le	-	-	-				

interlude:
DS'S' S'R'R' R'G'G' R'-S'-R'-----S'- D
G'P'G' G'G' G'P'G'
G'G' D'D' G'R' P'P' G'R' G'P'G' G'G' G'P'G'
G'G' P'D' P'G' P'P' G'S'R'

						R'	-	R'	R'	S'	-
						o	-	go	pi	yan	-
N	-	N	-	R'	-	-	-	S'	N	S'	N
ta	-	re	-	hain	-	-	-	chan	-	d	hai
D	-	-	D	-	-	-	-	R'	S'	S'	N
ra	-	-	dha	-	-	-	-	fi	r	kyu	hai
N	N	-	R'	-	-	-	-	N	N	S'	N
u	s	-	ko	-	-	-	-	vi	sh	va	s
D	-	-	D	-	-	-	-	R'	R'	R'	-
aa	-	-	dha	-	-	-	-	kan	ha	jii	-
R'	G'	R'	S'	S'	-	R'	G'	R'	S'	N	S'
to	-	jo	s	da	-	i	dh	r	u	dh	r
R'	-	R'	P	D	-	-	-	R'	R'	R'	-
dhya	-	n	r	he	-	-	-	ra	dha	be	-
R'	G'	R'	S'	S'	-	R'	G'	R'	S'	N	S'
cha	-	ri	ko	fi	r	a	p	ne	pe	kya	-
R'	-	R'	P	D	-	R	D	D	D	-	M*
ma	-	n	r	he	-	go	pi	yan	aa	-	ni
M*	-	P	G	R	-	R	D	D	D	-	M*
ja	-	ni	-	hain	-	ra	dha	to	m	n	ki

M*	-	P	G	R	-	R	D	D	D	D	-
ra	-	ni	-	hai	-	san	jh	s	kha	re	-
D	S'	S'	S'	S'	-	R'	R'	R'	R'	R'	-
ymu	na	ki	na	re	-	ra	dha	ra	dha	hi	-
S'	S'	D	D	R'	-	R'	S'	-	S'	D	-
kan	ha	pu	ka	re	-	oe	hoe	-	oe	hoe	-
-	-	P	P	D	-	D	S'	S'	D	P	-
-	-	ba	hon	ke	-	ha	-	r	jo	da	-
D	S'	S'	D	P	-	D	R'	R'	S'	D	-
le	-	ko	ee	kan	-	ha	-	ke	g	le	-
-	-	M	M	P	-	D	-	D	M	M	-
-	-	ra	dha	kai	-	se	-	n	j	le	-
R	-	M	M	P	-	D	-	D	D	S'	-
-	-	ra	dha	kai	-	se	-	n	j	le	-
-	-	M	M	P	-	D	-	D	D	D	-
-	-	aa	g	t	n	m	n	me	l	ge	-
-	-	M	M	P	-	N	-	N	N	N	S'
-	-	ra	dha	kai	-	se	-	n	j	le	-
D	-	M	M	P	-	N	S'	D	D	D	-
-	-	ra	dha	kai	-	se	-	n	j	le	-
D	S'	S'	S'	R'	R'	R'	G'	G'	R'	S'	-
na	dir	dir	na	dir	dir	na	dir	dir	din	na	-
R'	-	-	-	-	-	S'	R'	-	S'	D	-
ho	-	-	-	-	-	-	-	-	-	-	-
D	S'	S'	S'	R'	R'	R'	G'	G'	R'	S'	-
na	dir	dir	na	dir	dir	na	dir	dir	din	na	-
R'	-	-	-	-	-	-	-	-	-	-	-
ho	-	-	-	-	-	-	-	-	-	-	-
S'	S'	S'	D	D	D	M	M	M	G	S	-
na	dir	dir	na	dir	dir	na	dir	dir	din	na	-
R	-	-	-	-	-	M	-	-	D	-	-
ho	-	-	-	-	-	-	-	-	-	-	-

S'	S'	S'	D	D	D	M	M	M	G	S	-
na	dir	dir	na	dir	dir	na	dir	dir	din	na	-
R	-	-	-	-	-	-	-	-	-	-	-
ho	-	-	-	-	-	-	-	-	-	-	-

interlude: M P N N N N S' N D- D- 2
          S' S' D-M M G – S S R- M- D-2

								D	D	P	M
								m	n	me	hai
P	N	N	-	R'	-	-	-	N	N	S'	N
ra	-	dhe	-	ko	-	-	-	kan	ha	jo	b
D	-	-	D	-	-	-	-	N	-	P	M
sa	-	-	ye	-	-	-	-	to	-	kan	ha
P	N	N	-	R'	-	-	-	S'	N	S'	N
ka	-	he	-	ko	-	-	-	u	se	na	b
D	-	-	D	-	-	-	-	R'	-	R'	-
ta	-	-	ye	-	-	-	-	pre	-m	ki	-
R'	G'	R'	S'	S'	S'	R'	G'	R'	S'	N	S'
a	p	ni	a	l	g	bo	-	li	a	l	g
R'	-	P	-	D	-	-	-	R'	R'	R'	-
bha	-	sa	-	hai	-	-	-	ba	t	nai	-
G'	-	R'	S'	R'	-	G'	-	R'	S'	N	S'
no	-	se	ho	kan	-	ha	-	ki	y	hi	-
R'	-	P	-	D	-	R	D	D	D	-	M*
aa	-	sa	-	hai	-	kan	ha	ke	ye	-	jo
M*	-	P	G	R	-	R	D	D	D	D	M*
nai	-	na	-	hain	-	chhi	ne	go	pi	yon	ke
M*	-	P	G	R	-	R	D	<u>D</u>	D	M*	M*
chai	-	na	-	hain	-	kan	ha	ke	ye	-	jo
G	M*	P	N	PM*	GR	R	D	<u>D</u>	D	M*	M*
nai	-	na	-	hain	-	chhi	ne	go	pi	yon	ke
G	M*	P	N	PM*	GR	R	D	D	D	D	D
chai	-	na	-	hain	-	mi	li	n	z	ri	ya
D	S'	S'	S'	S'	S'	R'	R'	S'	S'	N	-
hu	ee	ba	v	ri	ya	go	ri	go	ri	si	-

N	N	D	D	D	M*	-	-	P	P	D	-
ko	ee	gu	z	ri	ya	-	-	kan	ha	ka	-
D	S'	S'	D	P	-	D	S'	S'	D	P	-
pya	-	r	ki	si	-	go	-	pi	ke	m	n
D	R'	R'	S'	D	-	-	-	P	P	D	-
me	-	jo	p	le	-	-	-	kis	li	e	-
R'	R'	-	D	P	-	S'	S'	-	D	P	-
ra	dha	-	j	le	-	ra	dha	-	j	le	-
D	D	-	M	MR	-	-	-	M	M	P	-
ra	dha	-	j	le	-	-	-	ra	dha	kai	-
D	-	D	D	D				P	P	D	-
se	-	n	j	le	-	-	-	kis	li	e	-
R'	R'	-	D	D	-	-	-	M	M	P	-
ra	dha	-	j	le	-	-	-	ra	dha	kai	-
D	-	D	D	D	-	-	-	M	M	P	-
se	-	n	j	le	-	-	-	kis	li	e	-
D	D	-	M	MR	-	-	-				
ra	dha	-	j	le	-	-	-				

```
M  MP    DD  DS'  MM    PD   D DS'
kisliye  radha jle  radha kaise n jle

M MP    NN  NN   M MP    DD  DD
kislie  radha jle   kislie  radha jle

DPDPDP--- PMPMPM-  MGMGMG-  RGMPD-
aa----------------------------------------

R'S'  S'R'G'-  R'S'S'ND-    DP PDS' DP PMGR
aa----------------          aa---------------- 2

MRM  DMD    S'DS'   R'S'R'
de-re  de-re   de-re    deren

M'M'  M'P'  G'R'  G'R'S'-R'    M'M'  M'P'  G'R'   G'R'S'-R'
dhan  dhan  dhan  dha---n      dhan  dhan  dhan   dha----n


R'R'  S'R'G'-R'  R'R'    NS'R'-S'
tan   dha-n     dhan    dha-n
```

```
S'ND    NDP  PDN    D  D  MR   GSR   MM
dha--   dha--- dha-t  di  di dhat  dha-n dha-t

S  R  MM     S  R  M--
di di dha-t    di di dha--

DD     S'R'  R'  R'R'  NN   NS'S'   N  DD   RM   DP   M   GR
radha kaise n    jle  radha  kai-se  n  jle  radha kaise n   jle
```

43. RUK JA O DIL DEEWANE

Film: Dil vale dulhaniya le jaayeinge (1995)	Music: Jatin Lalit
Lyrics: Anand Bakshi	Singer: Udit Narayan
Taal: Kaharwa	Chord: DR̲'G' PNR' S=C#

ruk ja o dil deevaane poochhoon to main zara
ladakee hai ya hai jaadoo khushaboo hai ya nasha
paas vo aaye to chhoo ke main dekhoon zara, ruk ja o dil….

dekhe vo idhar hansake bekhabar thaam ke dil ham khade hain
gumsum si nazar usaki hai magar honthon pe shikave bade hain
baat ban jae to main baat chhedoon zara

sharma vo gaee ghabara vo gaee mainne jo usako pukaara
ye dil le liya usane kar diya aankhon hee aankhon mein ishaara
jaan bhee jae to gam na karoon main zara

mahafil mein haseen too hee to nahin roothee too kisalie akelee
jis pe yoon fida ye dil ho gaya vo to hai teree ek sahelee
maan vo jae to baahon mein le loon zara

RUK JA O DIL DEEWANE

dhage	nti	nke	dhin	dhage	nti	nke	dhin	dhage	nti	nke	dhin	dhage	nti	nke	dhin
12	34	56	78	12	34	56	78	12	34	56	78	12	34	56	78

```
prelude:
D N R̲'D  N R̲' R'N  N R̲' R' G'
P'----- G'------  P'----- G'------
M*' G' R' R̲' NR' N-  G' R' R̲' N DN R̲'-
NR'D- NR'D- G'G'G'G'-
```

dhage	nti	nke	dhin	dhage	nti	nke	dhin	dhage	nti	nke	dhin	dhage	nti	nke	dhin
D	DD	-	-	-	R'	-N	-D	N	-P	-	-	-	-	-	-
ru	kja	-	-	-	o	-dil	-di	va	-ne	-	-	-	-	-	-

D	-D	-	-	-	R'	-N	-D	D	-	-	-	-	-	-	D
pu	-chhu	-	-	-	to	-main	-z	ra	-	-	-	-	-	-	are

D	-D	-	-	-	R'	-N	-D	N	-P	-	-	-	-	-	-
ld	-ki	-	-	-	hai	-ya	-hai	ja	-du	-	-	-	-	-	-

D	-D	-	-	-	R'	-N	-D	D	-	-	-	-	-	-	-
khush	-bu	-	-	-	hai	-ya	-n	sha	-	-	-	-	-	-	-

D	G'G'	-	-	N	G'G'	-	-	DN	-R'	R'R'	-N	N	-	-	-
pa	svo	-	-	aa	yeto	-	-	chhuke	-main	dekhu	-z	ra	-	-	-

interlude:
G' R'G' N NR'-
G'R' R' R' R'R' N- R'- 2
(DN R'R'R'R' R' R' R'R'R'R' R' R'
R' R' R' G' R' R' R'
NR' R'R'R'R' R' R' R'R'R'R' R' R'
R' R' R' M*' G' R' G'-) 2
G-P-P-D-N- D-N- R' R' NR' D-

R'	NR'	-N	-D	D	-	-	-	R'	NR'	-N	-D	D	-	-	-
de	khe-	-vo	-i	dhr	-	-	-	hns	ke-	-be	-kh	br	-	-	-

P	DN	-	-	NR'	-R'	-	R'	R'G'	-R'	-	-	-	-	-	-
tha	mke	-	-	dil	-h	-m	kh	de	-hain	-	-	-	-	-	-

R'	NR'	-N	-D	D	-	-	-	R'	NR'	-N	-D	D	-	-	-
gum	sum	-si	-j	zr	-	-	-	us	ki	-hai	-m	gr	-	-	-

P	DN	-	-	NR'	-R'	-	R'	R'G'	-R'	-	-	-	-	-	-
ho	thope	-	-	shik	-ve	-	b	de	-hain	-	-	-	-	-	-

N	G'G'	-	-	N	G'G'	-	-	DN	-R'	R'R'	-N	N	-	-	-
ba	tbn	-	-	ja	yeto	-	-	mainba	-t	chhedu	-z	ra	-	-	-

D	DD	-	-	-	R'	-N	-D	N	-P	-	-	-	-	-	-
ru	kja	-	-	-	o	-dil	-di	va	-ne	-	-	-	-	-	-

interlude:
R'R'G' R' R'- NR'R' N D- PDN R' N R'-
N R' R' R' R' R'- G'G'G'G'
R' R' G'R' R' R'- G'G'G'G'
R' G' M*' R' G' G'- G'G'G'G'
N G'N R'- R'-R'G' R'
N R'D N R'D R'R'R' R' R'-

R'	NR'	-N	-D	D	-	-	-	R'	NR'	-N	-D	D	-	-	-
mh	fil	-me	-hn	sii	-	-	-	tu	hi	-to	-n	hin	-	-	-

P	DN	-	-	NR'	-R'	-	R'	R'G'	-R'	-	-	-	-	-	-
ru	thitu	-	-	kis	lie	-	a	ke	-li	-	-	-	-	-	-

R'	NR'	-N	-D	D	-	-	-	R'	NR'	-N	-D	D	-	-	-
jis	pe	-yun	-fi	da	-	-	-	ye	dil	-ho	-g	ya	-	-	-
P	DN	-	-	NR'	-R'	-	R'	R'G'	-R'	-	-	-	-	-	-
vo	tohai	-	-	te	riik	-	s	he	-li	-	-	-	-	-	-
N	G'G'	-	-	N	G'G'	-	-	DN	-R'	R'R'	-N	N	-	-	-
ma	nvo	-	-	ja	yeto	-	-	bahon	-me	lelun	-z	ra	-	-	-
D	DD	-	-	-	R'	-N	-D	N	-P	-	-	-	-	-	-
ru	kja	-	-	-	o	-dil	-di	va	-ne	-	-	-	-	-	-
D	-D	-	-	-	R'	-N	-D	D	-	-	-	-	-	-	-
pu	-chhu	-	-	-	to	-main	-z	ra	-	-	-	-	-	-	-

44. TAAL SE TAAL MILAO

Film: Taal (1999)	Music: A. R. Rahman
Lyrics: Anand Bakshi	Singer: Udit Narayan, Alka
Taal: Kaharwa	Chord: GPN PNR' S=C

dil ye bechain ve, raste pe nain ve -2
jindadee behaal hai, sur hai na taal hai
aaja saanvariya aa aa aa aa
taal se taal mila ho..o.., taal se taal mila

saavan ne aaj to, mujhako bhigo diya
haaye meree laaj ne, mujhako dubo diya..aa..
aisee lagee jhadee, sochoon main ye khadee
kuchh mainne kho diya, kya mainne kho diya..
chup kyoon hai bol too, sang mere dol too
meree chaal se chaal mila
taal se taal mila o..o.., taal se taal mila

maana anajaan hai, too mere vaaste
maana anajaan hoon, main tere vaaste
main tujhako jaan loon, too mujhako jaan le
aa dil ke paas aa.. is dil ke raaste
jo tera haal hai, vo mera haal hai
is haal se haal mila o..o.., taal se taal mila ho..o
taal se taal mila

Vinod Kumar

TAAL SE TAAL MILAO

dhage	nti	nke	dhin	dhage	nti	nke	dhin	dhage	nti	nke	dhin	dhage	nti	nke	dhin
12	34	56	78	12	34	56	78	12	34	56	78	12	34	56	78
dhak	chik	nk	dhum	dhak	chik	nk	dhum	dhak	chik	nk	dhum	dhak	chik	nk	dhum

prelude:

flute: R' G' R' P' M' G' R' S' R'
        S' R' S' M' G' R' S' S' N

	nti	nke	dhin	dhage	nti	nke	dhin	dhage	nti	nke	dhin	dhage	nti	nke	dhin
	P	P	P	N	-	DN	P	-	P	P	P	N	-	DN	P
	dil	ye	be	chai	-n	ve-	-	-	rs	te	pe	nai	-n	ve	-
-	P	P	P	N	-	DN	P	-	P	P	P	N	-	DN	P
-	jind	di	be	ha	-l	hai	-	-	sur	hai	na	ta	-l	hai	-
-	R'	R'	R'	R'	R'	N	-	R'	-	S'	-	N	-	DN	P
-	aa	ja	san	v	ri	ya	-	aa	-	aa	-	aa	-	aa-	-
-	PS'	-N	-P	G	-	-M	-M	P	-	-	-	D	D	N	-
-	ta-	-l	se	ta	-	-l	-mi	la	-	-	-	o	-	-	-
-	PS'	-N	-P	G	-	-M	-M	P	-	-	-	-	-	-	-
-	ta-	-l	se	ta	-	-l	-mi	la	-	-	-	-	-	-	-

interlude:

violin: R' G' R' P' M' G' R' R' S'
         S' R' S' M' G' R' S' S' N

dhage	nti	nke	dhin	dhage	nti	nke	dhin	dhage	nti	nke	dhin	dhage	nti	nke	dhin
M*	P	D		P	-P	D	M*	-	M*	P	D	P	-P	P	-
sa	vn	ne		aa	-j	to	-	-	mujh	ko	bhi	go	-di	ya	-
-	P	D	S'	D	S'S'	S'	-	-	D	S'	G'	R'	-R'	R'	-
-	hay	me	ri	la	-j	ne	-	-	mujh	ko	du	bo	-di	ya	-
S'	N	D	-	P	-	-	-	-	-	-	-	-	-	-	-
-	-	-	-	-	-	-	-	-	-	-	-	-	-	-	-
-	M*	P	D	P	-P	S'	P	-	M*	P	D	P	-P	P	-
-	sa	vn	ne	aa	-j	to	-	-	mujh	ko	bhi	go	-di	ya	-
-	P	D	S'	D	S'S'	S'	-	-	D	S'	G'	R'	-R'	R'	-
-	hay	me	ri	la	-j	ne	-	-	mujh	ko	du	bo	-di	ya	-
-	S'	R'	G'	S'G'	-G'	G'	-	-	R'	G'	D	DG'	G'	R'	-
-	ae	si	l	gi-	-jh	di	-	-	so	chun	main	ye-	-kh	di	-
-	R'	G'	M*'	G'M*'	-M*'	M*'	-	-	D'	M*'	G'	R'	-R'	R'	-
-	kuchh	main	ne	kho-	-di	ya	-	-	kya	main	ne	kho	-di	ya	-
-	R'	R'	G'	S'G'	-R'	S'	-	-	S'	S'	R'	NR'	-S'	N	-
-	chup	kyu	hai	bo-	-l	tu	-	-	sng	me	re	do-	-l	tu	-

-	-	N	N	-	NR'	-R'	R'	S'	G'	-S'	-N	D	-	-	-
-	-	me	ri	-	cha-	-l	se	cha	-	-l	-mi	la	-	-	-
NR'	S'N	D	P	-	PS'	N	P	G	-	-M	M	P	-	-	PG'
-	-	-	-	-	ta-	-l	se	ta	-	-l	mi	la	-	-	-
R'	S'	N	D	P											
o	-	-	-	-											

interlude:
violin: R' G' R' P' M' G' R' R' S'
       S' R' S' M' G' R' S' S' N

	M*	P	D	P	-P	N	P	-	M*	P	D	P	-P	P	-
	ma	na	an	ja	-n	hai	-	-	tu	me	-re	va	-s	te	-
-	P	D	S'	D	S'S'	S'	-	-	D	S'	G'	R'	-R'	R'	-
-	ma	na	an	ja	-n	hu	-	-	main	te	re	va	-s	te	-
-	S'	R'	G'	S'G'	-G'	G'	-	-	G'	R'	S'	DG'	G'	R'	-
-	main	tujh	ko	ja	-n	lun	-	-	tu	mujh	ko	ja-	-n	le	-
-	R'	G'	M*'	G'M*'	-M*'	M*'	-	-	-	-	-	-	-	M*'	D'
-	aa	dil	ke	pa	-s	aa	-	-	-	-	-	-	-	i	s
M*'	-	G'	R'	-	-R'	R'		-	-	-	-	-	-	-	-
di	-l	ke	ra	-	-s	te	-	-	-	-	-	-	-	-	-
-	R'	R'	G'	S'G'	-R'	S'	-	-	S'	S'	R'	NR'	-S'	N	-
-	jo	te	ra	ha	-l	hai	-	-	vo	me	ra	ha	-l	hai	-
-	-	N	N	-	NR'	-R'	R'	S'	G'	-S'	-N	D	-	-	-
-	-	i	s	-	ha	-l	se	ha	-	-l	mi	la	-	-	-
NR'	S'N	D	P	-	PS'	N	P	G	-	M	M	P	-	-	-
o	-	-	-	-	ta-	-l	se	ta	-	-l	mi	la	-	-	-
D	D	N	P	-											
o	-	-	-	-											

Vinod Kumar

45. TUM PAAS AAYE

Film: Kuchh Kuchh hota hai (1998)	Music: Jatin Lalit
Lyrics: Sameer	Singer: Udit Narayan, Alka
Taal: Kaharwa	Chord: MDS' P<u>N</u>R' S=D

tum paas aae, yoon muskurae, tumane na jaane kya sapane dikhae
ab to mera dil, jaage na sota hai, kya karoon haay,
kuchh kuchh hota hai...

na jaane kaisa ehasaas hai, bujhatee nahin hai kya pyaas hai
kya nasha is pyaar ka, mujhape sanam, chhaane laga
koee na jaane kyon chain khota hai, kya karoon haay,
kuchh kuchh hota hai...

kya rang laee meree dua, ye ishq jaane kaise hua
baicheniyon mein man, na jaane kyon aane laga
tanhaee mein dil yaaden sanjota hai, kya karoon haay,
kuchh kuchh hota hai...

sad
jaan-e-vafa ho ke beqaraar, barason kiya mainne intazaar
par kabhee toone nahin ye tab kaha, jo ab kahaan
dil bebasee mein chupake se rota hai, kya karoon haay,
kuchh kuchh hota hai...

TUM PAAS AAYE

dha	ge	n	ti	n	ke	dhi	n	dha	ge	n	ti	n	ke	dhi	n
1	2	3	4	5	6	7	8	1	2	3	4	5	6	7	8

prelude:
S'------ S'R'S'<u>N</u> S'
aa------------------

 P D <u>N</u>-- D P M S
aa----------------

<u>G</u>------ R <u>G</u> M <u>G</u> M- R-
aa------------------

.NSR.<u>N</u>S   .<u>N</u>S .<u>N</u>S .<u>N</u>S RS-
aa----------   aa--------------------

```
RG S-  RG S-
S G D P-P PM G-P- -2
G'G'G' R' G' R' G' R'
R'R'R' S' R' S' R' S'
N S' R' S' N D P M P- P-


N   DP  MD   M N D
tum pas aaye  u----


N    DP MD     PM- S' NDP-
yun  muskurae  u--------
```

		N	-	-	D	-	P	M	-	D	-	-	-	-	-
		tum	-	-	pa	-	s	aa	-	ye	-	-	-	-	-
-	-	N	-	-	D	-	P	M	-	D	-	-	-	-	-
-	-	yun	-	-	mu	s	ku	ra	-	ye	-	-	-	-	-
-	-	P	D	-	P	-	M	G	-	P	-	S	-	-	-
-	-	tu	m	-	ne	-	n	ja	-	ne	-	kya	-	-	-
-	-	P	M	-	D	-	P	M	-	-	-	M	-	-	-
-	-	s	p	-	ne	-	di	kha	-	-	-	ye	-	-	-
-	-	M	M	-	P	-	D	R'	-	-	-	S'	-	-	-
-	-	a	b	-	to	-	me	ra	-	-	-	dil	-	-	-
-	-	M	-	-	P	-	D	R'	-	R'	-	S'	-	-	-
-	-	ja	-	-	ge	-	n	so	-	ta	-	hai	-	-	-
-	-	D	-	-	P	M	-	G	-	R	-	G	-	S	-
-	-	kya	-	-	k	run	-	ha	-	-	-	ye	-	-	-
-	-	P	M	-	P	M	-	M	-	M	-	M	-	-	MP
-	-	ku	chh	-	ku	chh	-	ho	-	ta	-	hai	-	-	-
D	-	D	-	-	P	M	-	G	-	R	-	G	-	S	-
-	-	kya	-	-	k	run	-	ha	-	-	-	ye	-	-	-
-	-	P	M	-	D	P	-	M	-	M	-	M	-	-	-
-	-	ku	chh	-	ku	chh	-	ho	-	ta	-	hai	-	-	-

```
interlude:
S- R-  (S'NDPx4)
S- R-  (NDPMx4)
flute: R'--- DD P  P M M R-
synthe: R RS R RS RSRMRS.N
flute: R' NN D D P P M-
synthe: M- R- MPDN-   S'NDPM-
```

D	-	-	N	-	-	S'	-	R'	-	-	-	N	-	D	-
na	-	-	ja	-	-	ne	-	kai	-	-	-	sa	-	-	-

P	-	-	D	-	-	N	-	S'	-	-	-	-	-	-	-
a	h	-	sa	-	-	s	-	hai	-	-	-	-	-	-	-

D	-	-	N	-	-	S'	-	R'	-	-	-	N	-	D	-
mi	l	-	ti	-	-	n	-	hin	-	-	-	hai	-	-	-

P	-	-	D	-	-	N	-	S'	-	-	-	-	-	-	-
kya	-	-	pya	-	-	s	-	hai	-	-	-	-	-	-	-

M	-	D	P	-	-	M	M	R	-	G	S	-	-	-	-
kya	-	n	sha	-	-	i	s	pya	-	r	ka	-	-	-	-

-	-	M	G	-	R	-	S	R	-	S	.N	-	-	-	-
-	-	mu	jh	-	pe	-	s	nm	-	-	-	-	-	-	-

S	-	-	G	-	-	G	-	G	-	M	D	-	-	-	-
chha	-	-	ne	-	-	l	-	ga	-	-	-	-	-	-	-

-	-	M	-	-	P	-	D	R'	-	-	-	S'	-	-	-
-	-	ko	-	-	ee	-	n	ja	-	-	-	ne	-	-	-

-	-	M	-	-	P	-	D	R'	-	R'	-	S'	-	-	-
-	-	kyu	-	-	chai	-	n	kho	-	ta	-	hai	-	-	-

-	-	D	-	-	P	M	-	G	-	R	-	G	-	S	-
-	-	kya	-	-	k	run	-	ha	-	-	-	ye	-	-	-

-	-	P	M	-	P	M	-	M	-	M	-	M	-	-	MP
-	-	ku	chh	-	ku	chh	-	ho	-	ta	-	hai	-	-	-

D	-	D	-	-	P	M	-	G	-	R	-	G	-	S	-
-	-	kya	-	-	k	run	-	ha	-	-	-	ye	-	-	-

-	-	P	M	-	D	P	-	M	-	M	-	M	-	-	-
-	-	ku	chh	-	ku	chh	-	ho	-	ta	-	hai	-	-	-

interlude:
DNS'-D- PDN-P- S'NDPM-

M GM GM GMPDP MGR
aa--------------------

G- RG RG RGMPD DPM
aa--------------------

piano: D S' N D P M D

```
PD—PD    MR-   MR-
he ------    hu----  hu---

SRS  D  P- M-    D P P M
aa--------------    aa-------

synthe: S' R' S' N S' R' G'-
R' S' R' M' R' S' N
S' – N S' N S' R' S' –
D—P D S' M-
```

D	-	-	N	-	-	S'	-	R'	-	-	-	N	-	D	-
kya	-	-	ran	-	-	g	-	la	-	-	-	yi	-	-	-
P	-	-	D	-	-	N	-	S'	-	-	-	-	-	-	-
me	-	-	ri	-	-	du	-	aa	-	-	-	-	-	-	-
D	-	-	N	-	-	S'	-	R'	-	-	-	N	-	D	-
ye	-	-	i	-	-	shq	-	ja	-	-	-	ne	-	-	-
P	-	-	D	-	-	N	-	S'	-	-	-	-	-	-	-
kai	-	-	se	-	-	hu	-	aa	-	-	-	-	-	-	-
-	-	M	-	D	P	-	M	G	-	P	-	S	-	-	-
-	-	be	-	-	chai	-	ni	yon	-	me	-	chai	-	-	-n
-	-	M	-	-	R	-	S	R	-	S	.N	-	-	-	-
-	-	na	-	-	ja	-	ne	kyu	-	-	-	-	-	-	-
-	-	S	-	-	G	-	G	G	-	M	D	-	-	-	-
-	-	aa	-	-	ne	-	l	ga	-	-	-	-	-	-	-
-	-	M	M	-	P	-	D	R'	-	-	-	S'	-	-	-
-	-	t	n	-	ha	-	ee	me	-	-	-	dil	-	-	-
-	-	M	-	-	P	-	D	R'	-	R'	-	S'	-	-	-
-	-	ya	-	-	den	-	sn	jo	-	ta	-	hai	-	-	-
-	-	D	-	-	P	M	-	G	-	R	-	G	-	S	-
-	-	kya	-	-	k	run	-	ha	-	-	-	ye	-	-	-
-	-	P	M	-	D	M	-	M	-	M	-	M	-	-	MP
-	-	ku	chh	-	ku	chh	-	ho	-	ta	-	hai	-	-	-
D	-	D	-	-	P	M	-	G	-	R	-	R	-	S	-
-	-	kya	-	-	k	run	-	ha	-	-	-	ye	-	-	-
-	-	P	M	-	P	M	-	M	-	M	-	M	-	-	-
-	-	ku	chh	-	ku	chh	-	ho	-	ta	-	hai	-	-	-

Vinod Kumar

46. TUMSE MILNA BATEIN KARNA

Film: Tere Naam (2003)	Music: Himesh Reshamiya
Lyrics: Sameer	Singer: Udit Narayan, Alka
Taal: Kaharwa	Chord: PN$\underline{G}$' RMD PNR' S=C

tumase milana, baaten karana, bada achchha lagata hai
kya hai ye, kyoon hai ye, kya khabar, haan magar, jo bhee hai, bada achchha lagata hai

teree chhotee-chhotee baat, teree har ek mulaakaat
tadapaaye mujhako, lamha-lamha tera saath-2
kya hai ye, kyoon hai ye, kya khabar, haan magar,
 jo bhee hai, bada achchha lagata hai

bahake-bahake mere din, mahakee-mahakee meree shaam
kore aanchal pe sada, main to likhoon tera naam-2
kya hai ye, kyoon hai ye, kya khabar, haan magar,
 jo bhee hai, bada achchha lagata hai

TUMSE MILNA BATEIN KARNA

dhage	nti	nke	dhin	dhage	nti	nke	dhin	dhage	nti	nke	dhin	dhage	nti	nke	dhin
12	34	56	78	12	34	56	78	12	34	56	78	12	34	56	78

prelude:
PD N N P P R- S'N D D N N P-
PD N N P P R- RG P P S' S' N-
PD N N P P R- S' N D D N N P-
S'N DP S'N DP ND PM ND PM

D P $\underline{G}$ $\underline{G}$ M D P--

													P	-	N
													tum	-	se
D	N	D	P	-	P	-	D	P	D	P	M	-	-	D	P
mil	-	na	-	-	ba	-	te	kr	-	na	-	-	-	b	da
$\underline{G}$	-	$\underline{G}$	-	-	MM	-D	-	P	-	N	S'	R'	$\underline{G}$'	-	R'
a	ch	chha	-	-	lg	-ta	-	hai	-	-	-	-	kya	-	hai
R'	$\underline{G}$'	-	R'	R'	$\underline{G}$'	-	R'	R'	-$\underline{G}$'	-	R'	R'	-R'	-	S'
ye	kyu	-	hai	ye	kya	-	kh	br	-han	-	m	gr	-jo	-	bhi
N	D	-	-	-	-	D	P	$\underline{G}$	-	$\underline{G}$	-	-	MM	-D	-
hai	-	-	-	-	-	b	da	a	ch	chha	-	-	lg	-ta	-

P	-	-	-	-
hai	-	-	-	-

interlude:

M'G' S' P'- M'- 2 G' G' M' G' R' N – 2 G' N R'—G'M'P'-
N N P P R MG R R N N D- S' N D D N N P-

														R'	S'
														te	ri
N	S'	R'	S'	N	-	S'	N	D	N	S'	N	D	-	D	D
chho	ti	chho	ti	ba	-t	te	ri	hr	ik	mu	la	ka	-t	t	d
N	N	D	P	G	-	R	R	G	G	P	P	P	-	R	R
pa	ye	mu	jh	ko	-	lm	ha	lm	ha	te	ra	sa	-th	lm	ha
G	G	P	P	P	-	-	-	-	-	-	-	-	G'	-	R'
lm	ha	te	ra	sa	-th	-	-	-	-	-	-	-	kya	-	hai
R'	G'	-	R'	R'	G'	-	R'	R'	-G'	-	R'	R'	-R'	-	S'
ye	kyu	-	hai	ye	kya	-	kh	br	-han	-	m	gr	-jo	-	bhi
N	D	-	-	-	-	D	P	G	-	G	-	-	MM	-D	-
hai	-	-	-	-	-	b	da	a	ch	chha	-	-	lg	-ta	-

P	-	-	-	-
hai	-	-	-	-

interlude: M'G' S' P'- M'- 2 G' G' M' G' R' N – 2 G' N R'—G'M'P'-
NNPPR MGRRNND- S'NDDNNP-

														R'	S'
														bah	ke
N	S'	R'	S'	N	-	S'	N	D	N	S'	N	D	-	D	D
bah	ke	me	re	din	-	mah	ki	mah	ki	me	ri	sha	-m	ko	re
N	N	D	P	G	-	R	R	G	G	P	P	P	-	R	R
aan	chl	pe	s	da	-	main	to	li	khu	te	ra	na	-m	main	to
G	G	P	P	P	-	-	-	-	-	-	-	-	G'	-	R'
li	khu	te	ra	na	-m	-	-	-	-	-	-	-	kya	-	hai
R'	G'	-	R'	R'	G'	-	R'	R'	-G'	-	R'	R'	-R'	-	S'
ye	kyu	-	hai	ye	kya	-	kh	br	-han	-	m	gr	-jo	-	bhi
N	D	-	-	-	-	D	P	G	-	G	-	-	MM	-D	-
hai	-	-	-	-	-	b	da	a	ch	chha	-	-	lg	-ta	-

P	-	-	-	-
hai	-	-	-	-

Vinod Kumar

47. TU CHEEZ BADI HAI MAST

Film: Mohra (1994)	Music: Viju Shah
Lyrics: Anand Bakshi	Singer: Udit Narayan, Kavita Krishna..
Taal: Kaharwa	Chord: S̲G̲P S=D#

PNS'---------- NS'PNMPMPPNS'N- -S'N- -2
PP-PNN-NN DD-D MM-M
PNDN DPDN S'NDS'NDP-
P N S'--- P R' S'---
too cheez badee hai mast mast too cheez badee hai mast (2)
(nahin tujhako koee hosh hosh - 2) usapar joban ka josh josh
nahin tera nahin tera koee dosh dosh,
madahosh hai too har vakt vakt

ko: too cheez badee hai mast mast too cheez badee hai mast - 2

aashiq hai tera naam naam – 2 dil lena dena kaam kaam
meree baahen meree baahen mat thaam thaam
badanaam hai too madamast mast
too cheez badee hai mast mast too cheez badee hai mast - 2

.NSGMPNS'G'R'---------- G'R'NDMG
GMDS'R'G'R'N-PS'—
S'- S'S'S'S'S' NNNN DDDD PNDP
MDMM GMGG RPRR SGSS .NSRGMPDN
S'-N-D-P- S'-N-D-P- S'-N-D-P
bol zara too jaane mahabubii mujhamen aisee kya hai khubii - 2
too ik resham kee dor dor, too ek resham kee dor dor
teree chaal pe aashiq mor mor
teree zulf ghanee, teree zulf ghanee chitachor chor
ghanaghor ghata mad mast mast
too cheez badee hai mast mast too cheez badee hai mast - 2

ko: PNS'------ NS'PNMPMPPNS'N- -S'N- -2
PP-P NN-N DD-D MM-M
PNDN DPDN S'NDS'NDP-
P N S'---- P R' S'----
ye dil teree aankhon mein dooba ban ja meree too mahabooba - 2
mat teer najar ke maar maar – 2 ye chot lagegee aar paar
aasaan, aasaan samajh mat yaar yaar ye pyaar bada hai sakht sakht
too cheez badee hai mast mast too cheez badee hai mast - 2

nahin tujhako koee hosh hosh usapar joban ka josh josh
nahi tera nahin tera koii dosh dosh madahosh hai tu har vaqt vaqt
too cheez badee hai mast mast too cheez badee hai mast - 2

aashiq hai tera naam naam, dil lena dena kaam kaam
merii bahen merii mat thaam thaam,
badanaam hai tu madamast mast
too cheez badee hai mast mast too cheez badee hai mast - 4

TU CHEEZ BADI HAI MAST

| dhage | nti | nke | dhin | dhage | nti | nke | dhin | dhage | nti | nke | dhin | dhage | nti | nke | dhin |
12	34	56	78	12	34	56	78	12	34	56	78	12	34	56	78
prelude: .N S'—G G R S -4															
P	-N	-	S'	-	-	-	-	NS'	PN	MP	MP	PN	S'N	-S'	N-
P	-N	-	S'	-	-	-	-	NS'	PN	MP	MP	PN	S'N	-S'	N-
PP	-P	NN	-N	DD	-D	MM	-M	PN	DN	DP	DN	S'N	DS'	ND	P-
P	-N	-	S'	-	-	-	-	P	-R'	-	S'	-	-	-	S tu
.N chi	SS zb	S di	G hai	R ms	RR tm	R st	S tu	.N chi	SS zb	S di	GR hai-	S ms	S t	- -	PP nhin
MP tujh	P ko	PN ko-	DN ee-	PD ho-	DP sh,ho	-P -sh	PP us	MP pr	PS' jo-	NN bn	D ka	PD jo-	DP sh,jo	-P -sh	S' nhin
S' te	S' ra	- -	- -	- -	- -	- -	S' nhin	S' te	S' ra	S' ko	S' ee	N do	ND shdo	-D -sh	PP md
PD ho-	DP shhai	P tu	M hr	G vk	GR tv	R kt	S tu	.N chi	SS zb	S di	G hai	R ms	RR tm	R st	S tu
.N chi	SS zb	S di	GR hai-	S ms	S t	- -	P aa	MP shik	P hai	PN te-	D ra	PD na-	DP mna	-P -m	PM dil
MP le-	PS' na-	N de	D na	PD ka-	DP mka	-P -m	S' me	S' ri	S' ba	S' hen	- -	- -	- -	- -	S' me
S' ri	S' ba	S' hen	S'S' mt	N tha	ND mtha	-P -m	PP bd	PD na-	DP mhai	P tu	MM bd	G ms	GR tm	R -st	S tu

.N	SS	S	G	R	RR	R	S	.N	SS	S	GR	S	S	-	
chi	zb	di	hai	ms	tm	st	tu	chi	zb	di	hai-	ms	t	-	-

.N S G M P N S' G' R'---------- G'-R'-N-D-M G-
G M D S' R' G' R' N-P S'—
S'- S' S' S' S' S' N N N N D D D D P N D P
MDMM GMGG RPRR SGSS .NSRG MPDN
S'- N-D-P-   S'- N-D-P-   S'- N-D-P-
music: as above

P	PS'	N	NS'	-	-	-	S'	N	S'R'	R'	S'	-	-	ND	P
bo	l,z	ra	tu-	-	-	-	ja	ne	mah	bu	bi	-	-	-	-
M	MD	D	D	-	-	-	-	N	D	M	MP	-	-	-	-
mujh	me-	ae	si	-	-	-	-	kya	hai	khu	bi-	-	-	-	-
P	PN	D	DN	-	-	-	N	S'	ND	P	M	-	-	GR	S
bo	lz	ra	tu-	-	-	-	ja	ne	mah	bu	bi	-	-	-	-
.N	.NR	R	R	-	-	M	-	M	GR	S	S	-	-	-	P
mujh	me-	ae	si	-	-	-	-	kya	hai-	khu	bi	-	-	-	tu
MP	P	PN	DN	PD	DP	-P	PM	MP	PS'	N	DD	PD	DP	-P	PS'
ik	re	shm	ki-	do-	rdo	-r	teri	cha-	lpe	aa	shik	mo-	rmo	-r	teri
S'	S'S'	S'	-	-	-	-	PS'	S'	S'S'	S'	S'N	N	DD	-P	PP
jul	f,gh	ni	-	-	-	-	teri	jul	f,gh	ni	chit	cho	rcho	-r	ghn
PD	DP	P	MM	G	GR	-R	S	.N	SS	SG	G	R	RR	R	S
gho-	rgh	ta	bd	ms	tm	-st	tu	chi	zb	di-	hai	ms	tm	st	tu
.N	SS	S	GR	S	S	-									
chi	zb	di	hai-	ms	t	-									

interlude: .N S'—G G R S -4

P	-N	-	S'	-	-	-	-	NS'	PN	MP	MP	PN	S'N	-S'	N-
P	-N	-	S'	-	-	-	-	NS'	PN	MP	MP	PN	S'N	-S'	N-
PP	-P	NN	-N	DD	-D	MM	-M	PN	DN	DP	DN	S'N	DS'	ND	P-
P	-N	-	S'	-	-	-	-	P	-R'	-	S'	-	-	-	-
P	PS'	N	NS'	-	-	-	S'	N	S'R'	R'	S'	-	-	ND	P
ye	dil	te	ri-	-	-	-	aan	kho	me	du	ba	-	-	-	-
M	MD	D	D	-	-	-	-	N	DP	M	MP	-	-	-	-
bn	ja	me	ri	-	-	-	-	tu	mh	bu	ba	-	-	-	-

P	PN	D	DN	-	-	-	N	S'	ND	P	M	-	-	GR	S
ye	dil	te	ri-	-	-	-	aan	kho	me-	du	ba	-	-	-	-

.N	.NR	R	R	-	-	-	-	M	GR	S	S	-	-	-	PP
bn	ja	me	ri	-	-	-	-	tu	mh	bu	ba	-	-	-	mt

MP	PP	PN	DN	PD	DP	-P	-	-	-	-	-	-	-	-	PP
ti-	rn	zr	ke	ma-	rma	-r	-	-	-	-	-	-	-	-	mt

MP	PP	PN	DN	PD	DP	-P	PM	MP	PS'	N	D	PD	DP	-P	PS'
ti-	rn	zr	ke	ma-	rma	-r	ye-	cho-	tl	ge	gi	aa	rpa	-r	aa-

S'	-	-	-	-	-	-	-	-	-	-	-	-	-	-	PS'
sa	-	-	-	-	-	-	-	-	-	-	-	-	-	-	aa-

S'	S'S'	S'S'	S'N	N	DD	-P	P	PD	DP	P	M	G	GR	-R	S
sa	ns	mjh	mt	ya	rya	-r	ye	pya	rb	da	hai	s	khts	-kht	tu

.N	SS	S	G	R	RR	R	S	.N	SS	S	GR	S	S	-	
chi	zb	di	hai	ms	tm	st	tu	chi	zb	di	hai-	ms	t	-	

P'-------- N R' M'---   P'M' G' R' P'--   R' S' N-- G' R' S'--
aa-------aa------   aa------   aa------ aa------

S'NS' NDN DPD PMP MGM GRG S
aa--------------------------------------

48. TERE NAAM HAMNE KIYA HAI

Film: Tere Naam (2003)	Music: Himesh Reshamiya
Lyrics: Sameer	Singer: Udit Narayan, Alka
Taal: Kaharwa	Chord: RMD GPN S=C#

tere naam hamane kiya hai, jeevan apana saara sanam
pyaar bahut karate hain tumase, ishk hai too hamaara sanam

udit naaraayan
gulashan bhee to ab veeraana lagata hai
har aapana hamako begaana lagata hai
ham teree yaadon me khoye rahate hain
log hamen paagal deevaana kahate hain
tere bina-2 naamumakin hai
zindagee ka guzaara sanam

laagee chhoote na, laagee chhoote na, laagee chhoote na
ishk ka dhaaga toote na

nainon se bahate ashkon ke dhaaron mein
hamane tujhako dekha chaand-sitaaron mein
viraha kee agni mein pal-pal tapatee hai
ab to saansen teree maala japatee hai
tere lie-2 is duniya ka
har sitam hai ganvaara sanam
tere naam hamane kiya hai...

alaka yaagnik
neendon mein aankhon mein pyaase khvaabon mein
too hee too hai yaara mahakee saanson mein
har bechainee rah-rah ke ye kahatee hai
har dhadakan mein teree chaahat rahatee hai
tere bina naamumakin hai
zindagee ka guzaara sanam...

dooree hai majabooree hai tanhaee hai
teree yaad hamen kis mod pe laee hai
apanee to manzil hai teree raahon mein
jeena-marana hai ab teree baahon mein
tere lie is duniya ka
har sitam hai ganvaara sanam
tere naam hamane kiya hai...

sad
mar ke bhee na vaada apana todenge
ik dooje ka saath kabhee na chhodenge
apana to sadiyon janmon ka naata hai
jaan se jaan ko kaun juda kar paata hai
tere siva is dariya ka
nahin koee kinaara sanam
tere naam hamane kiya hai...

TERE NAAM HAMNE KIYA HAI

dhage 12	nti 34	nke 56	dhin 78	dhage 12	nti 34	nke 56	dhin 78	dhage 12	nti 34	nke 56	dhin 78	dhage 12	nti 34	nke 56	dhin 78

prelude:

```
S' N R' N- N – 4
R G M P M- M- M-
N D S' N D- P- P-
R G M P P- P- P-
N D P M M-M G M R
S' N R' N- N -4
```

dhage 12	nti 34	nke 56	dhin 78	dhage 12	nti 34	nke 56	dhin 78	dhage 12	nti 34	nke 56	dhin 78	dhage 12	nti 34	nke 56	dhin 78
D	N	S'	D	N	-	-	-	R'	-	S'	-N	N	-	-	-
te	-	re	-	na	-	-	-m	la	-	la	-l	la	-	-	-
D	N	S'	D	N	-	-	-	-	D	-P	-M	M	P	M	-
te	-	re	-	na	-	-	-m	-	hm	-ne	-ki	ya	hai	-	-
G	-M	R	R	GP	-P	-P	M	D	-	P	-M	M	-	-	DP
-	-	-	jii	vn	-a	-p	na	sa	-	ra	-s	nm	-	-	ho-
MG	MG	R	R	GP	-P	-P	M	D	-	P	-M	M	-	-	-
o-	--	-	jii	vn	-a	-p	na	sa	-	ra	-s	nm	-	-	-
D	N	S'	D	N	N	-	-	-	D	-P	M	M	P	M	-
pya	-	r	b	hu	t	-	-	-	kr	-te	hain	tum	se	-	-
G	-M	RR	R	GP	-P	-	M	D	-	P	-M	M	-	-	DP
-	-	-i	shk	hai-	-tu	-	h	ma	-	ra	-s	nm	-	-	ho-
MG	MG	RR	R	GP	-P	-P	M	D	-	P	-M	N	-	-	-
o-	--	-i	shk	hai	-tu	-	h	ma	-	ra	-s	nm	-	-	-

```
R' N M    R' N P
la la la  la la la

R'S'R'  N PN
la--    la lala
```

iske bad tere nam hmne kiya .... ki tyun bjaen aur la la la me gayen.

interlude:

```
R G M P M- M- M-
N D S' N D- P- P-
R G M P P- P- P-
N D P M M-M G M R
```

dhage 12	nti 34	nke 56	dhin 78	dhage 12	nti 34	nke 56	dhin 78	dhage 12	nti 34	nke 56	dhin 78	dhage 12	nti 34	nke 56	dhin 78
D	N	S'	N	D	N	N	N	M	P	P	M	-	-	-	-
gul	shn	bhi	ab	to	vii	ra	na	lg	ta	hai	-	-	-	-	-
D	N	S'	N	D	N	N	N	M'	P	P		-	-	-	-
hr	ap	na	hm	ko	be	ga	na	lg	ta	hai	-	-	-	-	-

D	N	S'	N	D	N	N	N	M	P	P	M	-	-	-	-
hm	te	ri	ya	do	me	kho	ye	rh	te	hain	-	-	-	-	-

D	NN	S'	N	D	N	N	N	M	P	P	-	-	-	-	-
lo	gh	me	pa	gl	di	va	na	kh	te	hain	-	-	-	-	-

G'	-	S'	-D	D	-	P	-	R'	S'R'	-S'	D	N	-M	P	M
te	-	re	-bi	na	-	-	-	te	-	-re	bi	na	-	-	-

D	N	S'	-D	N	-	-	-	-	D	-P	-M	MP	P	M	-
te	-	re	-bi	na	-	-	-	-	na	-mu	-m	kin	hai	-	-

G	-M	R	RR	GP	-P	-	M	D	-	P	-M	M	-	-	DP
-	-	-	zind	gi-	-ka	-	gu	za	-	ra	-s	nm	-	-	ho-

MG	MG	R	RR	GP	-P	-	M	D	-	P	-M	N	-	-	
o-	--	-	zind	gi	-ka	-	gu	za	-	ra	-s	nm	o-	-	-

interlude:
R R R P- 3

R' R' G'-- M' R' N R'--
aa------aa --------

R' R' R' G' - M' R' N R'
aa-----------------

R'R' R'S' R' S'N NS'N R' S'N NS'N R' S'
lagi chhute na, lagi chhute- na, lagi chhute- naaa

S'S' S' NS' R' NPN
ishq ka dhaga tu te- na

D	N	S'	N	D	N	N	N	M	P	P	M	-	-	-	-
nai	no	se	bh	te	ash	kon	ke	dha	ro	me	-	-	-	-	-

D	N	S'	N	D	N	N	N	M	P	P	-	-	-	-	-
hm	ne	tujh	ko	de	kha	chan	dsi	ta	ro	me	-	-	-	-	-

D	N	S'	N	D	N	N	N	M	P	-P	M	-	-	-	-
vir	ha	ki	ag	ni	me	pl	pl	tp	ti	-hai	-	-	-	-	-

D	N	S'	N	D	N	N	N	M	P	P	-	P'	M'	G'	R'
ab	to	san	se	te	ri	ma	la	jp	ti	hai	-	-	-	-	-

-	G'	S'	-D	D	-	P	-	R'	S'R'	-S'	D	N	-M	P	M
-	te	-re	-li	e	-	-	-	te	-	-re	-li	e	-	-	-

D	N	S'	-D	N	-	-	-	-	D	-P	-M	MP	P	M	-
te	-	re	-li	e	-	-	-	-	is	-du	-ni	ya	ka	-	-
G	-M	-R	-R	GP	-P	-	M	D	-	P	-M	M	-	-	DP
-	-	-hr	-si	tm	-hai	-	g	va	-	ra	-s	nm	-	-	ho-
MG	MG	RR	-R	GP	-P	-	M	D	-	P	-M	N	-	-	
o-	--	-hr	-si	tm	-hai	-	g	va	-	ra	-s	nm	-	-	

G'	S'	N
te	re	nam -3

49. UD JA KAALE KAWAN

Film: Gadar (2001)	Music: Uttam Singh
Lyrics: Anand Bakshi	Singer: Udit Narayan
Taal: Kaharwa	Chord: RPN S=C#

ud ja kale kavan tere munh vich khand pavaan
le ja tu sandesa mera main sadke javaan
bagon me fir jhule pad gaye pak gaiyaan mithiyaan ambiyaan
ye chhoti si zindagi te raatan lambiyaan lambiyaan
o ghar aaja pardesi, ki teree meree ik jindadi

happy
chham chham karta aaya mausam pyar ke geeton ka
raste pe ankhiyaan rasta dekhein bichhde meeton ka
aaj milan ki raat na chhedo baat judaaii vaali
main chup tu chup pyar sune ba pyar hi bole khaali
o ghar aaja pardesi

sad
o mitra o yara yari tod ke mt jana
maine jag chhoda tu mujhko chhod ke mat jana
aesa ho nahin sakta, ho jaaye to mat ghabraana
main daudi aaoongi, tu bas ik aavaaz lagaana
o ghar aaja pardesi--

kitni dard bhari hai, teri-meri prem kahaani
saat samunder jitna apni, aankhon men hai paani
main dil se , dil mujhse karta, hai jab teri baatein
saavan aane se pahle ho jaati hain barsaaten
o ghar aaja pardesi…

Vinod Kumar

parvat kitne unche, kitne gahre hote hain
kuchh mat puchho pyar pe kitne pahre hote hain
ishq me jaane kya ho jata, hai ye rab hi jaane
tod ke saarii deevarein, mil jaate hain deevaane
o le ja mujhe pardesi, ki teri meri ik jindadi

udit
chham chham karta aaya mausam pyar ke geeton ka
raste pe ankhiyaan rasta dekhein, bichhde meeton ka
saari saari raat jagaaye mujhko teri yaadein
mere saare geet bane mere dil ki fariyadein
o ghar aaja pardesi…..

UD JA KAALE KAWAN

dha	ge	n	ti	n	ke	dhi	n	dha	ge	n	ti	n	ke	dhi	n
1	2	3	4	5	6	7	8	1	2	3	4	5	6	7	8

prelude aur interlude:
P P P DP P P P P SR   P P P DP P - - -   -2

1	2	3	4	5	6	7	8	1	2	3	4	5	6	7	8
P	-	P	-	P	-	D	-	P	-	P	-	G	-	S	R
u	d	ja	-	ka	-	le	-	kan	-	van	-	te	-	re	-
P	-	P	P	P	-	D	-	P	-	-	-	-	-	-	-
mun	h	vi	ch	khn	d	pa	-	van	-	-	-	-	-	-	-
P	-	P	-	P	-	D	-	P	-	P	-	G	-	S	R
le	-	ja	-	tu	-	sn	-	de	-	sa	-	me	-	ra	-
P	-	P	P	P	-	D	-	P	-	-	-	-	-	-	-
main	-	s	d	ke	-	ja	-	van	-	-	-	-	-	-	-
-	G'	-	G'	G'	-	G'	-	R'	-	G'	-	R'	S'	S'	-
-	ba	-	go	me	-	fi	r	jhu	-	le	-	p	d	g	ye
S'	S'	R'	S'	D	P	D	S'	S'	S'	S'	-	-	-	-	-
p	k	g	eeyan	mi	thi	yan	-	am	bi	yan	-	-	-	-	-
-	S'	-	S'	S'	-	S'	-	-	N	R'	S'	N	D	D	P
-	ye	-	chho	ti	-	si	-	-	zin	-	d	gi	-	te	-
-	M	P	P	P	P	D	-	M	P	P	M	G	R	R	S
-	ra	-	tan	lm	bi	yan	-	lm	bi	yan	o	gh	r	aa	ja

S	R	R	P	P	-	-	-	-	-	-	P	M	P	M	G
p	r	de	-	si	-	-	-	-	-	-	ke	te	ri	me	ri

R	G	R	S	S	-	-	-	-	-	-
i	k	zin	d	ri	-	-	-	-	-	-

P P P DP P P P SR P P P DP P - - - -2

P'----------- R', R' G' M' ------
ho-------------------------

G'------- R' M'--- G' R' S'
ho----------------------

G	P	P	-	P	D	D	-	D	N	N	-	D	-	D	-
chh	m	chh	m	k	r	ta	-	aa	-	ya	-	mau	-	s	m

-	G	-P	P	P	-	D	P	P	-	-	-	-	-	-	-
-	pya	-r	ke	gi	-	to	-	ka	-	-	-	-	-	-	-

G	P	P	P	P	D	D	-	D	N	N	-	D	-	D	-
r	s	te	pe	an	khi	yan	-	r	s	ta	-	de	-	khe	-

-	P	P	P	P	-	D	P	P	-	-	-	-	-	-	-
-	bi	chh	de	mi	-	to	-	ka	-	-	-	-	-	-	-

G'	-	G'	G'	G'	-	G'	-	R'	-	G'	G'	R'	-	S'	-
aa	-	j	mi	l	n	ki	-	ra	-	t	n	chhe	-	do	-

S'	-	R'	S'	P	-	D	S'	S'	-	S'	-	-	-	-	-
ba	-	t	ju	da	-	ee	-	va	-	li	-	-	-	-	-

-	S'	-	S'	S'	-	S'	S'	N	-	R'	S'	N	-	D	P
-	main	-	chup	tu	-	chu	p	pya	-	r	su	ne	-	b	s

M	-	P	P	P	-	D	P	M	P	-	P	M	G	R	S
pya	-	r	hi	bo	-	le	-	kha	li	-	o	gh	r	aa	ja

S	R	R	P	P	-	-	-	-	-	-	P	M	P	M	G
p	r	de	-	si	-	-	-	-	-	-	ke	te	ri	me	ri

R	G	R	S	S	-	-	-	-	-	-
i	k	zin	d	ri	-	-	-	-	-	-

G	P	P	-	P	D	D	D	D	N	N	-	D	-	D	-
ki	t	ni	-	d	r	d	bh	ri	-	hai	-	te	-	ri	-

P	-	P	-	P	-	D	P	P	-	P	-	-	-	-	-
me	-	ri	-	pre	-	m	k	ha	-	ni	-	-	-	-	-

G	-	P	P	P	-	D	D	D	N	N	-	D	D	D	-
sa	-	t	s	mn	-	d	r	ji	t	na	-	a	p	ni	-
P	-	P	-	P	-	D	P	P	-	P	-	-	-	-	-
aan	-	kho	-	me	-	hai	-	pa	-	ni	-	-	-	-	-
G'	-	G'	G'	G'	-	G'	G'	R'	R'	G'	-	R'	S'	S'	-
main	-	di	l	se	-	di	l	mu	jh	se	-	k	r	ta	-
-	-	-	-	-	-	-	-	R'	-	S'	D	P	S'	-	-
-	-	-	-	-	-	-	-	ho	-	-	-	-	-	-	-
G'	-	G'	G'	G'	-	G'	G'	R'	R'	G'	-	R'	S'	S'	-
main	-	di	l	se	-	di	l	mu	jh	se	-	k	r	ta	-
R'	-	R'	S'	P	-	D	S'	S'	-	S'	-	-	-	-	-
hai	-	j	b	te	-	ri	-	ba	-	te	-	-	-	-	-
S'	-	S'	S'	S'	-	S'	-	R'	-	S'	N	D	-	P	-
sa	-	v	n	aa	-	ne	-	se	-	p	h	le	-	ho	-
M	-	P	-	P	-	D	P	M	P	-	P	M	G	R	S
ja	-	ti	-	hain	-	b	r	sa	te	-	o	gh	r	aa	ja
S	R	R	P	P	-	-	-	-	-	-	P	M	P	M	G
p	r	de	-	si	-	-	-	-	-	-	ke	te	ri	me	ri
R	G	R	S	S	-	-	-	-	-	-					
i	k	zin	d	ri	-	-	-	-	-	-					

DS'---- S' D- P- -2
o--------   ho ho

G	P	P	P	P	D	D	-	D	N	N	-	D	D	D	-
p	r	b	t	ki	t	ne	-	un	-	che	-	ki	t	ne	-
P	P	P	-	P	-	D	P	P	-	-	-	-	-	-	-
g	h	re	-	ho	-	te	-	hain	-	-	-	-	-	-	-
G	P	P	P	P	D	D	-	D	N	N	N	D	D	D	-
ku	chh	m	t	pu	-	chho	-	pya	-	r	me	ki	t	ne	-
P	P	P	-	P	-	D	P	P	-	-	-	-	-	-	-
p	h	re	-	ho	-	te	-	hain	-	-	-	-	-	-	-
G'	-	G'	G'	G'	-	G'	-	R'	-	G'	-	R'	S'	S'	-
i	sh	q	me	ja	-	ne	-	kya	-	ho	-	ja	-	ta	-
R'	-	R'	S'	P	P	D	S'	S'	-	S'	-	-	-	-	-
hai	-	ye	-	r	b	hi	-	ja	-	ne	-	-	-	-	-

-	S'	S'	S'	-	S'	-	-	R'	-	S'	N	D	D	P	-
-	to	dke	sa	-	ri	-	-	di	-	va	ren	-	mil	-	-
-	M	P	P	P	-	D	P	M	P	-	P	M	G	R	S
-	ja	-	te	hain	-	di	-	va	ne	-	o	le	ja	mu	jhe
S	R	R	P	P	-	-	-	-	-	-	P	M	P	M	G
p	r	de	-	si	-	-	-	-	-	-	ke	te	ri	me	ri
R	G	R	S	S	-	-	-	-	-	-					
i	k	zin	d	ri	-	-	-	-	-	-					

50. YE BANDHAN TO PYAR KA

Film: Karan Arjun (1995)	Music: Rajesh Raushan
Lyrics: Indeevar	Singer: Udit Narayan, Kumar Shanu, Alka
Taal: Kaharwa	Chord: P̲NR' S=C

sooraj kab door gagan se, chanda kab door kiran se
khushaboo kab door pavan se, kab door bahaar chaman se
ye bandhan to pyaar ka bandhan hai, janmon ka sangam hai

tumheen mere jeevan ho, tumhen dekh-dekh jee loongee
main to tumhaare khaatir duniya ka zahar pee loongee
tere paavan charanon mein aakaash jhuka denge ham
teree raah me jo shole hon, to khud ko bichha denge ham
ye bandhan to pyaar ka bandhan hai...

mamata ke mandir kee hai too sabase pyaaree moorat
bhagavaan nazar aata hai jab dekhen teree soorat
jab-jab duniya mein aaen, tera hee aanchal paen
janmon kee deevaaron par, ham pyaar apana likh jaen
ye bandhan to pyaar ka bandhan hai...

ho insaan mara karate hain, vishvaas nahin marata hai
naamumakin ko bhee mumakin, vishvaas kiya karata hai
sapane sach ho jaate hain, har dua kaam aatee hai
vishvaas kee dor hai aisee, apanon ko kheench laatee hai
ye bandhan to pyaar ka bandhan hai...

Vinod Kumar

YE BANDHAN TO PYAR KA

dha 1	ge 2	n 3	ti 4	n 5	ke 6	dhi 7	n 8	dha 1	ge 2	n 3	ti 4	n 5	ke 6	dhi 7	n 8

prelude:
flute: S' S' R'
R' S' <u>N</u> P <u>N</u>
aa----------

flute: R' P'M' R'-

<u>G</u>' R' S' <u>N</u> S'
aa----------

N S' N S' NS'
aa---- aa--- aa—

flute: S' M' R' S' <u>N</u>-
guitar: <u>N</u> M P- <u>N</u>   <u>N</u><u>N</u> M P – <u>N</u> -2

<u>G</u>' R' <u>N</u> P M
ho---------

R' S' <u>N</u> P M
ho----------

S'-- <u>R</u>' S'<u>R</u>'S' <u>N</u>-
ho----------

PMP – S'-- <u>R</u>' S'<u>R</u>'S' <u>N</u>-
aa-----aa-- ------- -2

dha 1	ge 2	n 3	ti 4	n 5	ke 6	dhi 7	n 8	dha 1	ge 2	n 3	ti 4	n 5	ke 6	dhi 7	n 8
														S' su	- -
<u>N</u> r	<u>N</u> j	<u>N</u> k	<u>N</u> b	<u>N</u> du	- -	- r	D g	M g	- n	P se	- -	- -	- -	S' chn	- -
<u>N</u> da	- -	<u>N</u> k	<u>N</u> b	<u>N</u> du	- -	- r	D ki	P r	- n	<u>N</u> se	- -	- -	- -	S' khu	S' sh
<u>N</u> bu	- -	<u>N</u> k	<u>N</u> b	<u>N</u> du	- -	- r	D p	M v	- n	P se	- -	- -	- -	S' k	S' b
<u>N</u> du	- -	- r	<u>N</u> b	<u>N</u> ha	- -	<u>N</u> r	D ch	P m	- n	<u>N</u> se	<u>N</u> ye	<u>N</u> bn	- -	S' dh	- n
S' to	R' -	- -	- -	- -	- -	- -	- -	- -	- -	- -	S' pya	- -	S' r	<u>N</u> ka	P -

```
N   -   S'  R' | S'  -   -   -  | -   -   -   -  | N   -   S'  -
bn  -   dh  n  | hai -   -   -  | -   -   -   -  | jn  -   mo  -

S'  R'  -   -  | -   -   -   -  | -   -   -   -  | S'  -   P   S'
ka  -   -   -  | -   -   -   -  | -   -   -   -  | sn  -   g   m

S'  N   -   -  | -   -   -   -  | -   -   -   -
hai -   -   -  | -   -   -   -  | -   -   -   -
interlude:
N M P-M   NN M P- M -5
S' S' S' S' R' S' N P   S' S' S' S' R' S' N N  --2

                                                 N   -
                                                 tu  m

N   -   S'  -  | N   -   G'  -  | R'  -   -   -  | S'  -   N   N
hi  -   me  -  | re  -   jii -  | vn  -   -   -  | ho  -   tu  mhe

N   -   S'  N  | -   N   G'  -  | R'  -   -   -  | R'  -   -   -
de  -   kh  de | -   kh  jii -  | lun -   -   -  | gi  -   -   -
music: P'-M'- R' M' R' P' M'-
       R' M' R' P' M'- R'- S'R'S'R'N-
N   -   S'  S' | S'  -   S'  -  | N   S'  -   N  | D   P   P   P
main -   to  tu | mha -   ri  -  | kha -   -   -  | ti  r   du  ni

P   -   D   D  | P   -   S'  -  | N   -   -   -  | N   -   S'  -
ya  -   ka  z  | h   r   pi  -  | lun -   -   -  | gi  -   te  -

N   -   N   -  | N   -   D   -  | M   -   P   -  | -   -   S'  -
re  -   pa  -  | v   n   ch  r  | no  -   me  -  | -   -   aa  -

N   -   N   N  | N   -   D   -  | P   -   N   -  | -   -   S'  S'
ka  -   sh  jhu | ka  -   den -  | ge  -   hm  -  | -   -   te  ri

N   -   N   N  | N   -   D   -  | M   -   P   -  | -   -   S'  -
ra  -   h   me | jo  -   sho -  | le  -   hon -  | -   -   to  -

N   -   N   N  | N   -   D   -  | P   -   N   N  | N   -   S'  -
khu d   ko  bi | chha -  den -  | ge  -   hm  ye | bn  -   dh  n

R'  -   -   -  | -   -   -   -  | -   -   -   S' | -   S'  N   P
to  -   -   -  | -   -   -   -  | -   -   -   pya | -   r   ka  -

N   -   S'  R' | S'  -   -   -  | -   -   -   -  | N   -   S'  -
bn  -   dh  n  | hai -   -   -  | -   -   -   -  | jn  -   mo  -

R'  -   -   -  | -   -   -   -  | -   -   -   -  | S'  -   P   S'
ka  -   -   -  | -   -   -   -  | -   -   -   -  | sn  -   g   m
```

```
S'    N    -    -  |  -    -    -    -  |  -    -    -    -  |
hai   -    -    -  |  -    -    -    -  |  -    -    -    -  |
```

interlude:
M P N N N N N P D P M
M P S' N R' S' S' N N N N -2

N S' M'- G'- R' S' R' G' R'
aa--------- aa--------
M P S'----S' R' P P S' N
aa-------------- flute:

| | | | | | | | | | | | | | | N | - |
| | | | | | | | | | | | | | | m | m |

| N | - | S' | - | N | - | G' | - | R' | - | - | - | S' | - | N | - |
| ta | - | ke | - | mn | - | di | r | ki | - | - | - | hai | - | tu | - |

| N | - | S' | - | N | - | G' | - | R' | - | - | - | R' | - |
| s | b | se | - | pya | - | ri | - | mu | - | - | - | rt | - |

music: P'-M'- R' M' R' P' M'-
R' M' R' P' M'- R'- S' R' S' R' N-

| | | | | | | | | | | | | | | N | N |
| | | | | | | | | | | | | | | bh | g |

| N | - | S' | S' | S' | - | S' | - | N | S' | - | N | D | - | P | P |
| va | - | n | n | z | r | aa | - | ta | - | - | - | hai | - | j | b |

| P | - | D | - | P | - | S' | - | N | - | - | - | N | - | S' | - |
| de | - | khen | - | te | - | ri | - | su | - | - | - | rt | - | j | b |

| N | - | N | N | N | - | D | - | M | - | P | - | - | - | S' | - |
| j | b | du | ni | ya | - | me | - | aa | - | yen | - | - | - | te | - |

| N | - | N | - | N | - | N | D | P | - | N | - | - | - | S' | - |
| ra | - | hi | - | aan | - | ch | l | pa | - | yen | - | - | - | jn | - |

| N | - | N | - | N | - | D | - | M | - | P | - | - | - | S' | - |
| mo | - | ki | - | di | - | va | - | ro | - | pr | - | - | - | hm | - |

| N | - | N | N | N | - | N | D | P | - | N | N | N | - | S' | - |
| pya | -r | a | p | na | - | li | kh | ja | - | yen | ye | bn | - | dh | n |

| R' | - | - | - | - | - | - | - | - | - | - | S' | - | S' | N | P |
| to | - | - | - | - | - | - | - | - | - | - | pya | - | r | ka | - |

| N | - | S' | R' | S' | - | - | - | - | - | - | - | N | - | S' | - |
| bn | - | dh | n | hai | - | - | - | - | - | - | - | jn | - | mo | - |
```
```

R'	-	-	-	-	-	-	-	-	-	-	S'	-	P	S'
ka	-	-	-	-	-	-	-	-	-	-	sn	-	g	m
S'	<u>N</u>	-	-	-	-	-	-	-	-	-				
hai	-	-	-	-	-	-	-	-	-	-				

51. ZINDAGI BAN GAYE HO TUM

Film: Kasoor (2001)	Music: Nadeem Shrawan
Lyrics: Sameer	Singer: Udit Narayan, Alka
Taal: Kaharwa	Chord: P<u>N</u>R' S=C

jo meri rooh ko chain de pyar de
vo khushi ban gaye ho tum
zindagi ban gaye ho tum

jism se jaan tak paas aate gaye
in nigahon se dil me samaate gaye
jis hansi khab ki thi tamanna mujhe
haan vahi ban gaye ho tum
zindagi ban gaye ho tum

har kisi se jise main chhupati rahee
bekhudi me jise gungunati rahee
maine tanha kabhi jo likhi thi vahi
shayari ban gaye ho tum
zindagi ban gaye ho tum

Vinod Kumar

ZINDAGI BAN GAYE HO TUM

dha	ge	n	ti	n	ke	dhi	n	dha	ge	n	ti	n	ke	dhi	n
1	2	3	4	5	6	7	8	1	2	3	4	5	6	7	8

prelude:
NDP NDP NDP
DPM DPM DPM
NDP NDP NDP
NDP NDP NDP

1	2	3	4	5	6	7	8	1	2	3	4	5	6	7	8
													P	-	N
													jo	-	me
R'	-	-	-	-	G'	-	R'	R'	-	-	-	-	P	-	N
ri	-	-	-	-	ru	-	h	ko	-	-	-	-	chai	-	n
R'	-	-	-	-	G'	-	R'	R'	-	S'	-	-	S'	-	S'
de	-	-	-	-	pya	-	r	de	-	-	-	-	vo	-	khu
N	-	D	-	-	D	-	D	N	-	-	-	-	D	-	-
shi	-	-	-	-	bn	-	g	ye	-	-	-	-	ho	-	-
P	-	-	-	-	-	-	-	-	-	-	-	-	P	-	D
tum	-	-	-	-	-	-	-	-	-	-	-	-	zin	-	d
P	-	M	-	-	D	-	D	N	-	-	-	-	D	-	-
gi	-	-	-	-	bn	-	g	ye	-	-	-	-	ho	-	-
P	-	-	-	-	-	-	-	-	-	-	-	-	P	-	S'
tum	-	-	-	-	-	-	-	-	-	-	-	-	zin	-	d
P	-	M	-	-	S'	-	S'	S'	R'	N	-	-	D	-	-
gi	-	-	-	-	bn	-	g	ye	-	-	-	-	ho	-	-
P	-	-	-	-	-	-	-	-	-	-	-				
tum	-	-	-	-	-	-	-	-	-	-	-				
													R'	-	R'
													ji	s	m
R'	-	S'	-	-	N	-	N	N	N	-	-	-	R'	-	R'
se	-	-	-	-	ja	-	n	t	k	-	-	-	pa	-	s
R'	-	S'	-	-	N	-	N	N	-	-	-	-	N	-	D
aa	-	-	-	-	te	-	g	ye	-	-	-	-	in	-	ni
S'	-	-	S'	-	-	S'	-	S'	-	-	S'	-	-	-	S'
ga	-	-	hon	-	-	se	-	dil	-	-	me	-	-	-	s

```
R'    -    -    -    |  -   G'   -   R'  |  R'   S'   N    S'  |  R'   P    -   N
ma    -    -    -    |  -   te   -   g   |  ye   -    -    -   |  -    ji   s   hn

R'    -    -    -    |  -   G'   -   R'  |  R'   -    -    -   |  -    P    -   N
si    -    -    -    |  -   kha  -   b   |  ki   -    -    -   |  -    thi  -   t

R'    -    -    -    |  -   G'   -   R'  |  R'   -    S'   -   |  -    S'   -   S'
mn    -    -    -    |  -   na   -   mu  |  jhe  -    -    -   |  -    han  -   v

N     -    D    -    |  -   D    -   D   |  N    -    -    -   |  -    D    -   -
hi    -    -    -    |  -   b    n   g   |  ye   -    -    -   |  -    ho   -   -

P     -    -    -    |  -   -    -   -   |  -    -    -    -   |  -    P    -   D
tum   -    -    -    |  -   -    -   -   |  -    -    -    -   |  -    zin  -   d

P     -    M    -    |  -   D    -   D   |  N    -    -    -   |  -    D    -   -
gi    -    -    -    |  -   bn   -   g   |  ye   -    -    -   |  -    ho   -   -

P     -    -    -    |  -   -    -   -   |  -    -    -    -   |  -    P    -   S'
tum   -    -    -    |  -   -    -   -   |  -    -    -    -   |  -    zin  -   d

P     -    M    -    |  -   S'   -   S'  |  S'   R'   N    -   |  -    D    -   -
gi    -    -    -    |  -   bn   -   g   |  ye   -    -    -   |  -    ho   -   -

P     -    -    -    |  -   -    -   -   |  -    -    -    -   |  -
tum   -    -    -    |  -   -    -   -   |  -    -    -    -   |  -
```

R'---- G'--- M' G' R'
aa----------------

S'N D N S' --- N
aa----------------

D P M P D – P—
aa--------------

```
                                                                 R'   -   R'
                                                                 h    r   ki

R'    -    S'   -    |  -   N    -   N   |  N    -    -    -   |  -    R'   -   R'
si    -    -    -    |  -   se   -   ji  |  se   -    -    -   |  -    main -   chhu

R'    -    S'   -    |  -   N    -   N   |  N    -    -    -   |  -    N    -   D
pa    -    -    -    |  -   ti   -   r   |  hi   -    -    -   |  -    be   -   khu

S'    -    -    -    |  -   S'   -   S'  |  S'   -    -    -   |  -    S'   -   S'
di    -    -    -    |  -   me   -   ji  |  se   -    -    -   |  -    gun  -   gu

R'    -    -    -    |  -   G'   -   R'  |  R'   S'   N    S'  |  R'   P    -   N
na    -    -    -    |  -   ti   -   r   |  hi   -    -    -   |  -    main -   ne
```

R'	-	R'	-	-	G'	-	R'	R'	-	-	-	-	P	-	N
t	-	n	-	-	ha	-	k	bhi	-	-	-	-	jo	-	li
R'	-	-	M'	-	G'	-	R'	R'	-	S'	-	-	S'	-	R'
khi	-	-	-	-	thi	-	v	hi	-	-	-	-	sha	-	y
N	-	D	-	-	D	-	D	N	-	-	-	-	D	-	-
ri	-	-	-	-	bn	-	g	ye	-	-	-	-	ho	-	-
P	-	-	-	-	-	-	-	-	-	-	-	-	P	-	D
tum	-	-	-	-	-	-	-	-	-	-	-	-	zin	-	d
P	D	M	-	-	D	-	D	N	-	-	-	-	D	-	-
gi	-	-	-	-	bn	-	g	ye	-	-	-	-	ho	-	-
P	-	-	-	-	-	-	-	-	-	-	-	-	P	-	S'
tum	-	-	-	-	-	-	-	-	-	-	-	-	zin	-	d
P	-	M	-	-	S'	-	S'	S'	R'	N	-	-	D	-	-
gi	-	-	-	-	bn	-	g	ye	-	-	-	-	ho	-	-
P	-	-	-	-	-	-	-	-	-	-	-	-			
tum	-	-	-	-	-	-	-	-	-	-	-	-			

52. SARGAM YA ALANKAR YA PALTE

S R G M P D N S'
S' N D P M G R S

SS RR GG MM PP DD NN S'S'
S'S' NN DD PP MM GG RR SS

SSS RRR GGG MMM PPP DDD NNN S'S'S'
S'S'S' NNN DDD PPP MMM GGG RRR SSS

SR RG GM MP PD DN NS'
S'N ND DP PM MG GR RS

SRG- RGM- GMP- MPD PDN- DNS'-
S'ND- NDP- DPM- PMG- MGR- GRS-

SRGM RGMP GMPD MPDN PDNS'
S'NDP NDPM DPMG PMGR MGRS

SRGMP RGMPD GMPDN MPDNS'
S'NDPM NDPMG DPMGR PMGRS

SG RM GP MD PN DS'
S'D NP DM PG MR GS

SM RP GD MN PS'
S'P NM DG PR MS

SP RD GN MS'
S'M NG DR PS

SD RN GS'
S'G NR DS

SRSRG– RGRGM– GMGMP- MPMPD– PDPDN– DNDNS'-
S'NS'ND- NDNDP– DPDPM– PMPMG–MGMGR– GRGRS-

SRGSRSRG RGMRGRGM GMPGMGMP
MPDMPMP PDNPDPD DNS'DNDNS'
S'NDS'NS'ND NDPNDNDP DPMDPDPM
PMGPMPMG MGMGMGR GRSGRGRS

```
S
S R S
S R G R S
S R G M G R S
S R G M P M G R S
S R G M P D P M G R S
S R G M P D N D P M G R S
S R G M P D N S' S' N D P M G R S


S'
S' N S'
S' N D N S'
S' N D P D N S'
S' N D P M P D N S'
S' N D P M G M P D N S'
S' N D P M G R G M P D N S'
S' N D P M G R S R G M P D N S'


S-SRG- R-RGM- G-GMP- M-MPD- P-PDN- D-DNS'-
S'-S'ND- N-NDP- D-DPM- P-PMG- M-MGR- G-GRS-


RS GR MG PM DP ND S'N R'S'
NS' DN PD MP GM RG SR .NS


SGR RMG GPM MDP PND DS'N NR'S'
S'DN NPD DMP PGM MRG GSR R.NS


.P P  .DD  .NN  SS'  RR'  GG'  MM'
M'M  G'G  R'R  S'S  N.N  D.D  P.P
```

bhairav:
```
S R G M P D N S'
S' N D P M G R S
```

kafi:
```
S R G M P D N S'
S' N D P M G R S
```

aasavari:
```
S R G M P D N S'
S' N D P M G R S
```

bhairvi:
```
S R G M P D N S'
S' N D P M G R S
```

bhopali
```
S R G P D S'
S' D P G R S
```

shivranjani
```
S R G P D S'
S' D P G R S
```

yaman

S R G M* P D N S'
S' N D P M* G R S

malkauns

S G̲ M D̲ N̲ S'
S' N̲ D̲ M G̲ S

53. OTHER BOOKS OF VINOD KUMAR

- "Mukesh 51 Songs' Sargam" Part 1, 2,
- "Lata 51 Songs' Sargam",
- "Kishore 51 Songs' Sargam", Part 1, 2,
- "Md. Rafi 51 Songs' Sargam" Part 1, 2, 3, 4,
- "Asha 51 Songs' Sargam"
- "Singe Sachindev Burman and Yesudas 51 Songs' Sargam"
- "Manna Dey 51 Songs' Sargam"
- "Composer Sachindev Burman 51 Songs' Sargam" (In this book different singers songs sargam are available)
- "Kumar Shanu 51 Songs' Sargam"
- "Superhit 51 Gazals' Sargam"
- "Mahendra Kapoor 51 Songs' Sargam"
- "Sabad and Punjabi Songs Sargam, Part-1"
- "Bhajan Swarlipi" Part-1, 2, 3, 4,
- "Suman Kalyanpur 51 Songs' Sargam"
- "Md. Rafi Superhit Songs"

These Books are also available in English SRGM and Western CDEFG style at notionpress.com and amazon.in and at Flipkart.com

For English SRGM books search… (Singer name) 51 Songs' Sargam, book.

For Western CDEFG books search… (Singer name) Songs' Western Notes, book. If you like the books, pl. tell others. If any suggession, pl. mail me.

Vinod Kumar (vinod66vk@gmail.com)

51 SONGS' SARGAM
JEETA THA JISKE LIYE
Song Lyrics in English and Notations in SRGM
S R G M P D N S'
VINOD KUMAR
ASHA
51 SONGS SARGAM
Love Songs
Sad Songs
More Ang Lag Ja Baalma
SRGMPDNS'
LATA
51 SONGS' SARGAM
S R G M P D N S'
VINOD KUMAR
SUPERHIT 51
GAZALS'
SARGAM
chitthi na koi sandes
tum itna jo muskura rahe ho
Gazals' and Nazams' Sargam
S R G M P D N S'
VINOD KUMAR
MD. RAFI KE 51
GEETON KI SARGAM
SRGMPDNS'
Song Sargam or Swarlipi Book
VINOD KUMAR
Md. RAFI
51 SONGS' SARGAM
Part-2
Unke khayal aaye to aate chale gaye
S R G M P D N S'
VINOD KUMAR
Md RAFI
51 SONGS' SARGAM
Part-3
Main ik Raja hun Tu ik Rani hai..
S R G M P D N S'
vinod kumar
MD RAFI
51 SONGS' SARGAM
Part-4
Songs Lyrics in English and Notations in SRGM
S R G M P D N S'
VINOD KUMAR
KISHORE
51 SONGS' SARGAM
Singer Kishore Songs Lyrics in English and SARGAM with Taal
S R G M P D N S'
VINOD KUMAR
KISHORE
51 SONGS' SARGAM
Part-2
Songs' Lyrics in English and Notations in SRGM
SRGMPDNS'
VINOD KUMAR
MUKESH
51 SONGS SARGAM
Mukesh Songs lyrics in English and Notations in SRGMP
S R G M P D N S'
MUKESH
51 SONGS SARGAM
Part-2
Songs' Lyrics in English and Notations in SRGMP
S R G M P D N S'
VINOD KUMAR
MANNA DEY
51 SONGS' SARGAM
Love Songs
Bhajans
Songs' Lyrics in English and Notations in SRGM
S R G M P D N S
VINOD KUMAR
Composer
S.D.Burman
51 Songs' Sargam Part-1
Deewana Mastana Hua Dil
Songs' Lyrics in English and notations in SRGM
S R G M P D N S'
VINOD KUMAR
S D BURMAN
&
YESUDAS
51 SONGS' SARGAM
Mere saajan hain uspaar
Tu jo mere sur mein sur mila le
Songs' Lyrics in English and Notations in SRGM
S R G M P D N S'
VINOD KUMAR
Sahad and
PUNJABI
SONGS' SARGAM
Part-1
suhe vacheere waleya main kahni aa
S R G M P D N S'
VINOD KUMAR

Scan below QR Code from your mobile to get Vinod Kumar's (Singer name) 51 Songs' Sargam books from Flipkart.com site .(Hindi, English, Western all)

Scan below QR Code from your mobile to get Vinod Kumar's (Singer name) 51 Songs' Sargam books from Amazon.in site .(Hindi, English, Western all)